THE BURGLAR'S DOG

ALTERNATIVE GUIDE TO DRINKING IN NEWCASTLE UPON TYNE
Revised and Updated Edition

by Mark Jones

tonto press

www.tontopress.com
www.theburglarsdog.co.uk

A catalogue record for this book is available from the
British Library

Cover illustration by Garen Ewing
Interior images by Mark Jones

Based on the website www.theburglarsdog.co.uk

The opinions expressed in this book are those of the author
and do not necessarily reflect the views of the publisher

Printed & bound in Great Britain by Cox & Wyman Ltd

Tonto Press
Newcastle upon Tyne
United Kingdom
www.tontopress.com

THE BURGLAR'S DOG

'An incredibly funny, read-bits-out-to-your-mates, statement of truth' - **Robert Meddes, *The Crack***

'Funny and vitriolic' - **Coreena Ford, *Sunday Sun***

'An irreverent, riotous guide to the best and very worst of Newcastle's infamous pub scene' - **Dan Sheridan, *Accent***

'Every review in this book is hilarious' - **Claire Dupree, *NARC***

'Had me in stitches' - **Andrew Watson, *Upfront***

'If you like phrases like "tattooed, pickled and rough as a nympho's knees" then buy this book' - **Myles Hodnett, *Hexham Courant***

'Beautifully written, and it's very, very funny' - **Ian Robinson, *BBC Radio Newcastle***

'Refreshing, no nonsense and totally independent' - **Thomas Bagnall, *NEON***

'Weighty and well researched tome' - **Peter Dixon, *Informer***

'Expletive-spliced' - **Tony Henderson, *The Journal***

'It's a blast' - **Craig Conway, actor, *Journal* interview**

Thanks

This book is indebted to Burglar's Dog co-founder John Egdell. Website designer, technical advisor, unstoppable publicity machine; he is all of these things and more, and his presence rifts through these pages like last night's kebab.

Special love and thanks are long overdue to Karen Benfold, without whose patience, understanding, dedication and extra long lie-ins, none of this bellyaching would ever have been written up.

Thanks also to Paul Brown and Stuart Wheatman at Tonto Press, and to the following: Sally Adams, Parveen Ali, Naveed Aslam, James Atkinson, Thomas Bagnall, Rachel Baxter, Lorna Bell, Ian Bell, Lee Connor, Craig Conway, John Conway, Chloë Corkhill, John Deary, Kathleen Devlin, Peter Dixon, Simon Donald, Anita Duffy, Claire Dupree, Michael Egdell, Gemma Finney, Coreena Ford, Darren Gladstone, Julia Graham, John Gray, James Grey, Anna Griffin, Michael Harrison, John Hart, Tony Henderson, Myles Hodnett, Phil Hoffmann, Jason Hopper, Darren Hubbard, Beverly Hurst, Marie Jones, Laura Lancaster, Rachel Lancaster, Jonathan Linklater, Wayne Mason, Robert Meddes, Kelly Mounsey, Ray Nesbitt, Neil, Barry & Ian at the Newcastle Arms, Niall & Biffa at nufc.com, Paddy Parker, Laura Peart, Anne Potter, Narbi Price, Jennie Redmond, Ian Robinson, Paul Sharkey, Dan Sheridan, Gemma Snowden, Joanne Stuart, Gary Taylor, Mitya Underwood, Paul Wappat, Ann, George & Michael Wardle, Richard Warren, Andrew Watson, Allan Weir, and to everyone who has contributed to The Burglar's Dog website over the years.

The Burglar's Dog is based on an original swift half by Jones and Egdell.

Contents

Introduction   9

1. Quayside   13

2. The Burglar's Dog Stag & Hen Special   54

3. Central Station   60

4. The Burglar's Dog UEFAEuro2008™ Special   116

5. City Centre   120

6. Hang the DJ   172

7. Haymarket & Gallowgate   177

8. Ouseburn & City East   215

9. The Dog in the Bog   234

10. Gay Scene   237

11. The Gate   254

12. Bigg Market   273

Index   294

Introduction

This is the 'revised and updated' version of The Burglar's Dog Alternative Guide to Drinking in Newcastle, *with more ch-ch-ch-changes – hence the laughable Bowie pictures above – than you can shake a stick at. All the bars that have died a death since the first version have been taken out, the newly opened ones (plus a few extras) have been written up, and a fistful of pubs that maybe weren't kicked hard enough the first time round have been re-reviewed. That's not bad, is it? It's more than you'd get from the likes of* Time Out *or* Dorling Kindersley, *anyway...*

Newcastle upon Tyne is regularly voted as the best place in the country for a night out. With its world-famous Bigg Market, its plethora of relaxed lounge bars and its thriving gay scene, Newcastle guarantees a warm welcome for all and a tremendous evening's entertainment. There's a drinking venue to suit every taste, from boisterous and fun-loving, to quiet and contemplative and, young or old, large or small, you're certain to have the time of your life. Open any guide to Britain and you'll see it there at the top of the page: Newcastle is the place to be.

Cobblers. Why? Because – frankly – that whole idea is a sham. It's a clichéd, cynical, tourist board lie, like Paris as a city of romance, or the Golden Viennese Heart. We've all been sneered at by the surly French, and you need no more than half an hour in Vienna to fully understand how Hitler could only have been Austrian. But as long as 'Newcastle! Party City!' looks good on paper the media will churn it out and stupid people will swallow it. Aye, Newcastle is a party city, but it's a party that's been gatecrashed by absolute idiots; someone's puking in your fish-tank, there's a couple fornicating on your kitchen sink, and what that dirty beggar is doing upstairs with your mother's knicker drawer you really don't want to know. People flock to Newcastle for one reason, and one reason only: they think that if Bigg Market lasses are daft enough to wear next to nothing when it's minus five then they're daft enough to chew on their flaky cocks if they tell them it's a sausage roll. And don't try to tell me otherwise. Are our pubs as they stand really part of a great Geordie tradition? Are our tacky chain bars so much better than the tacky chain bars elsewhere? Like hell are they. It's the dubious promise of a quick scuttle down an alleyway that hauls in the tourists, and that's crystal clear.

Have you ever wondered exactly why every publication from every other city in the country is so keen to promote Newcastle's drinking circuits above their own bars and pubs? It's because they want you, you drunken oaf, to come and wreck our city with your appalling behaviour and leave their carefully tended Britain in Bloom town squares in one piece. Did you know that Newcastle's council has the largest budget in the European Union for street cleaning services? No, of course you didn't, because it's not true. But that doesn't matter. The facts about drinking in Newcastle are really quite simple: you're going to get served swill, you're going to be soundly ripped off and, at the end of the night, someone is going to try to kick your teeth out.

The Burglar's Dog aims to stick a whopping great monkey wrench in the works. We refuse to perpetuate the myth of the happy, smiling city, and when someone tells us what a snook is, you can be sure we'll be cocking it. If you're expecting to read things like, 'The walls are blue and the carpet is brown and a DJ spins most nights. Happy hours 5-8', then this probably isn't the book for you. The Burglar's Dog has no time for any of that nonsense. There will be no glossy featurettes and no eight-page spreads of underdressed inebriates pulling stupid faces.

We will simply say it as we see it. The fun pubs are our worst nightmare, the student hovels make us wince, and those indistinguishable, extortionate luxebars for berks with more vanity products than IQ points are going to get what's coming to them. We are pig-sick of reading the same stock phrases pulled from the ridiculous hat of style-mag journalism, and we won't be using any of that guff in our reviews. Chilled, smooth, designer, swanky, sumptuous: utter rot, all of it. We will not try to convince you that it's somehow chic to dribble your overpriced pint onto laminate flooring, no matter what those liars insist. We will not attempt to sell you mediocrity packaged as sophistication. And we fully understand how disappointed you're going to be when you realise that having a black napkin under your drink doesn't necessarily turn you into a VIP.

I can hear what you're saying. What about the bars themselves? Won't they be a tad perturbed by your irascible comments? It makes absolutely no difference to them, believe us. They'll still be packed to the rafters every night regardless of whatever cantankerous pasting this book has dished out, and I'm sure they could give a splattery cack about what some sanctimonious old bastard thinks about their establishments. Besides, there is no favouritism at The Burglar's Dog. None of the bars reviewed in this book have been singled out for abuse, so it's no good them getting the lip on because we've insulted their business; we've taken extra care and attention to slag off the whole bloody lot of them. It's a level playing field. If we've hammered one, then we've hammered its competitors, too. We'd like to make that abundantly clear.

You're probably expecting a disclaimer somewhere down the line, and this is it. Obviously we didn't spend all-night-every-night for a week in each of Newcastle's pubs to give a balanced view: objectivity is someone else's job. Nor did we have a drink in every bar the day before this book was sent to the printers, hurriedly typing up the reviews through a 150-pint hangover to meet the deadline. With the best will in the world and even with the lightning turnaround of modern publishing, things will have changed, usually and deliberately for the worse. This won't be here, that won't be there, and they'll have shifted that other thing out from behind the piano. But the atmosphere, the ethos and, most importantly, the people will never change. You still won't be able to get past the pinstriped, braying buffoon at the bar, and that twitching bag of bones in the fake sports gear will still be by the bandit. She'll still be looking at you like you're dirt, and he'll still be waiting outside to glass you.

But don't let us put you off. Just because we hate almost every pub in Newcastle and are all too aware that our tolerance of the rest is based on tearful nostalgia for an age that never existed; just because we have a range of personal issues that would have Sigmund Freud crying off with stress; and just because, clearly, there is something wrong with us, there's no reason why YOU shouldn't have the wondrous time that seems to pass us by every weekend. And every working day. And every Bank Holiday Monday.

Our reviews are all just opinion and observation. And stuff we've made up. In sticking our jaundiced heads above the parapet, we've opened ourselves to just as much ridicule as the bars we've lampooned. And ask yourself this: who is the bigger fool? The penniless critic or the publican with the yacht?

We like to think you'll find something you recognise in our interminable rants, even if it's only a crudely sketched caricature of yourself. We also hope you'll find some of this stuff amusing, as one man's heartbreak is another man's comedy hour. And we know all there is to know about heartbreak.

But we think it's only fair to warn you before you start reading: there might be one or two cuss words.

Quayside

'The rejuvenated Quayside is the flagship of the neighbouring areas of Newcastle and Gateshead. With a wealth of historical buildings, spectacular views, and the river's famous old crossings contrasting with the mechanical and design marvel of the 'blinking eye' Millennium Bridge, this is a place to make any local proud. The redevelopment of this once run-down area has seen the emergence of the magnificent Sage building and the nearby Baltic gallery for contemporary art, plus a whole host of restaurants and cafés.' – Norman Undercroft, Historian.

Akenside Traders
The Side, NE1 1PQ
'It's really packed, so it must be good'

Every single office night out from my work for the last 2,000 years has followed the same depressing route. Bar 42, The Lodge, the Akenside and Buffalo Joe's. Honestly. And since I detest every one of my colleagues, their friends and all members of their families past, present and future, my appearance record makes Michael Owen look like an ever-present, so it'd be fairly safe to say that the Akenside is not one of my favourite haunts. Oh, I dunno, call me a dripping wet blart if you like, but I do quite like being able to breathe when I'm supping my pint. The thing about this place is that people, being naturally as thick as the thickest pig's thickest shit, see it from the outside and think, 'It's really packed, so it must be good', but fail to understand exactly why there's a queue six deep all the way along the bar: because the service is fucking terrible. Me, I just take one look at the number of parched, angry punters, desperately waving tenners and getting redder and redder in the face, and head straight back down to the door. I'm not alone. There's something I've noticed in the distant past, standing alongside idiot middle management while they try to pull rank with the doormen about the age of the office junior. (You can call that a show of solidarity; I call it 'I'm not fucking going in there if she's getting out of it.') And what I've noticed is this: imagine you're plodging on the beach at Whitley Bay, and you spy a used Durex floating on the brine. The waves bring it in, and the waves take it back out, but even if you splash further along the sand, the fucker keeps coming at you. No, it won't bite you or give you a jellyfish sting, but it's still deeply unpleasant and you'd prefer if it kept the hell away from you. In their tides of exasperation and departure, each of the Akenside's customers is that rubber johnny. Of course, abusing the flotsam and jetsam of the clientele is just a way of getting me off the hook when it comes to describing the mass of fools at the bar, although plankton is a word that springs to mind. With this being a pub review book, I'd imagine you're expecting to find a comprehensive description of the decor at some point. It isn't going to happen, I'm afraid, but – over the crush and buried behind the promotions posters – I think I could make out a vague shipping theme, hence the tiresome nautical references in this piece. I'm going to say it straight: I hate this place and everything it represents. I've got nothing but bad memories of terrible nights out amongst imbeciles and of ricking my ankle on those stupid fucking steps. And if you've ever seen me here, looking close to suicide, I can guarantee I was either pissed senseless, or at knifepoint. Or both.

For: Cheap beer and plenty of frottage potential.
Against: Doesn't matter where you stand, there's always some-one grunting at you to move.

I want to get this out of the way as soon as possible, even if the Akenside doesn't serve it: how is Foster's 'head tap' legal? How come trading standards haven't jumped on their case yet? How can they get away with saying, 'Well, your pint's shite and we're sorry about that but, to make you think you're getting a better quality product, we're gonna stick this dollop of foam on the top so it looks more authentic'? It's criminal, it really is.

Blue

Mansion House Chambers, Quayside, NE1 3RE
'A particularly savage divorce'

Formerly Julies 2 night club - the one that got bollocked for sticking an ugly sign on an historical Quayside building - this place has reopened with longer hours and more emphasis on the bar side of things while still keeping the club angle for later on. Don't ask me for a review of the club part; I'm too old to bother, I refuse to embarrass anyone with my dancing, and - as all my previous forays into clubbing have ended in tears - it's best for all concerned if I avoid it altogether. Consequently, I can't tell you anything about whether the much-rumoured presence of Premier League footballers in that bit is actually true. What I can say is that, up to about nine bells of an evening, the bar part is abso-lutely swarming with middle-aged blokes in pastel shirts, all of them looking pained and defeated and clearly coming to terms with a particularly savage divorce. I hope they're not looking for love in here since, judging by the clip of the women we saw sprawled around, they'd just be making the same stupid, yes-dear mistakes as they did last time. And what the fuck are those old boilers doing, anyway? Sit up straight, you lazy, fat puddings. See when travel companies buy buses with seats facing each other, yet are surprised when people put their damned feet all over the upholstery? The seating layout in the window in Blue is going to leave them wondering how all their lovely - blue - stools are covered in mud and chewing gum and gravel and dog shit at the end of the night. They'll learn. Switching seats to the VIP / champagne area - where people with no grasp of reality can pay £200 for a bottle of Cristal fizzy wine - I can see the reflections in the mirrored bar of a carpet more suited to covering a corpse sliding down a quarry side, and the spotlit chandelier that keeps changing colour, from blue to blue, and then all the way back to blue again. The wallpaper is black and flowery, the booths red and leathery, the seating around the white plastic tables is fuck-knows-what-ery, and it's all starting to hurt my eyes. I am not having a good time. I doubt whether I'll ever set foot in here again, but I'll tell you this: it's not because of the people, the staff or the atmosphere. It's not even because of the prices. My problem is the decor. I've seen it all before, and I can carbon date it. I want to state this quite clearly here: I've lived through one 1980s already. And it was fucking shite.

For: The shining silver bazaar curtain at the back...
Against: ...hides the bogs, which, in the age of the designer toilet installation, looked to me just like a swimming pool changing room, complete with wall-to-wall foot pool. I'm going to take it as read that something was bust in there, unless getting pissy water all over your best kecks is some sort of new Quayside trend.

It's one thing second guessing your target customers - we do it often enough with the sweary cobblers we bung together for our punters - but a bar pandering to the extent that they've called a cocktail a 'Newcastle United' is just plain tragic.

Bob Trollop

Sandhill, NE1 1PG
'Everyone knows that beagles are the heavy smokers'

'Vegetarian Pub of the Year', says the sign on the window. Fine, I've got no problem with that, but explain this to me: on the wall in here they've got a picture of a terrier smoking a pipe, so do you think they're saying it's alright to leave the poor animals riddled with lung cancer as long as you don't actually eat them? Besides, they're miles off the mark with that terrier: everyone knows that beagles are the heavy smokers. The main theme of Bob Trollop seems to be the ramshackle 19th Century boozer experience, and they've done it pretty well, even if they did have a head start in this row of National Trust 'keep it tatty, the tourists love it' buildings. The place has low-beamed ceilings that look like they're falling apart and is stuffed with chandeliers, horse brass and knackered old clocks, setting it at least an inch apart from the planned-scruffiness of a fake-Irish theme bar. On top of that, the beaten-copper tables and rickety chairs seem to have been just thrown together instead of picked from a catalogue, although I'm a little concerned about the arse-ache seating: had haemorrhoids not been invented in 1862? The pub is split into two areas with the bar in between and you need to go out into the alleyway and try not to fall over the milk churns if you want to change rooms. The bit at the front has huge windows looking over the Guild Hall, Tyne Bridge and general Quayside carnage, but unfortunately that means that you'll have to put up with pissed-up passers-by laughing at your couscous and courgette casserole if you're stuffing your face, while the back room is more dark and depressing. One thing to watch, though, is that Bob Trollop shares its bogs with the Red House next door, so try to remember which way you went after you've emptied your bladder, or you'll end up red-faced and bewildered and in the wrong pub. I've done it dozens of times and I'm warning you out of genuine love and affection. So, Bob Trollop, then. Nowt remarkable overall, but nothing to start stamping my booties about. Depends what you're after. If you fancy slumming it with the beards and cardigans and deniers of the basic realities of the food chain, then get in early on, but if you think vegetarians are deviants who should be beaten and starved and tortured with sausage butties, go a bit later when the more typical Quayside crowd arrives.

For: The beer and food in here are excellent. No, really.

Against: The back room stunk of puke on our visit. Also: no, really.

Not that you'd know it from my ashen face, my appalling mood swings, my disciplinable sickness record and my pan-blocking turds, but I'm a vegetarian too. Thirteen whole years without animal flesh passing my lips. And, FUCK ME, I'm hungry. I could eat a scabby horse and go back for seconds.

Buffalo Joe's
Pipewellgate, Gateshead, NE8 2BJ
'Oozing post-coitally'

Pornography's a great leveller. No matter what the personality, background or interests of the wide-eyed adult industry starlet, each one will end up in exactly the same position: butt naked, on her knees, giving an inane, thumbs-up grin to the camera, with semen dripping off her chin. And while not everyone is lucky enough to have their back doors kicked in for money and the evidence posted on the internet, Buffalo Joe's provides a similar yet only slightly less degrading experience for Newcastle's young ladies. Every giggling wench with an eye for 'fun' and a clutch bag full of fivers finishes the night in here, caged and humiliated and wearing a fucking sparkly pink cowboy hat. Mandatory 'mystery' destination on every Comic Sans, clip-art-champagne-bottle office night out poster ('10.30pm - 2.00am Wherever???!!'), Buffalo Joe's has long been one of the most depressing bars in what the geniuses at the neighbouring councils would like you to call NewcastleGateshead, and its mornings-after the prime instigator of calls to the Samaritans. See it for yourself. Witness gang after gang of frustrated fools oozing post-coitally along the Quayside to this 'amazing Western fun theme bar' to piss the pittance they've earned over a hot photocopier up the nearest fake-saloon wall. See barmen dressed as Native Americans in lieu of getting a fucking proper job, groping soggy-knickered puddings in the cage until they're splashing around in batter. Watch the nightly snake pit of writhing, bottle clutching idiots chucking themselves around to a filling-loosening kick drum and muse on how much of a pity it is that we - and not the Germans - won the bloody war. Take it from me; the hanged man at the top of the stairs got the best deal. In his place I'd have run to the scaffold and thrown my head in the noose: anything to get away from this awful, awful bar. And if I ever hear that you've bought one of those stupid bastard hats, I'm going to punch you squarely in the face until my knuckles break. Have a nice day, y'all.

For: It's cruel and inhumane, but you can always join in the pointing and laughing and the poking with sticks by clicking on the image gallery on www.buffalojoes.co.uk. You'll soon see I'm not making it up.
Against: I hate people being young. I hate people going out. I hate people getting drunk. And I hate people having a good time. There: I've said it.

And while I'm on the subject of pornography, I'd like to ask this: how is it that there are thousands upon thousands of people only too eager to perform naked for goggle-eyed masturbators, yet there's a maximum of three people doing the voiceovers for all porn films ever? Surely it's not that bad a job. I used to work for a well-known utility company - whose name I won't mention because the cunts aren't getting any free publicity out of me - and my daily routine consisted of telling people 'Hello? No, sorry, you'll need to speak to British Gas. Goodbye.' I'd have gladly chucked that in to read out a script saying 'Fuck yeah! Fuck yeah! Oh fuck yeah! It's so good! Fuck yeah!' for eight hours a day. I could do it in three languages, too. No problem.

Chase
10-15 Sandhill, NE1 3JE
'Mussolini's mother behind the counter'

It's one of my favourite ironies that the Managing Director of the Ultimate Leisure group is called Mark Jones. He is, I swear. My few remaining friends ask me, 'Is it you? Can you lend me a tenner?' while strangers insist that I'm using a cruel pseudonym. The truth is that we both use our real names, and we both aim to get rich via the pub industry. That's where the similarity ends, mind, since he earns millions while I'm worth fuck all less tax and NI, which is why I am going to compensate by ripping the piss out of another one of his bars. Childish, that's me. Formerly an authentic fin de siècle bar – that's fin de the *last* fucking siècle, when everything was turquoise and yellow and shining like a shilling in shite, rather than a 1900s café with handwritten signs, clanking tills, and Mussolini's mother behind the counter – Chase has recently been refurbished and reopened to great hullabaloo. Conceived as a design statement and tailored towards the successful and debonair, boasting a style-conscious interior and carefully selected sounds, in reality this place is no more than another anonymous pick-up joint, routinely stuffed with the gawping and the pea-brained, each with all the conversational ability – plus the sonorous tones – of free range chickens. The DJs might as well play fucking 2Unlimited the entire night for all that the customers have their fingers on the pulse or indeed give anything approaching a shit, because Chase – like every other Quayside bar - is a raging tidal flow of hen and stag parties, sloshing in, disgracing themselves, ruining everybody's night, and depositing broken glass and plucked feathers on their way out. Oh man, I really used to like this place, back in the days when it first opened and was crawling with beauties who wouldn't so much as hockle on this ugly bastard for less than a billion in cash. What the hell happened? One of us has fucked something up pretty badly over the years. My money's on the Jones boy.

For: The enclosed outdoor terrace with the patio heaters; global warming be damned.
Against: Coming in through the back way, from the eastern end of the Quayside, you have to avoid all the seagull shite under the Tyne Bridge. Those beaky bastards have no shame.

Call it coincidence if you like, but I've had more mentalist episodes after drinking in Chase than in anywhere else in town. Last time, I got home very drunk and even more maudlin after some trivial misunderstanding, and I decided to sulk away my worries with some late-night melancholy music. Stumbling around in the dark, I stuck the headphones on and sat down with a whisky and the remote control. Thing is, I couldn't for the life of me work out why the music sounded so muffled no matter how much I pissed about with the settings, and it was only when I realised that the extra percussion was the neighbours braying on the windows that I understood what I'd done. Turns out that, instead of the headphone jack, I'd somehow managed to plug my shoelaces into the stereo. I'll be laying off the cocktails in future, I think.

The Cooperage

32 The Close, NE1 3RQ
'Salvaged from a shipwreck'

Looking for some quality beer in a ramshackle 17th Century alehouse, and one that's haunted to boot? The Cooperage is the place to go. With its tumbledown tilt and its splintered exterior, it's long been a wonder how the place is still standing. I read many years ago on a sign on the wall that the timbers used to build the Cooperage were salvaged from a shipwreck, and that's certainly true of most of the grizzled old bastards that have stared out the window at the passing Quayside revellers over the years. This pub hit a bit of a sticky patch a while back, with any amount of vultures circling over and trying to kill it off once and for all. There was never anything as drastic as a refit, you understand, but more a deliberate neglect so they could get the designers in to inflict a 'much-needed' makeover and leave it looking polished and contemporary and utterly bereft of soul, like some million quid church conversion in one of those ghastly weekend pullouts. Thankfully, none of that shite ever materialised. Now resurrected and rescued, they seem to have finally got the balance right between the traditional and the trendy, with the dusty dungeon on the ground floor no longer taking second place to the thumping nightclub-stroke-venue upstairs; each seems happy to coexist alongside the other, the 'amusing' sex-aids machine next to the bogs downstairs being the only hint at the debauchery above. The slow, creeping death has been reversed, and the neglected no-man's land that once held the pool table and later a half-arsed attempt at an old-time-daytime café has been spruced up to give a welcoming extension to the main bar. I still harbour concerns for this place, viewing it like a sandcastle against the tide. But hopefully, thanks to the joys of listed status, this knackered old building will always be the same, although peril is never too far away. There'll forever be some fucking lunatic looking to knock it down to build more executive apartments, encouraging people to get a mortgage ten times their salary for purpose-built 'luxury', and then sending them a catalogue full of eighteen-inch sofas to fit in their two-foot wide living rooms. But I think this place will be alright. There's something heroic about the Cooperage's struggle to appeal to the average meathead Quayside drinker without farting in the face of its old die-hards, and with it being surrounded by the likes of Jimmyz, Casa, Blue and Chase, plus that wretched superclub Sea over the way, that's no mean feat. It's good to see that, amongst the premium bottles and the multicoloured bitchpiss of the area, there's a place here for a full range of real ales. Fair enough, at the moment I'd rather drink my own jizz after a fortnight eating nowt but creamy Philadelphia than even ask for a half of Pedigree, but I still like to see it there as an option for when my nads touch my knees, my taste buds go on a Saga holiday, and I don't mind a pint that looks and smells like something I forgot to flush.

For: The students at the next table are actually communicating by voice instead of text message.
Against: If you must make untruthful boasts about your drug experiments to impress your equally dishonest mates, it helps to remember that heroin doesn't come in pints.

The Cooperage's ghost is that of Henry Hardwick, 16th Century cooper who, after failing to escape from pressgangers, was nailed to the back door of the Cooperage, had his eyes gouged out and his testicles severed. His spectre has been seen walking along Newcastle Quayside, with eyes just bloody sockets. Wait a minute: a bloke, on the Quayside, face covered in blood and holding his groin? And you're telling me that's a GHOST? I think someone's been pulling your pisser.

Crown Posada

31 The Side, NE1 3JE
'Shoddy'

If you ever look at an official guide to Newcastle, and check under 'bars', you're guaranteed to find the Crown Posada being hailed as a fine example of a Northern pub. That's a bit strange, really, because - at a time when the rest of Newcastle is stocking up on the alcopops and the imported premium draught - it's anything but. For a start, you'll not find many Geordies in here, unless they've been dragged in on a work's night out by the office bore. What you will find, though, are legions of guidebook-clutching foreign tourists, gazing in awe at the surroundings. And with good reason; it's not very often you find a pub round here with stained glass windows and a cravat-wearing landlord, let alone one with an old record player spinning Billie Holiday 78s (that's ancient vinyl, by the way, mp3 kids). There's no shoddy drinks promotion posters clogging up the walls, no hen night atrocities, and time seems to have stopped here when 'DJ' meant Jimmy Savile and Tony Blackburn. I've thought long and hard about this: is this the most pretentious bar in the town, or does the fact that it has remained untouched for so long make it the very opposite of pretentiousness? I like their style, either way. How many other bars in this city are prepared to stick so rigidly to wartime opening hours? Name me another pub in town that understands that all you need to refurbish a bar is a pot of paint and a wipe down with a damp cloth. This is a bar I like so much, I'm not going to complain about the snug at the front always being full of bloody students. Even the beer, for bog standard Carling, is pretty good. Most people come for the real ales, which are supposed to be at their best here; I wouldn't know about that, but then I've always been suspicious of people who think that drinking warm, flat vinegar makes them an intellectual.

For: The guides are right. It is a damn fine pub.
Against: If I do have a complaint about the place, it's that it's too damn narrow - you get two lard-arses at the bar and you're stuck there all day. Not necessarily a bad thing, come to think of it.

Comparing the craftsmanship in the Crown Posada to the flat-pack shambles of my spare room 'study' makes me think about how hard it is to get a decent tradesman these days. You're either lumbered with some incompetent boob who calls himself a joiner simply because he managed to charve the chisels from B&Q, or you cough up for a time-served expert who knows how desperate you are and how much advantage he can take of you. OR you do it yourself. Principles and bank balances mean the first two are out of the question for me, so number three is all that remains. Sadly, I am absolutely fucking hopeless at it. I bought myself one of those cordless screwdrivers in an attempt to feel a bit more self-confident and manly, but can I hell get the hang of it? I line the bit up with the screw, press the button, and what happens? The screw stays still while I get spun round it, banging into walls and furniture, that's what. Where's those sodding instructions?

Egypt Cottage

117 City Road, NE1 2AN
'I'm pig bloody sick'

While I'm too young to claim to have ever been in the audience for *The Tube*, I could, if you asked me, tell you exactly where I was when Jools Holland called me - personally - a groovy fucker. Seeing the Egypt Cottage on the telly during *The Tube*'s star-in-the-bar interviews always made me feel like it was something legendary, and when my balls finally dropped it was one of the first pubs I wanted to drink in. Class, it was: authentic no-messing pub atmosphere, good jukebox and a decent pint. I will confess, however, that laziness and peer pressure forced me into other venues over the years; well, that plus the fact that I'd heard it had become a, quote, *poncy wine bar*. Strolling up from a sunny Quayside Sunday the other day, we decided to face our fears and check it out. Sad to say, the oldest licensed premises in Newcastle has now become just another DJ-centric bar, with what they tell me is smooth and deep house beats meets bongomania. I haven't got a fucking clue what that entails, to tell the truth. Nor am I likely to be impressed by their club tie-ins and queue-jumps, especially when I'm so pig bloody sick of seeing ugly flyers strewn over every pavement of a Saturday night. So, aye, it's two floors of the very latest design, all rag-rolled red and gold, with Sphinx statues and Nefertiti tables, plus huge fan-shaped leather seats in the back room. The lights seem to be made out of samosas and the haphazard MDF fittings with their particularly prominent screws just plead with you to take the whole lot out and make them put it back the way it used to be. I'm reading here that they put live music on as well as the DJ shite, so perhaps it's not all untold misery in the noise department. Unless you include the bloody buskers nights, that is. What's my problem, then? The Egypt Cottage isn't even that bad: the beer's alright and the people seem pleasant enough. I just find it really depressing to see history replaced by yet more bandwagon jumping, but maybe what I see as cynical cashing-in is just the taste of a generation I have no connection with, and I'm a sad, past-it, four-eyed, greying arsehole. Maybe there's not much call for Dickensian taverns these days. Never mind groovy: I feel like an ancient fucker more than anything. Next birthday I'll be 85.

For: The photos on the walls of the place when it was good.
Against: Becoming a miserable old bastard and being the last one to realise.

If you really want to get me started, ask me about the Rose & Crown that used to be across the road from the Egypt Cottage: now there was a class boozer, with spit 'n' sawdust and big picture windows looking right down the Tyne. And what's there now? A bloody car park, that's what.

Exchange
Premier Travel Inn, Lombard Street, NE1 3AE
'Polite and welcoming'

Do I have to do this one? Why? As far as I'm concerned this place doesn't even count, since it's just a hotel bar, and not even a separate one like Martha's at the Vermont. Let's make it quite clear from the start: you will see no locals here, only visitors (I mean fucking stag and hen parties really, but I'm trying to be polite and welcoming) who think the Quayside IS Newcastle. This bar serves no other purpose than a meeting point for pack upon pack of hotel residents, knocking back eight pints and an Apple Sourz while they wait for the slowcoaches. And I can understand the wait. I can see why the party boys need so long to get ready. It takes a lot of time and effort to splash around a bit of Hugo Boss and choose which of their shirts to pull on. Should it be the plain white one, the same as worn by half the group, or the checked white one, as sported by all the fucking rest? Sometimes I think they might as well not bother leaving the hotel, and instead just grab one of the cafeteria-style chairs over by the windows, from where they'll get a commanding view of all that NewcastleGateshead (8,9,10... and relax) apparently has to offer, namely the Sage, the bridges, and that goddamn Tuxedo Princess moored opposite. This way they could save themselves the trouble of being spat at by the indigenous population AND conserve energy for banging on every door on every floor from midnight until the cock crows. Seen from my position well away from the action, this bar is something special to behold. With the sickly colour palette of a tortured artist in the months leading up to suicide, the desperate yellows, oranges, and pale wood produce a disquieting effect unrivalled in any other bar in town, while the ornate ceiling seems to lower in parallel with the froth on my pint. And I'm watching in amazement as some fucking caveman pits his wits against the quiz machine, unaware that he'd be better matched in taking on the plantpots. 'Ey oop, Torrr-neh!' he yells to his mate, 'What's t'Queen's first name, eh?' Of course, every cloud has a silver lining; even a lollystick in a dog turd has a joke on it. And this bar's saving grace is the theme corner set to the left of the main entrance. This marvellous installation aims to take you away from the look of the national chain reception area and into the realm of the family-run establishment. The lobby they've modelled this on seems to be those of London's hotel trade, where any room cheaper than £200 a night is going to be in some grotty annexe; bring your own door and mind the rodents. And so skilfully is it rendered, so exact in every detail, that it even looks like they've employed some toothless old skank to play the role of bag lady, slumped on the gnawed settee and with a face that suggests she's emptying her bladder between the cushions. Look, I know it's not claiming to be anything grand, and I know it's my own fault for expecting better, but there's only one way to deal with this place, and that's to pretend it doesn't exist. Just tell people it's the staff canteen of the Slug & Lettuce in the same block and pray they believe you. And knock them out if they don't.

For: Quality rooms from only £63 per night.
Against: Think who'll be booked in next door.

You've got to admire the optimism of the Premier Travel Inn, helpfully pointing out the local art galleries, opera house and countryside trails for the benefit of their guests, in the hope that one day - if only for that day - the tanked-up cretins will find something more cultural to do than seeing which travels furthest from the third floor windows; Foster's piss or Corona puke. Clue: the secret's in the lime.

Eye on the Tyne

9-17 Broad Chare, NE1 3QQ
'Bog standard, government-issue, no imagination'

Replacing both the shit-stained shit with shit on of the Bonded Warehouse and the licensing trade in-joke that was the Wig & Pen, the Eye on the Tyne is a blend of the old and the new, with a contemporary ambience housed in an historical vaulted building. Huge arched windows and strategically positioned mirrors combine to give this bar-cum-restaurant a bright, spacious feel, and the wooden floor and exposed brickwork provide an exciting counterpoint to the modern colour scheme. At least that's the sort of dreary fucking cobblers they probably want your average pub critic to spout. Well they can piss off, unless they're prepared to slip me a few tenners or fund a three-hour stint with a Chinese hooker. And if they don't, then it looks like I'll be forced to tell the yawning world that this horrendous plundering of the tourist money belt, this shameless cash-in that makes the Angel View in Gateshead look dignified (on account of the fact that you can comfortably view the Angel from there, unlike the contortionism you need to spot the vista here), does nothing other than heap more saccharine into an already unpalatable Quayside cuppa. Whoever is responsible for this coma-inducing travesty of design should have whatever fake qualification they bought on eBay rolled round a screwdriver and poked into each eye. For a so-called professional to study every manual, attend every focus group meeting, tick every box and still make such a complete fucking balls up of it beggars belief. In trying to get every individual aspect of the modern drinking experience so textbook spot-on, they've somehow managed to get the whole sorry thing utterly wrong. The layout's wrong, the ambience is wrong, the approach is wrong, the scale's wrong, the decor is wrong, the woodwork's wrong, the stone craft is wrong and the fucking colour scheme is wrong. And that's because, for at least the twentieth time in the past two years, this appears to be a purple bar: a bog standard, government-issue, no imagination, purple bar. You heard me: purple, the official colour of chill. For fuck's sake. Am I the only one who fails to see the link between purple and chilled? Is there something wrong with my sensory perception? Apparently there's a decorating concept that matches colours and emotions for essential modern living; simply select the hue that best fits the room's desired mood from the list, then watch those vibes flow. Green, for example, is supposed to be calming. Well, that's bollocks for a start, since my office is painted dusty sage, yet I've never once managed to get beyond 8.05am without wanting to wring some fucker's neck. And as for red being the colour of passion; my bedroom is crimson, but our lass hasn't given me so much as a stiff piston crank in months, so you'll forgive me if I scoff at that laughable notion. So why are pisspot bars such as this oversized abomination so keen to slap the mulberry all over every inch of flimsy plasterboard? Because a fucking sales brochure told them to, that's why. Buy THIS from us and achieve THAT. When are people going to realise that the last opinion you can trust is that of someone who is trying to sell you stuff? Sod off with your mandatory 'optional' extras, will you? Why can't people stand up for themselves a bit more, not just in bars but in every second-rate emporium of tat? No, I don't want scuff guard for these shoes that'll come apart in six weeks; no, I don't want an extended warranty for this gaming platform that'll be obsolete before I get it home; and no, I don't want eighty tins of maroon emulsion just because your office junior fucked up the order by a factor of ten. Especially if it's going to saddle me with the sort of James Blunts, Steve Punts and *Life On Mars'* Gene Hunts that the Eye on the Tyne attracts.

For: I never thought I'd see the day when the best thing about a bar is the Tesco Express just up the road.

Against: If those bloody skatepunk kids clattering about on the adjacent Law Court steps don't fuck right off within the next ten minutes, I swear there'll be a murder. And I won't even bother scarpering afterwards. I'll just 'fess up straightaway. Yeah, I'll say, it was me. Any chance you can just open the doors, stick me in the dock and send me down until the newspapers campaign for my release? Don't bother with the brief: tell him he's got the night off. I don't mind doing a bit of stir if it means there's a few less grainy clips of slack-jawed morons in knee-pads to clutter up the internet.

Bars like this are a haven for past-their-peak women who make it their business to look as much as possible like arena-pop foghorn Anastacia. There'll be at least one of these horrors in your place of work - there's three in mine - who can't even get the teas in without an inch of foundation, immaculately-tipped hair, heavy-rimmed specs and ballcrusher heels. Imagine, though, if you were drunk or star-struck or just plain stupid enough to sleep with one of these tragedies. Picture it, if you will. Following the doctrine of Lazy Man Love, you're flat on your back with your stalk in the air, and your conquest is crouching over you with her hands out in front, as if she's holding an imaginary handlebar but, like, upside down. You think she's trying to get her balance and achieve the optimum thrusting position, so you close your eyes and wait for the warmth of those fleshy walls. Slowly, softly, yet deliberately, she gently leans forward and, with her nose nudging yours in a kittenish fashion, utters her bedroom thoughts: 'WAMMATTA LURV. SEMME FRAY. LEMME OWTHIZ MIZERAY!' Jesus Christ, woman. I tell you, if that was me, there'd be nowt the matter. She'd be 'Left outside alOHne', alright: down by the wheelie bins with a fucking broken arm.

Fever
Akenside Hill, NE1 3XP
'Think, man, think'

For crying out loud, how are you supposed to review a pub that leaves no lasting impression? Fever is a big room with walls and doors and a counter where drunk people are served with alcohol. Really, that's about it. Formerly The Newcastle Arms, The Pump House, Muse and now Fever, I've never been able to string together more than three sentences by way of an accurate appraisal. The beer's alright, the cocktails cheap enough to swill down your throat before you have to taste them, the decor makes cut-price look palatial and the punters are run-of-the-mill Quayside goers. Christ, I am really struggling here. Think, man, think. This place seems to follow the bizarre party-bar pattern of being absolutely heaving or howlingly desolate with no comfortable grey area in between; and either way it's not much cop. There's certainly nowt that would entice me in here if it wasn't for the fact that I NEED to write this garbage up for the sake of completeness. The music's an eclectic mix of shite and fucking shite, all served up in that mic-gobbling 'Yeeees indeedy, that's the sound of...' style so beloved of pot-bellied, amateur-hour DJs the world over, and if there is any sort of interesting theme to this bar then I'm damned if I can see it. They've got geometric patterns on the walls, a stack of circular mirrors at the far end behind some zebra skin stools, more terrible modern art than could ever be deemed necessary, plus a mirror-tiled ceiling that looks like it might be easy to repair, if nothing else. And those tiles might provide the clue to why there's never any effort put into doing this place up; why bother if it's just going to get wrecked by stag and hen nights anyway? Is this long enough yet? It's not? Balls. You'll be wanting more ranting, then. I never thought I'd ever type these words, but Fever is as entertaining as the stag do that's in it. And more astounding than that, I'm going to say that the last time I was in I found myself chuckling at the antics of a gang of lads-off-the-leash, even if I was laughing at the fucking pillocks rather than with them. In fancy dress so poor they have to tell people who they're meant to be, and throwing shapes to leave even the hardcore Quayside crowd looking mortified, the dancing turned to pogoing turned to somersaulting, like Obafemi Martins on tartrazine after nabbing a rollover jackpot. Call me cruel, condescending, toffee nosed or biscuit-arsed, but there's always a joy to be had in watching people debase themselves completely, to the point where they could get no lower, short of shitting in a bucket and wearing it as a crown. Think how much they've pissed away on their big night out. Add it all up: the costumes, the hotel, the train fare and the ale. The dry-cleaning, the bail, the solicitor and the back-quack. And balance it against what they've got to show for it: a thumping head, a regrettable tattoo, an embarrassing itch and a Boots CD of blurred snaps to remind them of their stupidity. 'Here's one of me... pulling a face! There's Dave... showing us his beer! Where's that? Who the hell's she? And why the fuck do we do it..?'

For: The quintessential Bigg Market bar.
Against: Except it's, like, on the Quayside.

Inevitably the fancy dress party moved on, and was replaced by a more typical crowd. It was at that point that I was subjected to my worst pub nightmare: everyone buggers off and leaves me to get the round in while they nip to the bogs, and I get lumbered with two huge hen night parties in the same bar. And what does the DJ try in his desperation to drum up some atmosphere? He gets them to out-squeal each other. What a fucking idiot. The doctors say I may recover some of the hearing in my left ear, but the right one is beyond help. Thanks for that, you porky bastard.

Flynn's

63 Quayside, NE1 3DE
'It was your fault they elbowed you in the kisser'

Like a trip to the clap clinic, we've been putting off revisiting Flynn's for years and, now that we've been in for another squint, we realise our hesitation was fully justified. Hurrying in for a swift one purely to get out of a sudden downpour, we quickly saw why Flynn's has acquired a reputation as a bar you either hate unreservedly or visit just to take the piss out of it; there's no way on earth you could actually like it, unless you were educationally subnormal and a nasty little git an' all. The exterior of this place seems to change every fortnight (along with the name of the damn place - see the Flynn's / Slice Bar / Flynn's again debacle for proof), but no matter how they dress it up, it's still one of the rottenest bars on the Quayside. I notice that the latest paint job states that they're calling it a 'bar diner' these days: I didn't see any menus lying about, but whatever they rustle up, I'd still rather go scrabbling around the bins with the rats than ever eat my bait in here. Why? For a kick off, I'm buggered backwards if I'm standing about eating my grub, since there are about three seats in the whole bar, and even those are brutally pockmarked with old tab burns. Secondly, Flynn's has a policy of pumping out '80s cheesy pop sounds from the moment it opens. And on top of that, the place is falling apart, hamstrung by the last corner-cutting spruce-up they attempted unravelling at the seams. There's tatty laminate flooring and the usual depressing modern colour scheme, with only a collage by the door of what seems to be Frankenstein's monster and random bits of cleavage to give it any character of its own. Fuck alone knows what they were thinking when they bunged that up. And while I'm aware that the layout of three levels and low ceilings is due to the pub's location in an old Quayside building, the whole experience reminded me of being stuck on one of those cut-price party boats down the Tyne, where there's nowt but steep stairs, terrible music and contemptible berks you can't seem to escape from. On a brighter note, there was nothing wrong with the beer, except that it seemed pretty expensive to me since Flynn's is such a battered dump. I'd expected to pay Wetherspoon's prices for my standard pint, and not get shafted by a luxebar premium; maybe they'd got word that that imbecile with the freaky eyebrows and his stumpy bird were in town with their smug matching notebooks and decided to charge us triple out of general spite. Unlikely, I know, but if writing bollocks like that is enough to pad out this so-called review, then I'm a happy man. I suppose that just leaves the punters to gripe about: from the dawn of time until Armageddon shatters the last bottle of Smirnoff Ice, Flynn's will attract knuckleheads and hinnies, spastic dancing and yelling and knocking you sideways in their lobotomised over-exuberance. And you will smile and apologise and wipe their sticky cocktails off your best shirt, because, clearly, it was your fault they elbowed you in the kisser. It really is rough. Aye, it might have been friendly enough at five bells when we forced ourselves to go and review the place, but I'd be damned if I'd go any later. In fact I'll be damned if I go again.

For: Nice view of the Sage and the Tyne bridges.
Against: It truly is shocking. Imagine a punishment cell with a view and you're almost there.

I tried looking up some of the history of Flynn's - or at least of the building that houses it - on the internet. Bugger all there, I'm afraid. What I did find out, though, is that Flynn's is a notorious pick-up joint for pathetic, middle-aged men preying on underage, underdressed teenage drinkers. Fuck, I wish I'd real-ised that at the time.

Jimmyz

48-52 Sandhill, NE1 3JF

'(sic)'

I've been studying journalism lately. I have. Well, I've been reading the Chronicle while I'm having my dinner, but it amounts to much the same thing. What I've become most aware of while I'm stuffing my fat face is the concept of give-'em-enough-rope, of letting people reveal themselves to be idiots by just standing back and allowing them have their say. From the dumb bint from Byker who pissed away a million quid of Lottery winnings and couldn't fathom why her new 'snob' neighbours would object to a millionaire trying to cadge a cup of sugar, to the boneheads trying to claim compensation (and a replacement pair of underkegs for the ones they shat) from some bar that 'made' them drink thirty pints in happy hour, it's all there in black and white. Turn the page through 180 degrees and you'll see the words 'you stupid bastard; you stupid tart' written between every line. It's a fascinating approach and it's one I'm going to take for Jimmyz Bar, liberally quoting from the blurb on their promotional website to give you the review straight from the horse's slobbering mouth. Here, in their own officially-sanctioned purple prose is what they think you want: Oppulence (sic), decadence and seduction. Style, cocktails and dreams. Conspiratorial corners. Chandaliers (sic). Champages (sic)... ah, fuck it. This feels really unkind, like refusing to help a single mother off the bus with her buggy. The truth is that Jimmyz always was, and still remains, a farcically expensive, desperately crass Quayside bar catering to bozos looking to fight with - or gold-digging sexual predators in sparkly tops aiming to fuck - overpaid, immoral, more-red-cards-than-brain-cells Premier League footballers. Bloody hell: that was a clunky sentence, wasn't it? But if you like bordello reds, laminate flooring and damn-your-eyes wallpaper, and you don't give a sloppy shit how much it costs, then maybe Jimmyz is the bar for you. Perhaps you consider 1940s photos of people necking on to be seductive and glamorous. It takes all sorts, I fully understand. When will people realise, though: there is no glamour in Newcastle, and there never will be. It is not a luxury destination, and people who have the cash to throw about in here pretending that it is should have their bank accounts raided and the money given to charitable causes. Jimmyz is the bar equivalent of a cocaine habit, a way of wasting money trying to kid yourself that you're not worthless shite, and if you drink there you're a fool. It's as simple as that.

For: Their idea that a happy hour game - press the silver button and look at a screen, basically - could somehow be 'decadent' fills me with mirth.
Against: We missed the happy hour and got absolutely shafted.

In typical newspaper style, I'm going to tuck away the apology at the end of the review, hoping your mind will have been set in its ways by the screaming headlines of the initial report. You know what I mean. Page 1 of Sunday edition says 'Evil Teacher Tortures Kids'; hidden away on page 17 of Tuesday's late night final, long after windows have been put through and tyres slashed you get 'We're sorry. We meant to say that he only gave a B instead of an A+' Where am I going with this? Oh aye, apparently it's a lot cheaper through the week and a vast improvement on the pre-refit state. I'm just bitter that I'm skint and always will be.

Martha's

The Side, NE1 8TD
'A happy finish off the Pope'

Pinching the service questionnaire from one of the booths in Martha's, the drab little bar of the Vermont Hotel, I notice from the website it directs me to, that this pub is a 'popular meeting place for the over 20s'. Well, aye, technically that's correct, but when they say over 20s, I can tell you without fear of contradiction they really mean the over 40s. And, by crikey, it's desperate. Martha's is an ideal blind date venue for love's second and third-chancers, each with a buttonhole of woe and dragging matching Samsonite emotional baggage along by its dodgy handle. 'H-how will I recognise you?' they'll nervously stammer beforehand. 'I'll be the blancmange in the corner, gawping at the myriad photos of the heroes of my heyday, all bunged on the wall in no real order except where they fit round the aircon vents.' Fucking hell, man: those photos are a joke. What are they getting at? Are they the sort of people they wish would turn up to give this place a bit of class? Ha! I've got more chance of getting a happy finish off the Pope - the last one, the dead one - than these bastards have of seeing Natalie Imbruglia in here. Why would any respectable celebrity patronise this horrible bar, whose only concession to the turn of the millennium was to ditch the embarrassing Blues Brothers dummies, the ones that looked like they'd been swiped from a high street amusement arcade? Has George Michael got a thing about distempered walls? Is Björk big on conservatory windows? Will Sharleen Spiteri's next CD have a pervading atmosphere of defeat and reflections on wasted life inspired by a night spent weeping in here? Of course not. They wouldn't come here in a million years, not even if there was a gram of coke and an inflatable sheep alongside the complimentary After Eight on their hotel room pillow. And I can't even hand out plus points for the courtyard outside, since it's right under the railway viaduct. You're sitting on a summer's eve, chilling in the breeze and snorking up the smells of the Quayside's restaurants, and what happens? A train thunders over, the seagulls start flapping and shitting with fear, and their dribbling, fishy poop falls straight into your pint. Doesn't sound like my ideal night out.

For: It wasn't - when we visited - as ferociously expensive as we'd found it on all the other times we'd been conned into going. However, joining up the dots on the drinks menus, there seems to be a black hole for Saturday night peak time prices, where I suspect even a plain pint of Foster's will be £POA.
Against: The mezzanine level. If you dive at the correct angle, and propel yourself with the right force, you'll snap your neck the instant you land and it'll all be over. The fucking mezzanine was locked.

Celebrities? Trains? I remember once standing on the platform of

Central Station and seeing this specky little fart that I vaguely recognised. Finally it dawned on me where I knew him from, so I said to our lass, 'Look - subtly - over my shoulder. Is that Paul McKenna over there?' Sure was: a quick peek at his tour schedule in the paper proved it. A couple of minutes later, though, the baldy bastard walks up behind me and mutters to the back of my head, 'Yeah. I am.' What an arrogant wanker. The thing that struck me as odd was this: if he's such a mindbender and king of the paranormal, why did he have to come and tell me I was right? Why couldn't the weasel have just stayed where he was and sent the news over by telepathy? Something funny going on there.

Offshore 44

40 Sandhill, NE1 3JF
'Rammed like Fudges in a fat girl's face'

Offshore 44 is a bar that looks like it can't decide what it wants to be. Is it a timber framed old grunter pub playing on its genuinely historical Quayside tradition, with nautical pictures and ropes around the bar and furniture? Or is it a thumping, wailing, shuddering fun bar for the newly paid and short of responsibility? I'll tell you what I think it is, and that's a fu... hang on a minute. How many times have I been in here? Dozens. Yet this is the first time I've noticed that it's supposed to look like a ship? Now why is that? Is it because, stripped through vanity of my jam-jar geps, I'm Mr Magoo before the trip to Ultralase? It's possible, aye. But it's more likely that it's because Offshore has always been rammed like Fudges in a fat girl's face every single time I've been piped aboard. With what sort of punters? I don't know, man. There's just a jumble of limbs, with the odd spaghetti-strap here and a bought-ripped jeans leg there. And, floating over it all, are horns and hair dye, wigs and willies, all the tell-tale signs of the stag and hen crowd marking off every bar along the quay like dogs pissing up the lamp posts. It's brimming, it's mobbed, it's overflowing, and it's packed. Any time after Second Dog Watch - that's 8pm to you - you can guarantee it. But why the hell it's so popular I'll never understand. Does anyone actually get the chance to drink in here, let alone get smashed and party? I doubt it, since if they're not pushing for the bogs, then they're pushing to get out. And if they're pushing to the courtyard, it's not the bloody burgers from the summer weekend barbecues they're after, it's just the heavenly scent of the cool night air. Christ, I thought I was going to die in there.

For: The thought that there's a pool table in the front room, and of the forty-a-side teams playing winner-stays-on.
Against: Here man. Watch where you're gannin', you fucking tit.

There is a ghost in this pub, and it resides by the bottom of the staircase to the upper bar. I know ghosts are meant to be frightening, but this spook's party piece just amuses me no end. Stand by the bandit or under the Offshore mosaic and watch it: In pile the screeching factory girls, and out comes the spectral tripwire. Thump, thump, thumpity-thump; another bulking great hippo falls flat on her jowls up the steps, blue cocktail slopping one way and decorum dribbling the other. Never fails, in all the times I've been here. Long live the undead.

Pitcher & Piano

108 The Quayside, NE1 3DX
'Worth the effort'

Architectural marvel and overpriced tourist hotspot, the Pitcher & Piano is like an Ikea store set in a greenhouse, but without the good bits of either. One of the first real movers and shakers in the dolling up of the Quayside - and handily right next to the Millennium Bridge - this place has been pulling in the cultural visitors to sunny Newcastle and fleecing them good and proper for a while now. And I still don't much care for it. Can't quite put my finger on why, though. Maybe it's the punters, all designer distressed clothing, twenty-minute tans and not a complete personality between them. Perhaps it's the depressing sight of the scruffy urchins outside, trudging through the broken glass and trying to scrounge tabs off all and sundry. Or maybe it's just the fact that there are now dozens of similar places in Newcastle where you can pay so much for so little, that it's hardly worth the effort of dragging yourself all the way along here. Plus, I've always found the beer to be nigh on undrinkable, the staff contemptible, and the experience of taking in all the redeveloped views from the beer terrace such a crushing disappointment. I've been in for food and it's always been burnt or tepid. I've tried meeting them halfway by dressing like one of those fucking 'metrosexuals', and still been ignored at the bar. I've even asked - politely - for one of their expensive cocktails and got a full jug of orange juice squirted 'accidentally' in my face without so much as an apology, unless pouting and snorting are the new sorry. Man, this place blows. I hate it, to be honest. Even if I was scratching around for a positive slant, I'd have to say something along the lines of, if there's something decent on at the Baltic over the bridge, you could pop in here afterwards for a swift piss and an even swifter half. But if your bladder was up to it, you'd be a fool to choose it over the likes of the Tyne or the Free Trade.

For: If you hotwired a Navy gunboat, this place would make an excellent target.
Against: Men's facial grooming products - moisturisers, conditioners, cleansers and toners - make it so much harder to land a decent punch.

If there's ever some big event on the Quayside and you think, 'Let's go to the Pitcher and Piano and watch it from the balcony', then forget it: the uppity twats from the BBC will have commandeered the place. Mind you, if Lara Rostron from the local news is up there - TV's foxiest werepig - they'll need more than bouncers to keep me out.

The Quayside

35 The Close, NE1 3RN
'Tripping up the joggers'

Although The Quayside is set in a 16th Century medieval ware-house, being one of the bars of the JD Wetherspoon Lloyds No.1 brand it caters to the more discerning, upmarket bland chain bar clientele rather than the traditional, rustic bland chain bar customers of its parent company. A face-slapping racket of thumping tunes, with beach parties out in the cobbled courtyard - or under the umbrellas, if wet - the bar is a popular destination for the unavoidable stag, hen and office parties, and there's not a night goes by without the appearance of a rotund executive done up (like a fucking kipper, I'd say) as Ali G or some other celebrity from the fancy dress shop's sale rail. Sightseers and lovers of industrial heritage among you may care to note that the raised level gives you a perfect view over the Tyne to the delights of the Ovoline Lubricants factory. Tremendous. I'm serious. And entertainment for the bored and agitated comes in electronic form, with as many flashing buttons as you can press before you're down to your pocket fluff, plus the usual range of plasma screens, minority sports channels seemingly password-locked into place. But that's all immaterial. The main real reason to come here - and jostle with the bastards who just fail to realise it was your idea first and that you alone should have the best seat available - is the beer garden facing the river. Aye, to you it might just be a load of concrete slabs and a few picnic tables, but to us it's the French Riviera, a gorgeous waterside retreat to laze away the hours until the sun sets over Scotswood then sneaks round the back before the toerags have had a chance to pinch its wallet. And, bless them, the management seem to have no absolutely no problem with you taking your beer out of the confines of the pub area, strolling down the quayside and tripping up the joggers. No bollocks about designated zones or plastic glasses here; just a bit of trust for the customer. And comprehen-sive insurance cover.

For: It's a Wetherspoon pub. Therefore it's cheap.

Against: Your fantastic view of the Tyne's bridges will be marred - until 2058, if they encounter any more unexpected hiccups - by the flapping great white tarpaulins along the High Level Bridge. Why can't they employ some bored graffiti artists to make a reasonable stab at spray-painting on an image of what's supposed to be underneath? And if a few of the fuckers fall to their doom in the process, that's just unfortunate.

Those lovely lads roaring past on their jet-skis are great, aren't they? Parading their wealth and their knobbly knees on a Sunday evening when you're having a couple of sunset jars. Of course we're rooting for them. Of course we wish them all the best. That's why we laugh like a gurgling drain and throw celebratory rocks at them when they fall arse over tit and get a gob-full of Tyne water. Smugness: karma will intervene.

Quilted Camel

36 Sandhill, Quayside, NE1 3JF
'Buggy-pushing scratters'

Possibly my least favourite and most infrequently visited pub on the Quayside, The Quilted Camel has had an extensive refit since the last time I braved a review and has become, as you'd expect from somewhere subtitled 'Honeyrooms', a tarts' bar. With a dubious Gothic fetish theme, the place has clearly been redes-igned to appeal to thick, buggy-pushing scratters who've finally twigged that they'll never, ever be a princess, but still want to live out some sort of hackneyed fairytale, even if it's just over a sickly cocktail on their night off from the kids. It's that sort of fantasy. I've got no idea when the refit was done, so I don't know whether they've based it on Perdu in the city centre or the other way round, but there are certainly similarities, what with the beaded dividers, the retro-space-age chrome fittings, the colour scheme that ranges from the darkest purple all the way up to black, and the general murk. There's an ever-changing lighting scheme, so subtle and useless that still gets overpowered by the

41

candles flickering to the beat of Backstreet Boys classics and, if that's still too bright for you then, at the back, they've got a pitch black room with a pitch black carpeted bed. It confused the fuck out of me, that thing: I must've looked like I was doing the can-can while I was edging round it, alternately kicking thin air and some sort of invisible solid mass, and all the while trying to balance four pints and a bag of late-night shopping. I tried the bed thing myself, just for gimmickry's sake, once I'd worked out what it was. And I really wished I hadn't; my self-disgust at rolling about in the dandruff and scabs and hockle and spilt drink of the average Quayside drinker who'd been there before me left me feeling more than a little disturbed, and it took a 45-minute shower when I got home just to scrub off the fucking filth. True story. And once we'd sacked off the bed thing and gone hunting for seats, we got a better look at the rest of the decor, especially the big, I dunno, fucking castle or something behind the main bar, made out of earwax. There's a roaring lion's head fire up the far end, glitter balls down the other, Medusa masks here and there, and every available surface is daubed in what appears to be their corporate logo, some sort of inkblot test. And if you visualise all that lot and add pictures of exotic strippers - as opposed to For Your Eyes Only dollops - and other scenes of associated debauchery you'll have an exact mental image of the Quilted Camel: an expensively-refurbished, pretendy-lavish, over-crowded, terrible bar for dunces. I trust I don't need to tell you to give it a miss.

For: If there's ever a pub that'll make you abandon the humiliating Quayside-crawling work night out and piss off home long before the inevitable slide along to Buffalo Joe's, then it's this one.
Against: Burlesque Glamour. What the fucking hell is Burlesque Glamour?

Seriously, though: that bed thing. For about a week afterwards I was plagued by zits and boils and rashes and itches, right around the back of my neck where I'd been lying on their scatter cush-

ions. *You can call it psychosomatic if you want; I call it deeply disturbing.*

The Red House
32 Sandhill, NE1 3JF
'Life slowly ticking away'

The Red House isn't exactly the former home of celebrated local trollop Bessie Surtees, role model for Newcastle's female Quay-side-goers, but it's in the same block and that's close enough for me. Equally a haunt for whistling pensioners and chirruping hens, from the outside the Red House looks like a tiny, rustic boozer, but once you get inside you find a million different rooms, corri-dors and bricked-up dead ends; I'm ashamed to admit that I've never yet managed to get from the snug to the front door without cocking it up somewhere down the line. The building is from Jacobean times - whenever they were - so I reckon we can safely say that the cellar effect in the back few rooms is genuine, and with its dark wood and orange lighting, the overall atmosphere is one of relaxing gloominess without the perilous descent into depressing. This, you'll agree, makes it better for a slow after-noon session than a night out with the lads. I just wonder what the designers were playing at the last time they gave this place a refit, since I have no frigging idea what the hell the theme is supposed to be in here. It's like they started on a few rough sketches and then never quite got their lazy, overpaid arses in gear for long enough to carry any of them through. I can imagine them sat round a meeting room table on a Friday afternoon, with the stopwatch eating away at their client's budget. 'Red House, yeah? Like, red, like, Russian, yeah? Like, a balalaika? Like, in a glass case?' Meanwhile some other tit is going, 'A cellar? Doesn't that just say 'railway carriage theme' to you?' Typically, nothing is finished and little gets done, and they just bugger off to the pub, or chop out a line, or draw dicks on each other's heads and charge it to the account, or do whatever else designers that I've just invented do on an afternoon. Getting away from all this stupid prattle and down the factual stuff about the damned bar, as I suppose I must at some point, the beer in here is pretty good, and the food - from the same kitchen as Bob Trollop next door, I understand - is decent enough, though I've felt my life slowly ticking away waiting for my Sunday dinner when I've been out with the folks. To be honest, I don't get in here that often, which is a pity because I quite like the place. If you're down on the Quayside and you prefer listening to the sound of your own heartbeat to the din of a DJ, then I'd thoroughly recommend it. But don't blame me if it all kicks off later.

For: It isn't the Quilted Camel.
Against: I've taken to carrying a ball of string with me, like him (or was it her?) out of that story where there's, like, this maze and this gadgie with a bull's head or something. Exactly like that, aye.

Bessie Surtees was the daughter of a wealthy merchant who lived on the Quayside in Newcastle in the eighteenth century. When she fell in love with a coal merchant's son, the match was frowned upon, so the headstrong Bessie climbed out of a first floor window and eloped to Scotland. An eyewitness was later heard to exclaim to reporters from the local Scrofula Times, 'She could have put her fucking bloomers on before she backed down that ladder. Jesus wept! It was like a thatched roof.'

The Slug & Lettuce
Exchange Buildings, Quayside, NE1 3DW
'The lunatic by the fireplace with a rifle pointed at my head'

Part of a national chain, the Slug & Lettuce wins the award hands down for Newcastle's blandest pub. In the age where homemakers are advised to neutralise everything to maximise sell-on value, this place has followed suit, ditched all that could even hint at a personality, and if it has any sort of mission statement then I'd expect it to be something like 'Let's not have too much character, eh?' And the trouble is, when a bar has so little to occupy the mind, you end up concentrating on the tiny details just to stop yourself from losing consciousness, like the teetering pile of grubby napkins just inside the doorway that reveals itself to be a standard lamp, or the angle between the cream wall and the salmon pink one, the bit that's painted as well as my spare room was the day after my last tequila marathon. You can't seriously tell me a professional did that. There's art for sale on the walls, but... quick, quick, let me hide this bit here while she's not looking. Call it my message in a bottle, my scribbled note through the cell window, or my desperate eye signals to the milkman about the lunatic by the fireplace with a rifle pointed at my head, but I need to communicate this cry for help. Reading the menu in the Slug & Lettuce, our lass tells me she's not keen on egg pasta, and only likes the wheat stuff. She seems to have it in her head that the fettuccini or whatever is only made from one ingredient – egg or wheat – right up until I point out to her that egg pasta with no wheat in it is a fucking omelette. Shit, she's coming back... but it's art that's been watered down and decaffeinated: Michael Jackson's moonwalking feet, Elvis, Diana Ross, Che Guevara, anyone whose iconic image can be stolen from a remainder shop calendar rack, painted over by a child and given a laughable price tag. It's the sort of shite most frequently seen alongside Closing Down Sale posters - usually in shops with names that have dot.com or an '@' sign somewhere in them - and I can virtually guarantee that you have pictures like that in your home, behind your settee with matching lamps, clock, plant pots, bookshelf and coasters, all in brown leather. A black and white digital 'painting' of your first-born's snotty face? How did I guess? I bet you feel really individual, even though you'll be throwing it out in shame this time next year. But I'm only having a pop at you because there's so little to work on in here. What the hell am I supposed to say about a place as nondescript this? I can't even just go for the default setting and say, 'Ho ho ho. It's like an Ikea store', since it's not even that remarkable. It's more like the dreary furniture pages in the Index catalogue or the Kays one or whichever glossy shite gets left on our front step to tell the burglary trade that there's no fucker home. The Slug & Lettuce is a pub for people who don't like pubs, playing music for people who don't like music, and serving up food to people who haven't the slightest comprehension of the trendy label that's been applied to it: this year's rustic being the same as last year's fusion, an itty-bitty burger on a fucking massive plate. I actually feel cheated that I've shelled out for an experience that I have no recollection of whatsoever, and if this is what passes for normality, I'd sooner take outrageous pretension any day of the week. Fuck, I'd even go to Boom.

For: Dull enough to sedate the stag parties, giving a half-hour window of peace, quiet and respectability before they start their pillage.

Against: For your benefit, I'm always checking out bar websites to ensure accuracy in the reviews. I'm confident you've noticed and are very appreciative. On the Slug site, there's a graphic that undulates the words 'slurp swill slurp swill' before your disbelieving eyes. What? They're charging you the earth for a pint, and all they can do is rip the piss out of it, and you? They've got some bloody sauce.

Being on the semi-residential Quayside, there's a notice inside the doorway in the Slug & Lettuce that politely requests customers to respect the neighbours. I wish to fuck there was one of those in my street, I tell you. What is it about drunken idiots arguing at three in the morning that makes them want to spell out their viewpoints at a volume that's not just loud enough for their opponent, but is sufficient to wake up half the bloody road, too? Do they really expect me to go, 'That's a very valid point, actually. You have every right to feel aggrieved. Please continue this contretemps with my blessing'? Or are they just daring me to reach for the bedside bazooka before ducking out of sight behind the nearest hedge? Shut up and get to bed, you daft cunt.

Stereo

Sandgate, NE1 4AG
'Utopian drinking experience'

When Stereo first opened, I stated quite boldly that the pub had been ruined, and that its only saving grace - a Perspex bubble chair hanging from a chain - would be broken within the month. Clambering up the stairs for a sneaky revisit, I find that 'ruined' doesn't even come close to describing what has happened here: in the past few years this place has been absolutely destroyed, and that flaming bubble chair is now the only thing left intact. Every seat has been slashed, every surface battered, every footstool hoofed about and, as with most derelict buildings, some fucker has snuck along during the night and pasted up fly-posters everywhere. The paint's peeling, decking planks are scuffed to buggery, and everything you accidentally touch has the sticky film of last night's happy hour. How has a pub been allowed to disintegrate so completely in such a short period of time? This to me is the perfect example of what happens when you're a clever shite and you think you know best, and every greedy get with even the slightest interest in updating a pub should be dragged in here by the ear, forced on pain of death to observe what is wrong, and be told, with no room for misunderstanding, that THIS is what their folly will amount to. Buff my bollocks and call me Barry, but the state of this place nowadays has me nostalgic for even the chain bar nonentity of the Fog & Firkin that it was previously, never mind the utopian drinking experience of the Barley Mow before that. There really is fuck all left to see in here, and the only good thing about the whole bar is the view of what's outside, the rejuvenated Quayside. And believe me - as long as you're brave enough to wipe the smears off the sliding glass doors first - you'll spend a long time looking at it. You'll need something to justify the ridiculous price of your lacklustre pint, anyway. This can't be right. There must be something I'm missing. Maybe the ruination was part of the plan all along. Could the theme here actually be some sort of post-apocalyptic fallout zone, set shortly after the MDF wars? Maybe to complete their vision, the futuristic shell of the pub needed the natural, organic collapse of its interior. It's all fitting into place. Look at those knobs out there, on the ledge of the bit that used to be the town's best beer garden before some jerk glassed it over. Look at them standing at the barbecue, like tramps around a brazier in a desolate wasteland. Maybe they're all in on the prank, and I'm the only sad bastard who doesn't get it. I certainly hope so, because the alternative is unthinkable.

For: Hey! At least I can't say it's bland anymore!
Against: Indie superclub Stonelove - responsible for every last one of those fly-posters - may possibly have the best music of any club in the land, but for using the word 'Djography' on their website, they should be kneed in the groin from now until Christmas. Unless you're reading this on Christmas Eve, in which case we'll say Halloween.

I picked up a flyer on the way out, advertising the Stereo Sunday Market, with stalls including vintage photography, records, jewellery and textiles. Add to that 'fixtures & fittings, pint glasses, competent bar staff, and self-respect' and everything suddenly becomes clear.

Tavistock
57-60 Sandhill, NE1 3RG
'Forgive me, Lord, but I would...'

I got up late this morning. I'm not going into the details of why my head was throbbing like a bastard, but by the time I got to the papershop my normal Sunday paper had sold out. Flicking contemptuously through the glossy pile of shite that fell out of my potluck replacement, I see that this season jeans 'will be skin-tight'. It's there, in print, in black on white, with a sketch of some dumb bint to illustrate the point. Not 'the public have chosen', but a simple statement of fact that you'll be able to buy nowt else in the shops this year, purely because some size zero gak-head cunt has decreed that it shall be so. And while you're watching yard-wide arses ballooning over inch-thick ankles, think about the similarities between the rag trade and the pub industry. Bluntly put, if you want to open a bar in this day and age, then it has to look like this place. No argument; you get this because this is all you can get. Picture a designer bar in your head, a luxury venue for the upmarket drinker. Fuck knows you've had enough examples lately. You done it yet? Tavistock is exactly what you imagined. It's purple; it has laminate flooring; it's got dark wood in abundance; and there are branches in pots spreading up the walls and over the ceiling. I knew it would look like this before I even got off the bus, never mind stepped through the pub door and, to make matters worse, I was half humming the bar's choice of tunes on the way there; hideous pasteurised jazz from the dismal likes of Bublé and Cullum and all the other soundtrackers of domestic death by dinner party. Round the corner sits Jools Holland's piano in a further nod towards polite background tinkling - though woe betide anyone who touches the fucker - and behind the tasteful wooden blinds lie bizarre corporate logos of sunbursts of forks. All very luxurious, all very now, and all sac-scratchingly dull. See the trouble is, if you're bored and a pedantic twat like me, you notice all the little things that they've fucked up, and you feel the need to rip the piss accordingly. It's no good, he said in the manner of that old bird with the blonde bob off Channel 5's *Hotel Inspector* (forgive me, Lord, but I would...), having a lavish setting, then pissing it away with a menu full of spelling howlers. And it isn't even remotely classy to list the exact quantities of the cocktail garnishes - three grapes, four cherries, five mint leaves - like it's some sort of special service. As for the punters, I haven't a fucking clue. Not because they defied description, but because there weren't any. Aye, I know it was early doors, six bells on a Saturday night, but for a three pint duration we were literally the only customers; I could understand it if the rest of the Quayside was dead, but when the nearby Akenside, Red House and Crown Posada were all respectably busy, it's cause for concern. Maybe it's the sign above the door, with the word 'Bar' lost between 'Restaurant' and 'Grill' that's putting off the punters; maybe it just looks too flash, leading people to expect another Perdu-style condescension; or maybe, like in the Akenside, people only appreciate a pub if they've had to wrestle their way to the bar. I almost feel sorry for them; the beer was pretty good, and the barman was only brushing up his bottle spinning to stave off the tedium. But in a saturated market it helps if your Unique Selling Point amounts to more than 'we're exactly the same as everywhere else'.

For: I can't be sure, but to me it looks like there's a pole dancing area by the downstairs bogs.
Against: Don't know about you, but the thought of Debbie from Direct Debits grinding away there after a night on the trebles doesn't exactly stiffen my staff.

I'm too skint for taxis, and the only time a limo will ever arrive at my house for a social occasion is for my funeral, so that's why I get the bus to town when I'm on the lash. And it's a thoroughly demoralising experience. I don't mind the sharp rise in CCTV coverage – I've got nowt to hide, plus I'd sooner log on to YouTube to see what drunken atrocities I've been up to than rely on equally hammered witnesses - but I'd prefer to see the footage later rather than real-time. I leave the house feeling like a god yet, thanks to the security-psychotic bus companies, wide-angle views of my bloated carcass and wonky head appear on the screen above the ticket bin every six seconds, shattering my confidence before I cross the Tyne Bridge. And how come nobody ever told me I walk like John Inman?

thirty 3i8ht

Exchange Buildings, Quayside, NE1 3DE
'Look at me! I'm a tourist tit!'

Like weeds strangling down a delicate rose, the ravages of time and the whims of the drinking public will often destroy a thing of rare beauty. And so it is with this bar. Once the sleekest of the sleek and the wankiest of the wanky, with minimal design so studied that they had bloody kumquats placed for maximum colour scheme effect, thirty 3i8ht has suffered punctured pretensions over the years and, in trying to ingratiate itself with dumb-fuck Quayside customers, is now no stranger to the humiliating climbdown. You can even see it from the outside, where they've had to stick up a sign reading 'Bar 38' for people too remedial-level to work out what the hell 'thirty 3i8ht' was meant to say. Inside is no better. The basic shell of the place remains, along with the fake portholes in the walls and the wavy benches, but all the eclectic arty stuff, like the mobiles - that's mobiles as in Alexander Calder and not Nokia (look the bastard up) - and whatnot has long since vanished. And the atmosphere has changed from a luxury venue into a fading student pub. Not good. Other elements missing in action? The front room lit from the floor tiles up is now buried beneath a slouch of scatter cushions, while the daft leather igloo thing in the corner is painted in back-of-garage green and bereft of the projections of blue skies and fluffy clouds that once graced it and the foreheads of the beautiful ones inside. And now who's sitting in it, that slashed, scarred, filthy relic from a bygone age? Why, that'll be the out-of-towners, of course. It's a dead giveaway: anyone dim enough to park their arse in there these days might as well wear a T-shirt - retro stencilled by the Duffer of St George, mind – saying, 'Look at me! I'm a tourist tit!' Even the indestructible designer bogs are looking scuffed and defeated; if I'd thought on and applied for some ludicrous research grant when the bar first opened, I could have documented the exact effects of Foster's piss on shiny stainless steel. Missed opportunity there, I reckon. Look, I'll be honest with you; I was no real fan of the manifesto beforehand, and Christ knows I've slagged off enough bars for doing what thirty 3i8ht did first, but it just seems so disappointing that they've buckled under. Let's face it, if you're going to act the cunt, then at least have the courage and the decency to stick to your guns.

For: Set between Fever and Exchange, it shines like a diamond.
Against: Before witnessing how badly the rot had set in I was mentally composing a review that was a triumph of smart-arsery, full of scathing social commentary, peppered with references to

Catalonian art movements and liberal quotations from 20th century literature classics. That's that fucked, then.

It would have been a breeze to do that research project, though. I'd have - quite literally - pissed £300,000 of taxpayers' money up the nearest wall before handing in my thesis of six words to front-page headline scorn. Those six words? 'Del Boy falling through the bar'. Well, fuck man; it's the answer to most in-depth studies these days. I fail to see why I should miss out on my slice of the pie.

The Waterline

96 East Quayside, NE1 3DH
'Cackle, and cackle, and cackle again'

Once a gloomy pub burdened with a tacky shipping theme, the Waterline is now one of the finest spicy wedges restaurant-bars in the whole area between the Law Courts and City Road. An abundance of creams and whites and neutral tones, not to mention a large glass awning projecting onto the East Quayside, have given the bar a spirit-drainingly dull look and, thanks to the massive wood burning pizza oven at the back, every day of the year is like a fucking inferno. The Waterline is very popular with tourists and Quayside strollers who fancy an average pint in an average bar to go with the average contemporary art they've just pretended to understand in the Baltic over the river whilst really only going there to play in the lifts. I know this to be true, because it's exactly what I've done on the rare occasions I've been here. And my lack of attendance - together with the complete absence of anything noteworthy to mock in the decor - is the reason why I'm going to spend the rest of this review expanding on something I half-noticed when the missus was prattling on in my ear. There's an annexe in an older part of the pub off to the right that holds a pool table and, if my eyes don't deceive me, a semi-private party, which is to say a gang of meat-headed lads in co-ordinating catalogue casual clothing, hollering like fuck and casting the odd lecherous glance in the direction of the occupants of the pub's left-hand side. This, as you can probably imagine, means hen party weekenders, stopping by and meeting up, suitcase in tow, on their way to the Travelodge out the back. 'Eeh!' they're all saying, 'Your hair's ever so slightly different from the last time I saw you! Isn't it amazing?!' Then they cackle, and cackle, and cackle again, until one of them ruins the mood and the whole weekend by saying something worthwhile. Only kidding: there's been nothing interesting said on any hen party since Eve went out for a few cocktails with the snake and thought, Stuff this talk about the meaning of original sin; I just want to blather on about the new colour scheme in the Garden of Eden. And about the size of Adam's knob. Hee hee hee! Look at the L-plate on me fig leaf! Ah, you can't knock them for wanting to get away for a while though, can you? Which right-thinking gentleman isn't secretly jealous of the perfect girlie weekend? Don't we all long for a pampering, a few chatty beers and then fourteen hours in casualty waiting to get the bits of Bacardi Breezer bottle removed from the back of our heads? Of course we do. And if that means our entire day is spent saying, I says she says I says she says eeh I says she says never in the world I says she says I says she says I says she says eeeh, just before bursting into tears, then that's the price we'll pay.

For: If you can grab a seat outside on a warm summer evening with the sun setting behind the Tyne Bridge then you'll be laughing.
Against: The fucking stretch limos cruising past, with their shrieking occupants and their trails of spilt alcopops leaking from the bottoms of the doors. Why do people STILL think these things are a 'good laugh'?

Our lass - who is a berk at the best of times - suggests that I ought to give special mention to the little bloke who sits out the back with the tub of spuds, painstakingly carving them into twister fries. I've got an appointment with the solicitor this very week. He'd better pull his fucking finger out.

2

The Burglar's Dog Stag & Hen Party Special

People from all over the nation send us e-mails. They say, 'Dear The Burglar's Dog. We are having a stag weekend and plan to visit your town like a biblical plague of locusts, destroy it, and then move on, but we're much too lazy to read all the words that you have so lovingly written. Please tell us everything we need to know about your city so that we can ignore what you say, and busy ourselves with shrink-wrapping our naked mate to a lamp-post and punching passers-by out cold. Oh, and any chance you could pull the birds for us too, and maybe get them moist since we're too bloody stupid and ugly?' It's not just thick blokes, either: myriad are the times we've been promised, 'Hee hee hee! We'll buy you a pint! Thanks hun!' by giggling, smiley-using bimbos for telling them where they can meet 'lush lads' who are just as dim as they are.

And why not? Party organisers have so much on their plates with sorting out Elvis costumes, devil's horns and comedy marital aids that there's very little time left to work out where the hell they're actually going to go. But it is with a gladsome heart that we reply to our correspondents - time and time again - with itineraries and facts, even though there's zero chance of them being followed. Happy-to-help-have-a-nice-day-please-call-again, that's us. After all, stag and hen nights provide a welcome boost to our city's economy, giving many, many hours of overtime to street cleaners, emergency glaziers and community police. And where would our ethnic restaurant and takeaway proprietors be without their weekly helping of ribald racism from pissed-up, kilt-wearing tourists?

Oh, we really love seeing stags and hens doing their stuff, we do. Don't know about you, but every time we see one of those smashing groups of people, we always think, hmm, they look like an affable bunch, think I'll go and talk to them and see what they've got to say about life. Never will you hear these words pass our lips: 'Oh for fuck's sake, not another bunch of tedious cunts. Who would marry that glakey fucker, like? Hope they burn the twat alive.' And those racy little nametags on hen nights! They crease us up! Let's hear it for Anorexic Angela, Burdened with six kids by seven fathers Brenda, Cum on my curtains Caroline, Desperate to diet Debs, Egotistical oestrogen deprived Yvonne, Fuck me in the lavatory I'm not getting it at home Fiona, Gargantuan gunted Glenda... we love 'em to bits, every last pig-squealing one of 'em.

But hey, just because we're honest, upstanding, respectful local citizens, it doesn't mean that they can't come to our city and let their hair down a little. There's no law against interlopers acting like complete tits, wearing stupid outfits and vomiting in our roads. Yet. And let's not forget all those shitty little print-Ur-own T-shirt merchants whose very livelihoods are dependent on slapping fuzzy photos of semi-naked holiday drunkards on ill-fitting, pauper-weight garments for such glamorous occasions. Imagine their fall in turnover if the words 'Billy Bollocks On Tour' were never again seen - in fucking Comic Sans font - in the city's streets, bars and holding cells. Hats off to these champions of industry: they're what makes Britain Great.

So, definitively, once and for all, the Burglar's Dog aims to give the low-down on the stag and hen scene in Newcastle. We'll tell you the places to go to keep out of our faces, the pubs that have a devastation-repair kitty factored into their operating budgets, and the bars where, clearly, Sodom and Gomorrah still thrive. Plus, we'll tell you what's HOT and what's NOT, using the very latest research from our terminally angry reporters.

STYLE AND DEPORTMENT

Acting in the correct manner is important to you, isn't it? You want to be seen wearing only the latest trends, don't you? After all, you wouldn't want to stick out like a sore thumb and have people think that you're an unruly, drunken, manners-of-a-sow travesty of human flesh, would you? These are the things that are currently - and will be forever thus - hot and not in the stag and hen party world. Get them right and we might not kill you; get them wrong and you'll be nailed to a plank and floated up the Tyne.

Hot
Decorum
Warm hands of friendship
Keeping the fuck out of our sight
What the Irish call 'the craic'
Respect for the moral standards of the local population
Only laughing at things that are actually amusing
Sensible shoes
Dignity
Checking in at the hotel before you start drinking
The ability to say 'Why aye, man' without sounding Welsh or Pakistani
Realising you're an complete and utter pain in the arsehole

...and Not
Bacchanalia
Unsolicited displays of genitalia
Being in any way visible
Screaming like a brutally-buggered baboon within our collective earshot
Banging the town bike over a bin
Cackling at your own 'jokes'
Ball and chain combinations
Drag

Leaving your suitcases all over the floor in O'Neill's
Being Scottish. Or Cockney. Or a country bumpkin
Thinking you're in any way cool, funny or original

WHERE TO DRINK
When it comes to the matter of ideal drinking circuits, there is
but one question to ask yourself: Do you want to hang around
with fuckwits, or do you want to hang around with fuckwits
wearing Burberry hats? Newcastle has two main areas catering to
the likes of you: The Bigg Market (hats on), home of the football
hooligan, the underage drinker and the habitual criminal; and The
Quayside (hats off), where the clothes are more expensive, the
'flap' a little more 'class', but the IQ no higher. These are the
places to be seen in your stupid Mickey Mouse ears or your spew-
spattered gorilla suit. These are the places where anything goes
and where dignity is just a shit song by Deacon Blue on Century
FM's '80s Hour. And these are the places where we absolutely
insist you go.

Sure, there are other neighbourhoods in town, but you really,
really don't want to go to them. They're full of lemon-sucking
miseries like us, who have ambitions no loftier than a nice few
pints and decent conversation, and would never dare to scale the
dizzy heights of drunken indecent exposure or pizza-clutching
doorway fellatio. Some people just don't know what 'fun' is. Not
like you crazy kids.

Cast your mind back to chapter 1 in this book and flick forward to chapters 11 and 12: these sections feature all the bars
we think you should visit. In fact, we insist you do. In each
carefully selected locale mentioned, we guarantee a surly,
grudging welcome, queues a mile long and beer within a nano-
second of its sell-by date. They're loud, they're expensive, and
they're far and away the fightingest bars in the Northern Hemisphere. Choose wisely.

And for last orders? Let's be honest here: like salmon returning to their native rivers to breed, so do party 'goers' head
inexorably for Buffalo Joe's on the Gateshead side of the Swing
Bridge looking for love, friendship, and maybe tops and fingers.
Fact: you will end up there. Fact: you will buy a fucking glittery

cowboy hat. Fact: we will hate you, unreservedly.

WHERE TO STAY

What are we, like: the frigging tourist board? How should we know? Why in the name of Jaheseus Christ would we pay good money to stay in a hotel when we can walk home from the city centre? If it's any help, we hear that the Jury's Inn is quite popular with 'visiting groups'. They apparently have a bit of a downer on loose morals, though: a mutual friend of ours was barred from taking his new lady friend to his room simply because she was an obvious last-orders-on-the-dance-floor case. Yeah, go on; try the Jury's. And make sure you go for a few pints in one of the numerous bars between there and the city centre, too. Those customers with tight T-shirts and handlebar 'taches are guaranteed to give you the warmest of welcomes, especially if you start spouting your inbred homophobic bollocks the minute you walk through the door.

Or, you could try the Premier Lodge in the centre of town: it's not too far to crawl back to your room from the clubs with a shattered pint pot sticking out of your neck. And the area around it already stinks to high heaven of piss and puke, so you need have no qualms about making it worse with your appalling conduct.

Where else is there? Oh aye, there's the Malmaison and the Copthorne at opposite ends of the Quayside, if you're feeling particularly flushed, and there's another Premier Lodge in the middle, across the river from that big slugalike Sage building, plus a Travelodge behind the law courts. And bearing in mind bad publicity is better than no publicity, I suppose we'd better rope in the Royal Station Hotel next to the, uh, station, and the Quality Hotel off the top of the Bigg Market.

Anywhere else, you're saying? I dunno, man. Have you never heard of the internet?

No matter which friendly establishment you choose as your resting place, we're sure that you'll find the utmost comfort in which to shave each others eyebrows off and take 'amusing' photos of the saggy genitals of the first of the group to pass out. Remember: it's especially hilarious if you chuck one of your mates, bollock-naked, into the corridor and let them holler vengeful threats into the wee small hours. Other guests will shake you firmly by the hand in the morning after hearing such wizard japes. Just before kicking your head in.

We hope you have found our guide to stag and hen parties in Newcastle upon Tyne useful. If you have any further queries, please do not hesitate to ask some other fucker before you bother us. And, as a friendly word of warning, we would like to make this crystal clear:

If you have used the word 'doo' instead of 'do' on any promotional literature, e-mail, or fckng sms txt msg for your event, we will hunt you down with dogs, and tar and feather each and every one of your party, their relatives, and their nodding acquaintances. And then we'll really fucking kick off.

Finally, we wish the lucky couple all the very best for their impending nuptials. We'll give it six months before she starts banging the window cleaner.

3

Central Station

'Fanning out from John Dobson's 1850 station edifice, the Central Station area is home to some of the city's most architecturally important buildings, and is flanked at each side by a magnificent cathedral; to the west, St Mary's with its statue of Newcastle's own Cardinal Basil Hume, and over to the east the cathedral of St Nicholas, the 15th century lantern tower of which is one of the best known landmarks of the city. The eastern side is also home to the castle built by Henry II between 1168-1178. One of the finest surviving examples of a castle keep in the country, it is this from which Newcastle takes its name.' – *Norman Undercroft, Historian.*

Apartment
28 Collingwood Street, NE1 1JF
'We'll miss you, Doris. You're a star.'

Progenitor of Newcastle's so-called 'Diamond Strip' and the place responsible for adding the word 'luxebar' to the city's illustrated dictionary, Apartment is designed around a Manhattan-style living space boasting plenty of warmth, comfort, and character. It's also the place where one of the employees - masquerading as a random punter - e-mailed the Dog to complain about our attitude to a bar that is simply 'attempting to change the perception of the North East and drag us kicking and screaming into the 21st century'. The tinker. So I'm sitting towards the back end of the pub trying to see what he meant, and shaking my head in utter astonishment that the pint and a half of Carling I have just bought has cost me coppers less than six quid. I'm thinking, hmm, raised wooden area, brickwork illuminated in sickly shades, and a load of grinning berks who've been told to dress in unobtrusive black yet are desperately over-emoting in an attempt to be noticed. Then it strikes me where I've seen this before: Monday to Friday, 4.15 to 5pm, Channel 4. This layout is a kick in the arse off the set for *Deal or No Deal*, and while there may not actually be a Bakelite telephone in the middle of the room, there is definitely some cunt with poorly judged facial hair and a terrible shirt repeating what the voice on his phone is saying for benefit of the sycophants around him. And instead of entering into the spirit of the evening, chanting 'Blue! Blue! Blue!' or tearfully intoning, 'We'll miss you, Doris. You're a star', I'm trying not to lose my temper and I find myself wondering whether I can buy teargas on the internet. Or napalm. Or maybe a sachet of Agent Orange. Fuck me forever and a day: THIS is what you get for your money? THIS is Newcastle's cultural future? I'm talking to someone who knows the place well, and I'm being told that far from being a mish-mash of Next Directory clutter, each of the areas connected by the Benwell back lane concrete floor actually has a different theme: there's a bedroom, a gallery and, for all I know, a frigging larder and a scullery, too. I'm also hearing that you can take advantage of the exclusive Front Room Cocktail Lounge Card or, as the lowly rank and file among us may see it, pay £400 a year to sit in the fucking window. Fancy it? Application forms are available from the staff if you feel confident enough in your 'look' to approach one of them. Failing that, you could just nail your scrotum to the table: it'd be far less painful and at least you'd get the attention you crave. This bar is unspeakably awful. I wouldn't care so much if you got what you paid for, someone from the celebrity world to gawp at. But all I can see around me is the overspill from the Bigg Market or the dregs of the social club scene, all praying that this fucking farrago will give them some sort of higher status. Look at her over there; her with the balloons. Here, woman: you are sixty-three years old, have biceps like turkey wattle and, in all probability, genitalia like thrice-chewed Wrigley's. There is absolutely no need for you to totter about in your white stilettos and your BacoFoil dress when I am trying my level best to nurse some value out of this pint. What the fuck am I even doing here? Every single person in this building is an idiot, and I include myself in that for noticing the bongos on the stage and still failing to spin on my heels back to the doorway. What is wrong with people? Where is the fucking sense in scrimping every penny you earn in your menial job only to piss it away on overpriced mediocrity just to make it look like you haven't had to scrimp every penny? And what is the point of paying membership fees for a place that lets you in for nowt anyway? Bloody hell, man. What is the world coming to? And what was it Groucho Marx said about not wanting to join any club that would have him as a member? Oh, aye, he said, 'Apartment? Wankers. Fuck 'em.' And I, for one, can't argue with that.

For: Ha ha ha. Just been on their website, and it's full of absolute gems. They've actually used the phrase 'to die for' to describe their service! Brilliant.
Against: Does anyone have the faintest idea of what 'people action' is, though? Or the verb 'to couch up'?

I can fully understand you gents who don't want to wash your hands after using the toilets in Apartment. After all, as soon as you lob your cocks out you're entering into an unwritten contract with the pillock by the sinks to hand over a quid for half a squirt of something noxious and a rap on the knuckles with a serviette. But if you must be such a slave to 'your style, your way', is there any chance you could invest in some strong-hold gel or some industrial wax to get your barnet set before you leave the house, instead of rubbing your pissy hands through it after each slash?

@Home

36-38 Mosley Street, NE1 1DL
'In three words: fucking strip joint'

This is a temporary review. And that's because @Home is a temporary bar. Why? I'm not one to blow my own trumpet, but here's a quote from the piece I did just after this place opened: 'I'm afraid that it'll be a matter of months before their minimalist facade becomes plastered with Red Bull cocktail posters like the rest of the city's bars, and not much longer 'til Titty Tuesdays make a regular appearance.' And wouldn't you believe it, that's exactly what is planned for here, albeit under a different name. It's going to be The Navy Bar and Officers' Mess, apparently, a label that aims to conjure up images of gentlemen in white uniforms letting off steam after three months in an iron hull without sight of a woman, gleefully hooting and a-hollering at the Forces Sweetheart and the occasional glimpse of a stocking top. It could, however, be better summed up in three words: fucking strip joint. But it hasn't quite happened yet, mainly because there's a massive ding-dong about the licensing. The council, the Chronicle, the cathedral out the back - and every fucker who just likes a good squabble - are all beating their breasts about the depravity of lap-dancing and the sensitivity of the area, despite the fact that you can see far, far worse – in public – across the road in the Bigg Market than behind these closed doors. The battle rumbles on, with objections and appeals and sidesteps and uproar, which is why @Home is still lingering despite every mention of it in print being prefixed with 'the former'. I mean, it's there as I write, and it would be remiss of me to exclude it, but it's got its suitcase packed and keeps impatiently looking at its watch, and it'll be gone before you can say 'Is that a ship's monkey in your pocket, or are you just having a glop?' Just thought I'd keep you informed.

For: One less bar with an @ sign in it has got to be good news.
Against: Fucking hurry up and sort it out, man.

You know why the @Home name was ditched? Because they forgot to register it as a trademark, leaving the way clear for a Gateshead furniture shop to use it. And if Gateshead High Street – nine takeaways, three charity shops, a handful of pensioner pubs and half a mile of dereliction, basically – starts aping your cutting-edge designer concept, then you're really in the shit.

The Attic

25-27 Mosley Street, NE1 1YF
'The goody bag of a particularly inept paedophile'

I remember we went in to The Attic when it first opened, were rightly appalled, and swore blind never to return, preferring instead to scowl at it from the other side of the road whenever we're in the vicinity. But, like kids in a horror film checking out the old barn, curiosity forced us in for a revisit to mark and mock the changes. Once notorious for their groundbreaking sloping bar, the one that deposited expensive drinks onto expensive trainers, they've seen sense, backed down, and replaced it with the kind of traditional, level, SAFE counter that's done alehouses proud since beer was invented. That, as far as I can tell, is the only positive thing to have happened over the years. Everything else seems to have taken a turn for the worse and thrown away the bloody map. Glancing around I get the feeling - and I may be wrong, but fingers, toes and testes crossed - that the bottom has fallen out of the luxury bar market. Let's fucking hope so. That would explain why everything I can see in this place seems to have been done on the cheap, from the grubby-looking pictures knocked up on a photocopier with a knackered cartridge to the bargain-bin frames on the walls; just frames, nowt in them. There's plastic ferns dressed in Christmas lights, tables made out of old cornflake packets and sticky-backed plastic, and spray-painted sticks in pots. Even their feature wall of tiles - from a distance like something they've pinched from Notre Dame - reveals itself on closer inspection to be made out of tacky plastic too. And fuck me 'til I fart and follow through, their colour scheme is abysmal. What the hell are they supposed to be? Candy stripes? The only time you'd get candy that depressing is in the goody bag of a particularly inept paedophile, one who's stocked up on Werther's Originals, Mintoes and a couple of Caramacs to tempt the kids to see his puppies. And if that isn't enough, then look at the state of that carpet; it was criminal when it was still on the loom, never mind mashed and trampled with years of dog ends, drink and hockle. Don't bother taking the spiral staircase in the corner, either: it just leads to more of the same gloomy shite upstairs, but with curtains nailed haphazardly to the ceiling and a few lonely mirror balls. Unsurprisingly, the Attic is still a cocktail bar, but one with the notion that the clown doing the stirring is the attraction, rather than the drink they're making, so you can still see the inevitable 'practice session' if you get in early enough, plus suffer the surcharge passed on to you for what the twats slop down your their bloody shirts when they do it for real. I'm sorry; I still hate this bar and everyone who drinks in it. I have never been impressed by their questionable claims of greatness or their list of VIP visitors, and I'm certainly not going to be told that a bar is in any way luxurious - despite all the attempts at tarting it up - when the first thing I see when I walk through the door is the fucking goods lift staring dejectedly from the other side of the room.

For: One of the Windsor kids hauled his royal arse in here once. Not sure if it was the baldy one or the ginger one but, either way, it's the kiss of death for credibility.
Against: As far as I can tell, there's only one set of (non-disabled) bogs, and they're down in the basement. So if you're supping upstairs, it's round and round the spiral staircase, through the lower bar and down another flight before you can relieve yourself. I'd guess you'd be gasping for breath by that point, but I'd advise against it, since the whole toilet level still reeks of mould and decay after all this time.

I never understand fashion at the best of times, but what the hell is going on with the kids' haircuts these days? Sticking up at the back, wonky at the sides, huge chunks missing from the fringe, and it's exactly what they fucking well asked for! Look at

*them as they leave the salon, grinning like Harold Shipman at a
tea dance and tipping the stylist a tenner. It wasn't too long ago
when, if they'd walked out of the hairdressers looking like that,
they'd have cried for a month and phoned Mr Justice. Gullible
turds.*

Bernaccia

1 The Side, NE1 1PR
'Confusing and befuddling'

I'll stick my neck out here: I'll say you're probably too young to
remember the Sellafield nuclear plant when it was called Wind-
scale. Grand, it was: pumping out irradiated filth into the Cum-
brian air, causing ecological imbalance and genetic stupidity, not
least making the poor mutants believe it's a good idea to build
Carlisle housing on a flood plain. But you will recall that MAFF,
the Ministry of Agriculture, Fisheries and Food – a department so
desperate for staff that they once practically begged me to take
a job despite my accidentally using the f-word in the interview –
became DEFRA after the Foot and Mouth debacle. What I'm trying
to say here, in my usual laboured way, is that if things aren't
going to plan, then the most popular solution seems to be to
change the name, with the intention of confusing and befuddling,
whilst doing fuck all in the way of sorting the problems out. And
so it is with this place. Only four months after becoming Kuba,
another name change and furniture shuffle arrived to mystify the
hell out of the casual punter. I wouldn't care, but there wasn't
even that much wrong with Kuba, or Agora as it was before that,
and if I've whinged about it in the past it was only because I was
so bloody cheesed off with having to come up with 500 freshly-
minted words on the back of another pointless rebrand. I just
don't understand why it keeps changing moniker and management so often. Is it haunted? Is there some sort of tax dodge
going on? Is it viewed in the industry as a junior starter pub for
trainee landlords, where they can tinker and meddle a bit before
fucking off elsewhere? Really, the difference here is infinitesimal.
They've got the same chandeliers, the same dark wood, and the

same studied gloom. They've also got the same fucking prices and, if our visits are anything to go by, the same lack of paying customers. If there is a difference, it's that the bands they feature on the stage in the window have been toned down, clearly to reinforce the smooth, chilled and relaxed atmosphere that every damned new bar in Newcastle thinks its punters can't live without. These days it's all polite acoustic strumming, a far cry from, say, the time that Chippewa Falls emptied the place of poseurs and Vodkats in the first thirty seconds of their deafening set. But seriously, that's about it. I'll stick my neck out again, finally. I'll give my prediction for how long before the next daft name goes above the door: eight months.

For: The valiant stance that refuses to let it slip back into the thumping Bigg Market hellhole that it was when it was the Empress or Zoots. Anything that keeps the fucking maggots out is fine by me.
Against: Seven months and twenty days. Seven months and nineteen days. Seven months and eigh...

Chippewa Falls are a Newcastle-based post-rock instrumental trio, and they make one hell of a racket when the mood takes them. But this bit isn't about them; it's about those flaming Vodkats, poster children for the drink of the same name and template for the modern drinker in Newcastle. Remember them? Remember their adverts with some tit in jacket 'n' jeans standing on the verge of tears while a load of lippy harridans crow about how their cloppers are worth more than the one on the next lass? Her: 'I'm not high maintenance. I just deserve better.' Him: 'Hunh?' Their website claims, 'There is nothing false or fake about a Vodkat. Real people with real attitude', before telling you how they discarded thousands of 'unreal' people until they found the ones who fit their profile. 'The kind of person that walks in the room and everyone knows about it...' apparently. If you came in my bar with an attitude like that, you'd get the soda siphon up your fucking nostrils and a boot up the jacksie on your way to the pavement. And EVERY fucker in the room would know about it. 'You've got to be one to drink one' have you? They must have spent a lot of time supping at the furry goblet, that's all I can say.

The Bodega

125 Westgate Road, NE1 4AG
'The best way to creosote a fence'

I think it's fairly safe to say that I'm approaching the crossroads of life. I'm sitting in a staid leather booth in one of the most drearily decorated bars of the Sir John Fitzgerald empire – and fuck knows there's stiff competition for that crown – listening to the steady creak of time echoing round the hall. And I really like it. I find myself gazing at the stained glass domes in the ceiling with an appreciative smile, even though my inner youth says they look like nowt so much as tacky tiffany lamps, the ones that stare out from angrily flapped Argos catalogues when the T-Bar 'Mum' bracelets have sold out yet again. Every single person in the bar is wearing specs: not big Joe 90s in some ironic statement, or belligerent museum curator-style like you'd see in Tilleys down the hill, but simple, unflattering geps from the Vision Express sale bin. There's a morbidly obese man in the next booth to me, shoving porky scratchings into his swollen red face. He's eight grams of fat off a heart attack, and I don't know whether to raise my concerns with the bar staff, or sneak up behind the gluttonous fuck with a pin and a balloon. And what's worse is I can't even be sure it's a glass partition between our booths: his slouch, his clothing and his body language of defeat seem to match mine so closely, I'm starting to think there's a mirror there. Not wishing to stare my own coronary in the face, I hurriedly sacrifice a quid in the quiz machine and switch seats to the other end, the bit with the custom-designed wallpaper. It's not tasteless gift-wrap like in a pounding DJ bar, or gilded flock from the land of luxe; it's not even the collages of fucking Whigfield and the Simpsons you get in Boom!, but banjos and balalaikas and lyres and lutes. All around me are groups of middle-aged men, miserable, mis-shapen, and droning out the drivel. They have zero sense of humour and even less insight, and they seem to be gesticulating towards me. And while I know they probably just want to dish out advice on the best way to creosote a fence, to me they look like pale, spectral visions, their siren call beckoning me in, shortly before my plums are grated for all eternity. This may be impossible to resist. I have a powerful urge to corner a stranger, state the bleeding obvious and expect them to be impressed. My lager is suddenly 'too fizzy' and the appeal of some lukewarm piss brewed in a sheep-dip grows by the second. I'm ecstatic that my belly is huge since, what with my rapidly disappearing arse, it's the only thing keeping my bloody jeans up. And I'm not even sure I could give a dysenteric dump anymore, to tell you the truth. My choice at the crossroads seems to have already been made. I look around for the last time at the best years of my life, and sigh theatrically. This is it, then? This is what I have to look forward to each weekend from here on in? A no-frills, no-fun, no-fucking-about boozer in an old music hall? I can put up with that.

For: One of the most noted real ale pubs in the city, and winner of just about every CAMRA award going, at least until the Newcastle Arms waltzed in and tiddled in their tankard.
Against: The ring road just up the hill from the Bodega has been christened St James' Boulevard by the council. Boulevard? Ha ha ha. Six lanes of traffic snarls and a few spindly trees and they think it's Hollywood.

Why has there got to be such a flaming song and dance about real ale? It's only a quid and a bit a half, man. It's not a bloody Lamborghini. If you want to try it, just take the plunge and buy a standard measure. And don't do what I saw six blokes do in a bar not a million miles from here: each take a swig and a swirl from a whisky tumbler of cloudy swill before agreeing to a purchase. They were, however, at least gallant enough to step aside and allow me to be served while they cogitated. Getting into the spirit, I tried the same stunt myself, except I asked for a sample of Foster's. Nobody laughed. Not even me.

The Bridge Hotel

Castle Garth, NE1 1RQ
'Chair-gnawing awfulness'

Also owned by Sir John Fitzgerald Ltd and far more of a flagship than the snooze and dribble-fest of the bar on Grey Street that bears the company name, The Bridge Hotel is easily one of the finest old pubs in Newcastle. In fact, the only thing I don't like about it is how really, really difficult it is to find something I don't like about it. Overlooking the castle keep and helpfully located right next to a bridge - the High Level, the one that'll be wrapped in swaddling for the next twenty years while they work out what the bloody hell's wrong with it - this is a pub like they used to be made, with leather lounge seating, snugs at the front, wood panelling and bookshelves and stuff. And while the stained glass pictures of bridges and historic scenes dotted about are hardly going to have York Minster bricking it, they're still good enough for this whingeing twat. I'd say The Bridge is a bar for all seasons, if I didn't think I'd get walloped for writing such hack-neyed bollocks. Look at it this way: would you, amid the relent-less trudge of winter, head for a snooty lounge bar to sit and freeze in the glow of designer candles puttering ineffectually to the beat of some git-boy's white label collection? Or would you snuggle down in here next to the three-bar fire that's hot enough to melt your britches to your shins? It's a tough choice, I know. Summer means it's time to tiptoe down the back stairs to the beer terrace between the old city walls, where there's views to the riverside and across the water, with the legendary - to dickless film buffs who don't have to look at it every day - Gates-head multi-storey car park rotting in the distance. And all year round, upstairs has the function room with its photos of jazz greats and its planky stage, usually featuring acoustic-something-or-other. Pull up a stool or perch on the windowsill, and see for yourself the canyon between belief and talent, between the greatness of the concept and the chair-gnawing awfulness of reality. But you can't grumble, even if you're guaranteed that, whichever night you choose to go, the one act you could ever tolerate played their final show there the day before. And taking the bar as a whole, you can't really complain about any of it, unless you're desperate to pull or bursting to gyrate like an undead kebab to the latest sounds of maxed-up Corsa land. If that's what you're after you can get it down the hill or back in the Bigg Market. And you can also, make no bones about it, fuck off. I'm not going to deny that everyone in here is a fart, a bore, a fogey and a scruff. But I mean that in a good way. The Bridge is class.

For: Even the crappiest of crappy lagers can usually be relied upon to taste halfway pleasant and not leave you feeling inferior to the snobs sipping single malts or gargling and sluicing on Oggle's Green Cockrot.

Against: Here's the one thing that gets on my nerves: the terrace and the bogs are on the same level, but to get between them you have to go up the stairs to the main level, and then down again to empty your back.

This is how unlucky I am: when I was standing outside like a tit in a trance trying to get the photo for the Dog website, the function room was crammed with loud-shirted lads roaring at some sort of spectacle. A photographer's life is a cursed life: you see the world through a tiny viewfinder, and by the time you've got the frigging camera to focus you've missed most of the event you wanted to record. And so it was that I caught sight of the disappearing bare shoulder of the young stripper who was up there with them, just as they'd realised I was there and dropped their kecks for a full moon. Goddamn it.

Centurion
Newcastle Central Station, NE1 5DG
'Humphrey Bogart'

Picture the scene: it's 7pm on a cold winter's night; you're waiting for your one true love to arrive back in town and meet you in the bar in the station's lovingly-restored, Grade I Listed, first class passenger lounge. You're excited, hopeful, apprehensive even, but, slumped in the armchair facing the bar, you try to give off an air of studied nonchalance, scanning the newspaper supplements while sipping nervously at your drink, glancing occasionally at the arrivals board on the screen above the counter, and at the grandeur of the historic Burmantoft tiling. The gentle flicker of the flaming lanterns soothes your soul, while the strains of Barber's Adagio recall the fireside evenings spent in warm embraces. Suddenly the door opens, your beloved enters and, instead of a Humphrey Bogart tear-stained reunion, she drops her case on your foot, starts complaining about the spot on her chin and the breast-feeding bitch at her table who hectored her all the way home, while some glakey bastard hollers, 'SHUT THE FUCKING DOOR, IT'S FREEZING IN HERE, MAN.' Then it hits you: this place, like your hopes, like your very life, is a sham. You're in a train station bar with backpackers leering through the door, the flames aren't real, the beer is overpriced and the target customers - YOU - are complete wankers. I mean, look at you, man. What sort of a fucking fool do you feel like now? You sit there, with your toffee nose in the air, like there's a 30 year-old cognac in your hand and not a scabby pint of Foster's, waiting for the Flying Scotsman to come back into service. So you pinned all your hopes on some black and white matinee dream, did you? You wanted *Brief Encounter*, but instead you got *What the Butler Saw* with all the mucky bits cut out. Am I right? Go on, you simpering mug. Give her a kiss like you're at least halfway happy to see her; grab her case like the gentleman you'll never be, and haul your sorry carcass to the taxi queue in shame. You cad.

For: I say, darling. Would you mind awfully if I slipped you a length?
Against: *(slap)* You bounder! How dare you?! And tell me, sir: Is that your cologne or the faint-yet-unmistakable aroma of man-piss wafting through the bar?

The cad in the review was me, in case you couldn't tell. I've always wanted a train station scene that didn't involve Glaswegian drunks or the smell of Burger King, and, behind your post-

ironic exterior, so have you. Nostalgia is the new rock 'n' roll, I'm telling you. And that's why I prefer to write about that instead of the abomination that Centurion has become. Take it from me; even the good-bad bits of the original design are history. The fake flames have disappeared, along with the sumptuous café-bar atmosphere and most of the tasteful comfy chairs. In their place is a room full of neglect and echoes, with tacky lighting effects clashing with the tiling, and a range of pouffe seating that's only one step up from the bags on a left-luggage floor. It's crystal clear what's going through the minds of the management: they're cursing the very idea of listed buildings and the restrictions they put on DJ sets. And it's plain to see they've got as much love for those tiles as they would for a ginger stepchild.

Clear

Pudding Chare, NE1 1JE
'Safe from the bad man'

Brought to us by the people behind the Telegraph, Clear is the poor relation, the delinquent little brother, the kid in the callipers in every possible way. Just take a look at the place, if your peepers can stand it. The Telegraph - obviously first to the trough - took the soothing shades from the family paint box and left the runt of the litter with the rest to slap around in his clumsy, juvenile manner. And when Mummy came back from the shops and saw the mess that the brat had made in trying to copy his big brother, she wasn't very happy. But there'll be no smacked bottoms today, because a child that matches purple walls with a bilious green doorway and artwork is clearly a special needs child who requires understanding and tolerance. The Telegraph is an adult now, a working man, and he has the skills of a time-served joiner; little shitboy here, meanwhile, should hang his head in shame at the balls he made of those radiator cupboards when he found Daddy's tools at the back of the garage. If the Tele can have a grown-up rooftop beer garden, then junior is going to have his own, out in the yard and safe from the bad man. He's going to put up fairy lights and have metal tables to clang. And when he's bored with the clanging, he's going to go inside and make more noise; he's going to be like his brother the DJ, except he doesn't want to have guuuuuurls talking to him and kissing him and saying they'll put his doo-dah in their mouths if he plays their favourite song. Instead he's just going to press as many buttons as he can until he gets told off and starts to cry. You had enough of this junior theme yet? Are you going to beg me to drop it? Look, the only reason I've persisted with it is that it ties in neatly with the bar's main customer base, namely barely pubescent girls and angry youths, taking out their frustration at society's ills and their hormonal slavery by slashing the seats and wrecking the booths. Clear - for reasons I have yet to fully understand - is a haven for kids. It is, and that's something I can say confidently without fear of legal action, mainly because they're the ones always up before the beak and in the papers, getting in bother for serving underage drinkers. Beats me why it even gets that far, since I can't see how the damned staff can fail to notice the ages of the punters. Clear never seems full or even break-even busy. It's not like there's ever a crush or a heads-down-and-pour pandemonium at the bar. There's just a steady trickle of shifty teens wasting their pocket money trying to keep the place afloat. Do you go there? No. Me neither. Can't see this one making it to a ripe old age.

For: The entire front wall is made of glass, so you can see exactly what you're letting yourself in for.
Against: That 'For' means I owe the 'end a sentence with a preposition' tin another quid.

I ended the review talking about the lack of customers. The first time we visited Clear finally underlined why you should never trust officially sanctioned photos. We were just sitting there on a Monday evening when we heard all this hollering and 'supervision' going on. Christ, I thought, it can't be some Team Leader bossing around her army of headset-wearing phone monkeys after-hours, can it? Hell no. Rent-a-crowd, I'm telling you, shipped in by the management to make the place look busy for the Chronicle's promo launch photos. Straights. And you know what happened next? Once the snapper had done his business, they just slammed down their courtesy lime and sodas and pissed off. Ungrateful fucking hoors.

Coco.V

Bewick House, Forth Lane, NE1 5EF
'Recklessly unnecessary'

My bus used to stop outside Coco.V every morning, but since the routes changed following the High Level Bridge fiasco - not to mention the endless demolition projects around the Station - over time this place reverted in my imagination from schmoov bar back to the dull office block it was before. I couldn't give even a weak Wednesday wank about Coco.V these days, heading straight for the Forth every time I've walked this way, but returning for the review I found that it's more or less still laid out as the designers intended. Here's the buzzwords from the old Coco.V promo stuff: Leather and Soul. Cappuccinos to Cocktails. Relaxing Rhythms. Warm Vibes. And here's what you really get: Dansak-diarrhoea walls and lights that look like a hanging basket of used condoms. (Well, mine, anyway: the rest of you can just fill each of a dozen blobs with a glass and a half of full-cream milk and hang the fuckers on a hook.) There's a handful of booths with Ali-Baba curtains, handy for trapping the flies, and a zebra skin carpet near the doorway that is nothing but recklessly unneces-sary. Digging further into the decor, I see Moroccan lamps hanging in the windows, hidden nooks decked out like Arabian tents and, obviously for a 'laugh', plastic palm trees. This, I would have to conclude, is a souk bar theme, dangerously similar to the one that caused the ruin of Po Na Na. Do people never learn? A few pints in on the last time we were here we noticed a couple of blokes dragging out a big box into one of the raised areas. I'd hoped it was a magic show - maybe saw the barmaid in half, or something like that - but it turned out to be another fucking no-mark DJ plying his pitiful trade to a handful of uninterested early-evening punters. I think I've realised why superstar DJs are such a hit in places like this: it's because for ninety percent of the time self-appointed 'cultural high' bars play stuff that sounds like Curiosity Killed the Cat demos, and anything with half a tune is seen as a godsend. Fucking hell, man, the howls of a hyena inserting barbed wire suppositories would be preferable to the dismal 'b-duh-duh-tish-tish' background noise they spin in this place. And this is what the kids today aspire to? Never mind National Service, they should bring back chimney sweeping.

For: It's not too bad in the early evening, basking in the dying rays of the sun with a happy hour pint or two.
Against: Later on, this place will attract wankers like a Gateshead girl's g-string gets, uh, some sort of fly beginning with 'g'. Fucking hell, this alliteration business is hard work. Greenfly! That's the bastards!

Even though I'd rather wipe my hands on the wife in a fraudulent display of affection than wash my mitts in the sinks, I couldn't help but notice that above the taps in the bogs here are illuminated adverts that turn into mirrors when you approach them. How miraculous is that? And what's this? A machine that dispenses both condoms and breath fresheners for the bar's amorous and hopeful? If only there was an extra slot where they could stick in a £2 coin and get a fucking personality too, they'd be laughing.

Destination

Royal Station Hotel, Neville Street, NE1 5EW
'The world's shabbiest breakfast bar'

I think I know what my problem is with this place. The way I feel about Destination is pretty much the same as the way I felt about Cheryl Tweedy before she opened her mouth. From a distance, first impressions pointed to everything I'd ever wanted; my heart was racing, and I was thinking 'Yes. Yes! Tremendous'. Then the reality whacked me round the back of the napper with a rolled up Chronicle; Cheryl's a fucking charver dimwit encased in the face and body of an angel, and Destination's exterior hides a core of true evil. Well, maybe that's a bit strong, but it reflects my disenchantment: there's something about being promised great-ness and delivered mediocrity that pains you much more than expecting and getting shite. Situated downstairs in what used to be the world's shabbiest breakfast bar, of the Royal Station Hotel, Destination is yet another all-flash-no-soul experience, complete with the spirit-sapping colour scheme and other crap we've all come to expect from a modern bar. And although it has a wealth of history to draw on, Destination looks to have tried its gut-busting best to sully anything that might have been good about the period features. The original ceiling tiling has been lovingly exposed and then inexplicably obscured by highly un-original air conditioning pipes; the carvings on the pillars painted in a shade of mauve that infringes my human rights; and the walls clad in what looks like scratched plastic. Purple plastic, naturally. The carpet on the upper level will have dictionary committees redefining the word 'hideous', the signal for the expensive plasma screens renders every image like a sketch in cheap col-oured pencils, and the divider across the room looks exactly like the bar by the window in Delboy's Peckham flat. Judging by the punters when we were in, I'd say this place is popular with hen night first-pubbers, straight off the train and down the stairs, fidgeting in the window before the rest of the girls turn up with the devil's horns and amusing marital aids, and casually eyeing up the knobheads at the bar. That bar is nowhere you'd want to loiter for long. Maybe the staff are so sick of dealing with the stream of cocky clothes horses and feral she-cats that they've introduced a policy of making even the pint buying unpleasant: the barman and I concluded the deal with minimal interaction and a display of mutual contempt. On paper there's only one thing that makes Destination just about bearable, and that's the beer terrace outside, but even that crumbles when put to the test; you go out expecting a pleasant outdoor pint with a quick peek up a passing skirt, but instead you just get fag ends and gravel hoofed into your face. And fresh air? Forget it. Better get a taste for the taxi fumes as the greasy, fat twats with Matchbox cars fixed to their lugs slowly fuse themselves to their seats while they idle in the queue alongside the hotel. Look at the state of me. Look at the expression on my face. Post-work on a Friday, in the sunshine, pint in hand, and I still feel unhappy? That takes some doing.

For: Empty.
Against: The DJ in the corner or in a booth I can accept. The DJ set up on a podium in the middle of the dancefloor, like they're going to wheel the prick around on a forklift, is a different kettle of cod altogether.

The Royal Station Hotel is often host to wedding fairs, at which stressed-out brides-to-be can 'Ooh!' and 'Aah!' at all the ways they can be ripped off on their special day. We were talking about the whole wedding fiasco the other day and I was having problems understanding why, no matter what the bride's hair-style is for the rest of the courtship, come the big day she has to adopt the regulation wedding barnet. Whether she normally sports tumbling curls, a sleek modern crop, or even a bloody afro, on the happiest day of her life she'll have her hair scraped back in such a fashion that there's a force of 500 Newtons per square inch of scalp. Finally it dawned on me that these poor women don't do it to look good, but because it's the only way they'll be able to keep their rictus grin through eight hundred photos, the best man's speech and a brutal family punch-up. Now I understand. Could YOU look happy watching ten grand being frittered away so people you don't like can wear daft hats and go 'Eeh!'?

Dog & Parrot

52 Clayton Street West, NE1 4EX
'George fucking Formby'

Now back as the Dog & Parrot after all those years of being saddled with the stupid name of the Tut and Shive, this place remains popular with what's left of Newcastle's punk scene. There's not an hour goes by without some middle-aged, pot-bellied old soak propping up the bar in his Discharge leather jacket, having to convince himself at least once per pint that punk's not dead because, if it was, he'd look a right fucking fool with his leopard-skin tattooed head. Don't get me wrong; I've got nothing against a bit of fancy dress, but if these berks must adopt a look that's just a jump to the left of the Rocky Horror Picture Show, then it makes sense to be able to wash it off the next morning. Bless. For all its outside hints at Traditional Bar, on the inside the Dog & Parrot looks like nothing so much as a purpose-built dump, with old doors clagged to the ceiling, grimy paint-work and all manner of tatty crap on the walls. This is a good thing. There's a fire in the corner, a pool table on the upper level and, on a blackboard above the bar, there's this month's list of wave-chasing live acts. I haven't seen a band upstairs for a while, but it looks to me - judging from the gig stills they show on the plasma screens downstairs - as though the stage walls have gone from plain black to a backdrop of rock posters featuring the sort of legends they wish had cut their performing teeth in places like this. That's clearly a joke: never mind The Who and Led Zeppelin, George fucking Formby would have had problems with the D&P's farcically huffy sound limiter. But that's nitpicking based, probably, on hearsay and misheard sour grapes from people in bands that needed the plug pulling on them as a mercy killing. Looking back at our old reviews, I remember we gave this place a right old skinhead moonstomping when it was the Tut & Shive. But we've mellowed with age. As long as you're prepared to genuflect to Green Day every twenty minutes and don't mind looking at some knacker with a bolt through his nose while you're supping your pint, then there's plenty to recommend.

For: The big roaring fire and the retro rock on the jukebox.
Against: I still have nightmares about the upstairs bogs, where pissing your pants was a more hygienic option than wading about in the dark, ankle-deep in human waste and tripping face-first over the mop and into the trough.

I like to people-watch - or, more accurately, leer - in extreme bars like this. I find it most amusing to see the very moment at

which it dawns upon the emerging babe in the ripped fishnets
that her galumphing teens are giving way to shapely womanhood.
Look deep into her over-painted eyes and you'll see the realisa-
tion writ large. It says: 'Nirvana fucking, like, rock. Punk is here
to...hey wait! The puppy fat's disappearing! Hang on: what the
hell am I doing in here with these uggers?'

Fleet Street

14 Pudding Chare, NE1 1UE
'Wishy-washy-wanky'

If you turn on cable telly right now and channel hop until you find
a sitcom - the sort of offensively inoffensive guff made for times
of world catastrophe or when a Royal snuffs it – I can guarantee it
will follow this plot. Confused mother of dysfunctional yet lovable
brood has midlife crisis, dresses up in rebellious teenage daughter's clothes and make-up, and tries to regain lost youth, with
predictably disastrous results. Confused mother will then return,
ashen-faced but wiser, to her normal dowdy but respectable
state, just in time for the unexpected twist, probably involving
some sort of small, yappy-type dog and much canned laughter.
The moral to this is, obviously, that people will love you for what
you are, that you should know and be happy with your place, and
that whenever you feel blue you should just get your scriptwriters
to pinch ideas from *It's A Wonderful Life*. (Me, I just want to go
and kick the fuck out of my neighbours when I feel blue, especially when there's nowt on telly yet again). And so it is with
Fleet Street. Formerly and legendarily the Printer's Pie, and the
haunt of the drunks from the Chronicle offices next door, this bar
was subjected a couple of years ago to one of those wishy-washy-
wanky makeovers for no good reason that I could ever fathom.
Out went the old-time boozer decor and in came an autistic
child's version of a luxe bar, with terrible tongue-and-groove
cladding, loathsome lounge furniture and a complete cocking
absence of any individuality. And it stank. At some point since
then, though, the staff and customers have clearly caught sight of
themselves in a mirror, been horrified at what they have wit-

nessed, and changed as much as possible back to what they were before, with an unspoken understanding that the subject was never again to be mentioned. Dropping in for a pint before the match, it seems that the grumpy old geezers are back, the pictures of Chronny journalists and sellers are back and, instead of pointless black napkins spread along the bar, I can see huge plates of complimentary hotdogs and chips. Now that's better. The beer's comfortingly average, the haircuts reassuringly staid and unfashionable, and the DJ has – as you'd expect for a man of his age – a homely lack of discernable musical taste. And nobody minds because... because, well, we love you, Mum. Don't ever change. There's really only one thing that's troubling me, and that's what I've seen upstairs when I've staggered up for a piddle. Permanently chained up and empty, and spoken of only in whispers, is a fully-functional, lights-on-nobody-home designer bar, like some friendly but dangerously insane auntie in the attic. I'm not exactly sure what's going on there, but I suppose that'll have to wait for a later episode. Tune in tomorrow for more crazy goings-on in the Pourne-Starr household. Next tonight it's *Fuck My Uncle*, with Andi Peters and Abi Titmuss... *(sound of foot going noisily through TV and neighbours phoning police)*

For: The windows at the front open in summer.
Against: Those windows open out onto a minging back lane with the grunts from the Chronicle despatch leering at you all after-noon.

The standard of the Chronicle's journalism has really gone downhill lately; amongst the usual slipshod clangers last week there was a bit inviting people to a 'pubic' meeting. No word of a lie. You might come to notice that I'm always blathering on about misused apostrophes, partly because I'm borderline autis-tic, but mostly because it really gets up my bloody hooter the way that the English language is going to hell in a Humvee and nobody but me seems to give a shite. Get this, right: there's a fireplace shop along my way, where some bungler has made a sign for the front that says 'Fire's' instead of 'Fires'. A lazy slip of the brush I could accept - provided they sent me a letter of apology, of course - but this sign is in relief, so someone has obviously gone to the trouble of making a separate apostrophe, plus three extra pegs to hang it on. I was along there on Tuesday night, only a little bit drunk, trying to whack it off with a stick to do the shopkeeper and, indeed, the whole town a favour by correcting the signmaker's punctuation. And what happens? I'm the one who gets arrested! Can you fucking believe that?!

The Forth

Pink Lane, NE1 5DW
'Raspberry headfucker'

The Forth is a bit of a strange place in that it alternates between a relaxing, intimate, friendly, down-to-earth, modern bar with a great jukebox, and a cliquey, smug wankfest full of irredeemable cunts. No word of a lie. I've witnessed it many a time. Always a Dog favourite for at least one pint on a night out – apart from when it burned down a few years ago - The Forth has a good choice of exotic beers, plus economy lager for the student in your life. It's one of life's great hoots when you drag your work 'mates' in to see that pubs other than Pacific and Bar 42 do exist, let them develop a taste for some Belgian raspberry headfucker and then watched them shit blood when they've seen the price of their round. The latest post-blaze decor consists of massive chandeliers, some alarming wallpaper on (thankfully) one wall only, and work from local artists on the upper level: did they ever flog that painting of the Gateshead multi-storey car park? I certainly hope so, since it's bad enough having to pass it every day, without seeing it on the walls of the bar, too. There are big windows to illuminate that lunchtime session and to give you an unparalleled view of the dossers and crackheads in Pink Lane, and while the outside paint job seems to be stuck at the undercoat stage, I'm not entirely sure if that's permanent or not. What I really like about the Forth, though, is the way that, whatever design foolishness they care to throw at it, it always looks like a knackered old boozer. You can't buy qualities like that, you know. But, hell, it wouldn't be a Dog review without a bit of griping about something. And here it is: I despise, fail to understand and try to avoid DJs at all costs, as anyone will tell you. I'm a dismal old fart who's long past his peak, and I'm only a cardigan's throw away from shouting 'Turn that bloody racket off. Call that music? You want some Big Black on, something with a proper tune'. But what I will say is this: there is absolutely no need, ever, for the Forth's Sunday AFTERNOON DJ to ruin my day and my undercrackers by booming out shit-loosening bass under Top 40 standards. What the fuck were they thinking? But all this is just minor carping about a place I really like and end up in more often than not. Go on, give it a whirl. You might even like it. And if you're feeling a little uncertain about your freedom of expression and the individuality of your dress sense, then rest assured: there's always someone in here who looks more of a dick than you ever could.

For: One of the few bars in the town to still have a decent sized, fully functioning real fire.
Against: Said fire is always surrounded by total helmets who'll hog it all night, especially when you're frozen to the marrow.

It was a while back now when they did it, but The Forth was also one of only two bars to acknowledge The Burglar's Dog website, plugging it on their menus and on the boards in the doorway. The other pub was the closed-on-police-advice Cage Bar. I try not to think about that too deeply.

Gengis

Grainger Street, across from Central Station, NE1 5EN
'Stand up for the murderous tyrant'

The woman we bought our house from was a heavy smoker. And she was a lunatic, one who seemed to have dedicated her entire life to spreading Artex over everything and then sitting down with twenty Bensons to admire her handiwork. Her idea of the perfect living room ceiling was one with two-inch thick asbestos-peppered icebergs that laughed in the face of the smooth-over or the abrasive scrape, and were only prepared to talk business with the wallpaper steamer, the chisel and the fucking six-pound lump hammer. Weekend after weekend we spent up those damn ladders getting the poisonous shite off, the steam dripping boiling hot liquid nicotine down the backs of our necks, until we could finally relax with a battered - but healthy - starting point for our B&Q dreams. And that, the stained, cracked, riddled, distempered, tobacco-streaked shell of a room we were left with, is more or less what Gengis looks like. Sure, there's a couple of other features, like the wallpaper that's supposed to resemble peeling paint - the stuff with the comically fake studs glued to it - plus some oriental pictures and ornaments and other crap bought on the internet when they were desperate. Aye, there's a mix of wood and slate, and some laughably unconvincing flickering flames behind the bar. But what the fuck's that on the wall over there? Is it an exotic logo, or is it mould? I'm going to stand up for the murderous tyrant here because, let's face it, he gets a bit of a bad rep. I'm going to state quite boldly that the sheer ineptitude of the design concept in this bar is an insult to the memory of Genghis Khan, especially since they haven't even spelled his name right. What are they trying to imply? That, if he came back from a few months' hard marauding, the first thing he'd want to do would be come in here and relax with a gloopy cocktail or a business lunch? And there's a DNA statistic that I misheard once that says, like, 45% of the population of the western world are direct descendents of the Mongol Overlord. In that case there must have been a rogue gene on the loose somewhere down the line because, instead of being fiery warriors, the berks responsible for this bar were clearly not just effeminate, but bone bloody idle too. And if Genghis had known that this was his legacy, this tatty, cardboard haven for red-faced and silverhaired executives, he might have kept his pecker in his pants a bit more often.

For: At least they've had the decency to abandon their initial super-priced pretensions from when they first opened all those years ago.

Against: I haven't seen them switch on the - whoo! - flaming torches outside for a while. That might be because I haven't even glanced at the place for a while.

The Burglar's Dog on... studs. Slippy metal studs beside pedestrian crossings. Why? I'd assume it's for the blind, but I fail to see just how putting death traps in the pavements can be a positive step for the visually impaired. It's almost like they're saying, in some bizarre form of foot-Braille, 'Hey! Stevie Wonder! When you're flat on your face with your head in the bus lane, then you'll know you're at a safe place to cross.'

The Globe

11 Railway Street, NE4 7AD
'The best shag I've ever known'

Sometimes, when forced by friends with no taste, no bus fare and certainly no mercy, I can be seen supping on Gateshead's Low Fell. It hurts, but it's not life threatening. A couple of years ago the Fell's drinkers were witness to the debacle of Smart, where the scuzzy Gateshead Arms was modernised, refurbished and transformed into the sort of luxury bar that pub designers think everyone on the planet wants to chill in; erroneously, I might add. Heads were scratched and wallets kept firmly in pockets as Smart's owners tried to force the concept of the blissed-out lounge down the throats of people who simply could not give a monkey's, then watched in despair as their takings plummeted before giving in, shutting up, and changing it all back - name included - to the way it was before. Four months Smart lasted, if my memory serves me well. And I can see that sort of thing happening here. It's a shame, really, because the refurbished Globe is much better than Smart ever was, and certainly has a lot more going for it than some other spruced up bars I could care to mock. Why the worry? Mainly the site of the building, which does them no favours whatsoever; it's less location, location, location, and more oh-fuck, oh-fuck, oh-fuck. Stuck in the middle of nowhere, with the gay bars on one side, Benfield Motors across the way, and no more than a handbrake turn from Scotswood

Road up over, the Globe has got its work cut out to drag in the customers, unless they strike a deal with the Jury's Inn nearby, making it a compulsory condition of sale to nip in here for a couple. I'm not going to pretend it's revolutionary; black slate, black leather, wooden bar and floor. There are modern photos and artworks of the Quayside on the walls - purple, I'm afraid - with sections painted to look like polystyrene tiles. The carpeted area has the best shag I've ever known on a pub floor, and the lamps – I swear - have been made out of old black tights. And I'll warn you now before you're desperate: the bogs are up some stairs, through some doors, up some more stairs, through another set of doors, out through the yard, DOWN again, across the hall and up again. At least that's how I got there. But it's helpful that they've acknowledged the maze by sticking up arrows to take you back to your pint. That's it: no surprises, no wacky gimmicks, no horror show. It's a nice bar and I bear them no malice. When there's a gig on at the Arena round the corner they should hope-fully be coining it in, but I fear - and it's proper pants-pappering fear - that if the punters there prefer officially sanctioned Arena beer at twice the price of the Globe's, then it'll be bankruptcy and ruin, with dogfights on the pool table and the Scotchy charv-ers dancing triumphantly around the smouldering ashes.

For: Not only is the Globe cheaper than the Arena, but they let you drink out of glasses made of glass, and not pitiful plastic beakers with about as much rigidity as a bag of fucking goldfish from the Hoppings.

Against: I shouldn't be rocking at my age, let alone dodging the flying piss down the front. I'm starting to feel embarrassing, so fuck knows how long I've *been* embarrassing. You have my apolo-gies.

Whoa-whoa-whoa. Hang on: it looks like the Globe has found its niche. Dragged myself all the way down to the Arena box office yesterday to avoid paying a fiver-per-ticket online charge and another six quid to have some berk try to deliver them between the hours of 3pm and 3.05pm on days when there's nobody home (a signature, proof of ID and a fucking tap-dancing display is required). Popped in the Globe, and found that it's become a Polish ex-pat bar, complete with bilingual bar staff, red-and-white flags, and a full range of lethal and vowel-free bottled beers. I'll be discussing those beers later...

Gotham Town

Neville Street, NE1 5DF
'Better than a leper clanging on a bell'

You wouldn't really think that a mediaeval theme pub would thrive in Newcastle, would you? But you'd be wrong. Across from Central Station and a magnet for first pint gaspers, Gotham Town has been packing them in for as long as I remember, and attracts a loyal following both on match days and during the week. Fuck knows how, since when it comes to decor, this bloody ridiculous bar knocks even the Death Metal dungeon of Trillians into an overflowing chamber pot, with ornate pulpits, fearsome carvings, gloomy little alcoves and sweeping staircases just some of the features my eyes couldn't quite believe. And despite a full wall of windows onto Bewick Street – with the statue of Cardinal Basil Hume peering in and frantically praying for the customers' salvation – the lighting in here makes the murk of a torture chamber look like a sunny day's jousting. In mediaeval times – long, long before the invention of the plasma screens and mirror balls and bandits that dot Gotham Town – you had to make your own entertainment, and it's a thrill to see that the tradition carries on to this day, with the tavern's Pick At The Wallpaper tournaments making a right fucking mess of the gallery overlooking Pink Lane. I certainly prefer that to the acoustic sessions that take place here, though, with mandolin-molesters who think Newcastle's musical legacy began and ended with Lindisfarne droning out dirges only marginally better than a leper clanging on a bell. Taking leave of Milady and bowing and scraping downstairs to the privy, I find a four-inch thick heavy door that you need a fucking battering ram to open, and behind it a fake-stone hole-in-the-wall contraption that promises and fails to attend to my every ablutionary need. What witchcraft is this? When I've evacuated my night-soil, I just want a tap and some soap and possibly a friend's doublet to dry myself on: I don't expect to have to send a messenger to the Wise Woman in the woods to find out how the fuck I'm supposed to get cleaned up. Is it any wonder that disease is so rampant? Tragically, I find myself alone in even wondering, as most of the serfs here are just happy to go about their daily business oblivious to the health risks. Bacteria is passed from hand to pint to quiz machine. Microbes move from finger to bandaged mediaeval tattoos at the bases of spines, spines of peasants mimicking the princess yet too uneducated to realise that the princess has been covering up her own mutilation in shame since it went out of fashion three years ago. I'd like to see these jesters undergo a proper mediaeval experience. Stick them in a reeking alehouse with the rats and the typhoid and the dysentery. Shove them amongst real rowdiness where the plotting in corners turns to indiscriminate murder at the toss of a groat. Remove them from the protection of the theme and propel them into the reality. See how they get on then.

For: It filters off the lunatics straight from the station before they get as far as the Forth or Tilleys or the Bodega.
Against: Poisoned wells and shitting in the castle moat get a bad press. At least those smells were honest and natural, and not like the putrid stench coming in from the branch of 'sandwich artistes' Subway round the back of here, and at 50-yard intervals until the edge of the flat earth. Here be monsters. And High Street-strangling cunts.

Speaking of toilets, I got bollocked again at work this week. It wasn't the best half-hour I've ever had behind closed doors, but a man has to stand up for what he believes in. My supposed crime? As a frequent visitor to the gents – I haven't quite got the diabetes yet, but I can see them unloading it from the van – I am appalled at the sanitary habits of my fellow employees. I got in early on Tuesday morning, and printed out an A3-sized notice for the toilet walls, which read, 'NOW WASH YOUR HANDS', and underneath, in slightly smaller font, 'Wiping your pissy fingers on the doorknob is not an acceptable alternative'. The amount of dirty fuckers I see in there manhandling their choppers and digging in their arseholes before heading back to their desks without so much as a dibble under the cold tap beggars belief. All the virulent germs on the door furniture, all the bowel-vacating bugs I've picked up, and they say that I'm the one offending sensibilities?

The Head of Steam

2 Neville Street, NE1 5EN
'A good sprinkling of numpties'

Buried under a gruesome office block, and proving that you don't need to desecrate an important piece of local architecture to site a successful pub, the Head of Steam is Newcastle's number one bar for indie saddoes, emo kids, student wankers, call them what you will. It's also one of Newcastle's most popular small venues, and a damned fine boozer to boot. The punters on any given night are exactly the same: sullen kids dressed in the standard I'm-an-individual (and-so-are-all-my-mates-who-look-just-like-me) gear: heavy-rimmed glasses, too-small T-shirt, and a scarf indoors. The girls all wear men's shoes and the lads seem duty bound to sport women's bags, for some reason. Like, kewl. Me, I gave up reading the NME years ago - on account of trying to match up their praise of The Datsuns with the actual band called The Datsuns, mostly - but if you're looking for an indie rock ghetto, or somewhere to hear people squabbling about whether the latest over-hyped skinny white boys were better when nobody liked them, then this really is the place for you. In terms of layout, the pub is on two floors - upstairs and basement - with only the vile pissers and a windowsill full of jumbled-up club flyers on the ground floor. The upstairs bar - the main bit, if you like - is a laid-back, friendly, theme-free room done out in cream and red and with a load of paintings on the walls; stylistically I'd put them somewhere between Roy Lichtenstein and Julian Opie, but that's only 'cause I'm a git. Here you'll find the full range of the pub's cracking choice of beers, together with a good sprinkling of numpties of all persuasions at any time of day or night. And the downstairs bar -

open only when there's something on - is the venue where, together with what the pub management themselves tactfully refer to as 'entry level' live music, you can see any Newcastle band that will ever make it big. Well, by 'see' I mean 'be there when they play', since it's nigh on impossible to get a decent view of any band on a stage that's no more than a foot high, and if you're stuck round the corner you're doubly fucked. There you are, then: a halfway positive review, which is something the Dog doesn't do every day. I've got a lot of time for the 'Steamer' - as I've been told the kids call it - and if you catch me saying bad things about it, it's only 'cause most of the punters in here take one look at me and wonder whose fucking fatha I am. Cheeky little cunts.

For: Owain behind the bar used to work in the underground medieval prison in London called The Clink. I say used to, because Owain behind the bar was sacked for accidentally locking in two foreign tourists overnight in his hurry to get down the pub. Owain behind the bar is a living legend. 'Hapless museum worker', we salute you.

Against: Fair enough, they're accessible to the street as well as the customers so they get a heavy duty pounding, but the toilets are absolutely honking.

Picked up a flyer in the Head of Steam for an indie club night, which gave a long list of band names with the promise that they would actually play the groups they listed. I couldn't tell you which venue it was; when I said, 'picked up', that was immediately before crumpling it into a ball and launching it across the room. But it got me thinking about the competitors of that club night, the ones they find so appalling. Why WOULDN'T you play stuff by the bands on your adverts? Why would you lie? To haul in the punters and then - once you'd got their entrance fee - tell them, Sorry, the CDs are double booked?

Long Bar

39-47 Westgate Road, NE1 5SG

'Christ, I didn't think I was that drunk'

I was in the Cub Scouts when I was a boy. Don't like to talk about it, but it happened. Every FA Cup Final weekend - the cheapest weekend of the rental calendar - we'd trudge dejectedly to Gosforth Park to build huts out of brushwood and then try to set them aflame. The rain drilled holes in our heads, the games were insulting and the cooking was inedible, so the only highlight of the entire weekend would be a trip to the wooden shack they laughably called the 'tuck shop' to stock up on E-numbers and nutrition-free food. And that shack, give or take a few optics and a cash machine, was exactly what the Long Bar looks like to me. Genius. The Long Bar is named after the long-gone real pub around the corner from here called, uh, The Long Bar, that was used as a set in *Get Carter*, giving them license to clag up loads of stills from the film, blurred almost beyond recognition by some idiot with a hooky copy of Photoshop. It also looks fuck all like the long-gone real pub around the corner. If my tuck shop comparison left you baffled, then try conjuring up the image of a '70s Swiss fondue restaurant, maybe on a telly advert with Chris Tarrant ripping the piss out of it. Think bare wood, stone pillars, cacky browns and subdued lighting, with two whole walls of 'Christ, I didn't think I was that drunk' wonky mirrors, and you'd be bang on. Quite like the choirboy pew seating next to the downstairs bar, though. Reminds me of when the Bishop of [anecdote deleted following legal advice]. The bar upstairs seemed to be the more popular when we were in, though it's probably not a good sign if all the punters are ignoring your flashy decor and gazing ruefully out of the window at the Union Rooms, wishing they'd gone there for a better - and cheaper - pint instead. I was bunged up with flu and an ear infection, so I can hardly be relied upon in the Jilly Goolden stakes, but to me the beer tasted of... well... nothing whatsoever. Our lass says it was pretty average, though. Average food menu, average atmosphere, average prices, average everything, really. Overall, then, not impressed. And to think they closed a betting shop to make way for this? Disgraceful.

For: A reasonable standard of topiary outside.
Against: Is it safe to go in here yet? Last time I was in they had posters up of that flaming Ingrid woman, ex- of Metro Radio and now whoring her arse on the Postcode Lottery. I will take to my grave the trauma of seeing her on every wall, grinning like a hospice child when the Toon come visiting. Is she still doing it? Put your teeth away, girl. Your life's not that bloody joyful.

The Long Bar is popular with the after-work crowd, with suits aplenty. How come everybody in the world - except me - looks at least halfway decent in a suit? I pull mine out of the wardrobe, and I'm thinking Reservoir Dogs, I'm thinking George Clooney in Ocean's whatever, and I'm even thinking the fat kid out of The Hives. And what do I see in the mirror? Fucking Paddy MacDee, that's what.

The Lounge

8 Neville Street, NE1 5EN
'Love and hate across the knuckles'

Once upon a time I thought this place was half-decent. Call it youthful exuberance, the shock of something so unfamiliar to my codger-bar loving palate, or just plain stupidity. Returning five years later I find that, aside from the inevitable slide into tattiness that goes with any pub that doesn't have a spring clean every eighteen months, The Lounge has a problem and it's that fashion is leaving it behind. Without actually changing one little bit, the fixtures and fittings have crossed the line from arty to cheesy, never to return, and the purple paint that was the absolute must-have when it went up now looks as clichéd and dated as love and hate across the knuckles. And they know it, that's for sure. That's why I'm certain they're trying to soften the blow of losing their hip status while still hoodwinking the remaining few devotees, by using a drinks tariff that would make

British Gas blush: by the time you've worked out how much your cheap pint is going to cost based on what time you arrived divided by the number of staff on multiplied by the number of pumps no longer functioning, your beer has gone up another 50p. Look, I don't really want to hammer the place. It's no better and no worse than average and they serve a decent enough pint, but I can think of at least another five bars within a hundred yards of here that I'd sooner go to. Maybe it's just that, after spending so long writing bollocks about pubs and constantly having to look for new ways to be abusive about life's trivia, I now feel every cubic inch of the office block above weighing down on my soul. Maybe it's that I've really only been here lately in the daylight, and so I'm missing out on the bar's primetime, the after-10 hours when it turns into a nightclub (where the first 500 ladies get in free every weekend; get yourself a frock, lads, you'll save a fortune). Perhaps if I gave that a try instead of sticking so rigidly to the hipster bars or, more likely, lying tucked up in bed with my porn under the pillow waiting for our lass to drop off, I'd appreciate the finer points. Can't see it happening myself, though; can you?

For: The summertime terrace - or fenced off bit of the pavement, to be exact - outside.
Against: British weather, the traffic fumes, and the city's alcoholics and other assorted riff-raff, all of which will ruin your alfresco lunchtime pint on that very terrace.

Oh, how I laugh when I think of all those crazy students sitting at the tables along the massive window wall, plotting which amusing attachment they're going to add to the three public art sculptures that form the piece Man With Potential Selves (or, as you probably know it, Man with Traffic Cone On Head) that stand outside The Lounge. I could chuckle and chuckle, and chuckle some more, until every last breath is squeezed from their limp bodies and I can get on with digging another shallow grave in St John's churchyard round the corner. Knobheads.

Newcastle Hero

Central Station, NE1 5DL
'A genuine tuppenny whore'

Just as people don't often feel the need to go to their own city's tourist office, they very rarely see the point in drinking in their local train station bar. I'd never been in here before the review visit, and I see absolutely no reason to go again, unless failure to wave off a distant relative threatens my inheritance. Approaching the door of this place I expected nothing, and nothing is exactly what I got. Lots of it. The Newcastle Hero is a big, unremarkable room with no real distinguishing features worth ridiculing. There's just the bare necessities of any station bar; somewhere to sit, something to pump shrapnel into, and something on the walls to look at if you can be arsed. The threadbare collection of portraits of Newcastle heroes along the wall opposite the bar runs to the likes of Sting (honorary doctorate of everything, ever), Neil Tennant, and our old beige-bar friends, the fucking Lighthouse Family. And if you're skint, I'd advise you take along a screwdriver when you go, because their signed photo of the legendary Brendan Foster has got to be worth a mint on eBay. That comprehensive gallery won't keep you occupied for long though, so you're bound to find yourself gawping at the customers just for something to do. What you'll see is a whole range of people united in their need to be somewhere else; backpackers, laptop slaves, pensioners picking the peanuts out of their upper dentures, plus - when we were in - a genuine tuppenny whore awaiting the call for her next lonely punter. How am I so sure about this? I'll tell you: any half-attractive woman looking expectantly in my direction and retaining her gaze even after making eye contact with this beer-gutted, badly dressed, carrier bag-toting sack of shit loitering by the quiz machine, has got to be on the game. Simple when you can read the signs, even if those signs mean my youth has gone and I now look like a dirty kerbcrawler. But that's it; that's all there is to the Hero. I suppose it serves its purpose well enough, and it's at least a civilised alternative to the brain-dead hollering in O'Neill's, but there's really only a scabby pigeon's difference between a pint in here and sitting on the platform with a can of Stella.

For: Massive chandeliers...
Against: ...hanging from a polystyrene ceiling.

For all that The Lighthouse Family are up on the wall as Newcastle Heroes, it has to be made clear that they are adopted Geordies: the singer - the one that every fucker used to do on Stars In Their Eyes because you didn't have to put any effort in - and the other bloke that not even his mother would recognise were both born in London. And you can take that as evidence of the warmhearted nature of the people of Newcastle, since every other city would have had one listen to their anaemic, GI-diet soul pap and run the cunts out of town.

North
The Old Ticket Office, Neville Street, NE1
'Balls'

The tiny North bar in the Central Station is possibly one of the least inspiring boozers I've ever encountered. I don't mean that in a bad way, like; it's just that once you've clocked the 'theme', the posters and the stuff hanging from the ceiling there's not a whole lot left to deride. And that doesn't keep the wolf from this moaning sod's door, I'll tell you that. North lists its address as 'The Old Ticket Office' and having the bar counter in the middle set in what looks like - or might even be - a ticket booth can conjure up a feeling of nostalgia for the more personal days of rail travel before the keyboard-pummelling frustration of internet booking. It also makes it an utter bastard to get served when the damned barman can't see you past the corners of the booth. Mind you, it's probably halfway your own fault, since while he's shouting 'Next' you're too distracted by the porn film posters on every wall publicising American classics like *Debbie Does Dallas*, *The Devil in Miss Jones*, plus such home-grown favourites as *Now Then Mrs Armthorpe, Tha's Got Lovely Tits*. North's real claim to fame is that it holds the world record for having the most mirror balls in a bar. There must be, what, literally dozens of them, all different sizes and collecting different amounts of dust and dead moths. And, in a stroke of design genius, the mirrored theme is, uh, mirrored by the DJ enclosure in the corner, the one lined with peeling stick-on tiles reflecting the cardboard boxes and junk they're too chilled to chuck in the wheelie bin. I think that's your lot for North. No wait, there's a beer garden out the front, off to the side of the steps; I wouldn't say it was small, but if you're in it, it's full. Back in the bar and struggling for inspiration, I'm reduced to griping about the music, mainly because North's legendary 25-CD randomizer seemed to be stuck on default Red Hot Chili Peppers setting when we were in. Forty minutes straight of funk-rock stodge with that tit Kiedis going, 'Hut-AH hip-AH itty-itty-oop-AH' like he does in every fucking song they've ever released. Thanks for that, bartender.

For: The music for the rest of the time may be the usual DJ-centric crap, but at least they've got a written policy of keeping it at a level where you can hear what people are saying to you.
Against: I always head up the stairs, peer through the wrecked doorway and into the abandoned unit and wonder what the hell happened to North. That's usually shortly before realising I'm in the wrong place and the bar itself is another twenty feet along the road.

You can do a degree in porn films now, you know. Well, maybe not a full degree, but certainly a module or two as part of a media studies diploma. Media studies: possibly the most immoral course of all time. It's not just that it's such an unbelievable skive, getting a certificate for watching telly for three years, but more that these gits are guaranteed a cushy number at the end of it, with the industry creating jobs for suitably 'qualified' graduates whether they're needed or not. Another 20,000 2:2s with mitigating circumstances? Fine, we'll just set up a few hundred extra channels; there's bound to be an audience for BBC67. Where the hell is the talent these days? I'm sure that in the golden age of television, students had to produce no-budget projects just to get a tick from teacher. Now those projects ARE the fucking programmes. Here's an idea for primetime telly: take everyone pocketing their wages from the licence fee for doing naff all, tell them they've got an hour to auction off their AV equipment for at least half of what was paid for it, or they'll get an icepick between each vertebra for every quid they're short. I'd watch that. Will there be an omnibus edition?

O'Neill's

38 Neville Street, NE1 5DF
'I am a Jarrow Marcher'

There was an advert when I was kid for, I dunno, McEwan's Best Scotch or something, which implied that, no matter where you may have roamed, their bubbling, tasteless piss was the 'One you gotta come back for.' This pub, this terrible Irish theme bar opposite the Central Station is the exact inverse of that, in that it's the last place people go before they get the hell away. This is what I imagine limbo to be like, lost souls awaiting their final destination, only with Van Morrison as every other song over the PA. The first thing you'll notice, kick and curse when you venture into O'Neill's is the huge pile of bags all over the floor. And the second thing to strike you will be the complete lack of anyone from Newcastle, since O'Neill's is almost exclusively home to ex-pats, stag weekenders, sectarian sympathisers and other assorted idiots tearful for the aul country, as if their piddle-poor Irish chain bars are so much better than ours. Night after night you'll see dickheads in their Celtic tops, waving their pints, hollering their rebel songs and promising each other 'tiocfaidh ar la'. It's not the rebel songs I mind - anything that drowns out the frigging Cranberries is fine by me - but more the cast iron guarantee that these fuckers would shit treacle and go running to Ma at the first sight of a black balaclava. Oh aye, they're happy to act the bad boy here, far from home and safe from harm, but they're clearly no more part of a post-ceasefire Republican splinter group than I am a Jarrow Marcher. Just fucking grow up, you imbecile. Quit glorifying some cause you read about on a gable end. We're not terrified of your dubious connections or your kneecapping glances, you tit. We just find you tragic. Now sit there quietly while you wait for your train. Have a little nostalgic weep to yourself at the hurling sticks, the tricolours and all the bollocks about 'craic' daubed on the walls. And shut the fuck up and behave yourself, like you'll have to when you get home. There's a good little boy.

For: At least O'Neill's have woken up to the notion that if someone broke a fiddle in a pub in Ireland they'd put it in the bloody bin and not in a glass case behind the bar.
Against: The place has far and away the most repellent Gents toilets in the civilised world. The open-air troughs in the old Gallowgate End at St James' Park were better than the ones in here.

I have absolutely no gripe with the Irish, honestly. One of my best mates comes from Strabane and he's sound, even if I can only understand one word in five he says. I tend to view him more as a representative of his nation than the fuckpigs we encountered in O'Neill's. My problem is with anyone - from anywhere - who's away from home and who puts themselves forward as their country's voice simply because they can't handle their ale and like shouting shit. I'm aware that right now in an English theme pub somewhere there will be an equally vile bunch of retards yelling 'No surrender to the IRA' before scuttling back to their meek hometown chain bars. And I fully understand that you can't judge a country on its travellers. National stereotypes - wherever you're from - are what come about when our scum meet their scum, scampi-faced and rat-arsed beside a pool in Benidorm. National stereotypes have got fuck all to do with 99% of the population, and anyone who believes any of that cack should be beaten soundly. Just thought I'd clear that up.

Perdu

20 Collingwood Street, NE1 1JF

'Wrong, wrong, wrong'

When a bar first opens to great hullabaloo, you have to assume that what is offered at that time is what they really want to provide. Whatever atmosphere, attitude, game plan or gimmick is foisted upon the customers – the people helping to establish the business, let's not forget – must be seen as the long-term intention, and must be the thing for which they are ultimately held to account. After all, a serial killer up in Acklington may be all shame-faced and repentant now, but he still committed his catalogue of crimes; he still thought he could get away with it despite society's views to the contrary. This is why, despite many minor changes to Perdu since its opening night, it should forever be branded criminal. The barmaids wearing stupid lace collars like Victorian dandies may have dressed down to branded polo shirts, the wall full of framed 'interesting' bits of the wallpaper may have been removed to extend the drinking area, and the psychiatrists' couches struck off, but this remains a pub that is so far up its own arse that any kind of enjoyment can only be permitted if it fits in with the colour scheme. It's difficult to know where to start in pulling the piss out of this ridiculously toffee-nosed establishment, but I think I'll just jump right in regardless. From the pretentious French name (it means lost, as in dignity and your entire night out budget, more than likely) to the *soi-disant* (ha!) opulent chandeliers that make your office Christmas deccies look tasteful; from the minimalist lighting in the bead-curtained booths to the slouching areas by the window (cushions on the floor to you and me), it's all a load of contemptible bollocks and woe betide anyone who cracks a fucking smile. I treasure to this day one of their stupid booklets that I pinched in the week this place opened, just to keep on file as evidence. Get a load of this risible guff: 'His neck lowered in a phrase, his heart sways to her rhythm, as she lifts an amber glass and falls into a smiling cloud'. Hoo hoo hoo! David Blunkett with a box of fridge poetry could hardly come up with worse, and at least he'd have the sense to not get it printed and stuck in front of the public. Ah man, you've got to see the place, just to see how fucking utterly wrong, wrong, wrong it all is. I don't care if they've branched out from the seamless - i.e. the same beat all frigging night - mix of DJ grooves and smooth jazz to a broader scope incorporating Soul on Sundays or tepid indie rock. Nor could I give a rodent's rear end if they've tried to lift at least some of the gloom by opening an Astroturf-lined beer garden out the back in the bit where the bins used to go. This bar remains a perfect example of how to feel disenfranchised in your own town, and any visitor hot off the train is going to think we're all a bunch of desperate, aspirational morons in utter denial of our city's own character, and that THIS is what we want. I'm still shaking my head in disbelief. Absolutely horrendous.

For: They now have a much-trumpeted happy hour.
Against: Fuck the happy hour and its mortifying 'games'. Sod the humiliation of pressing some grubby button or whatever other embarrassment they force you to endure. There is no joy – unless you're of limited intelligence and recovering from a breakdown – in 'only' being charged the English full price instead the Scandinavian one.

You can never have enough rants against pub DJs, I feel. In the same way that Britain is piss poor at sport because of the idiot notion that winning is irrelevant and it's the taking part that matters so everyone must get a prize, the year two-thousand-and-whenever-you're-reading-this has been the worst for British music simply because any two-bit arsehole with some decks and a record bag is allowed to call themselves a musician. And because they're abundantly available, they're cheap, so the punters get stuck with them whether they like it or not. It's a shocking state of affairs, it really is. If you're shit, you're barred: that's the way it should be.

Rafferty's

29-31 Pink Lane, NE1 5DW
'Burn it'

Now sandwiched together under one name for convenience but still effectively two separate bars, in either guise this place has always had a reputation for being a bit rough. The right hand side of this building - the old Rafferty's - is a haven for old codgers in overalls, while the left hand - the old Quin's - caters for the younger customer. Clutching our pints we chose left, not out of any preference for decor or jukebox selection or any of that nonsense, but simply to get away from the snogging couple in the right, slavering and licking and gnawing on each others jawbones at five o'clock on a Friday afternoon. And because it was so early, we made a conscious attempt to do the review properly, instead of digressing into the usual tangential ranting. These are our findings or, more specifically, How to do a bar the Rafferty's way. We've all been in bad Italian restaurants, haven't we, chowing down on tomato-based mush with no real taste but which leaves you with garlic breath for a week and a half. Picture your local pizzeria, with its pretend taverna roof under the real woodchip ceiling, with fake beams and pillars, and with Artex swirls six inches thick. Imagine the lies they tell you to make you feel like you're in rural Tuscany and not above a hardware shop on some dilapidated backwater High Street. Is the image fixed in your mind? Yes? Right, now set it on fire. Burn it, char it, blacken it. And leave it for a couple of years. Trust me on this. Now throw up some plastic - I'm guessing - honeysuckle round the roof, clag some old adverts and Far Side cartoons on the walls, and get busy with the dullest paint colours you can find; trying to recall it this morning our lass says terracotta, while I say goose shit green. Add a few rails, a jukebox and a quiz machine, and you're almost ready. OK, fling open your doors to any old nutters, drunks, passers-by and basket cases, serve them cheap beer and let them get on with it. And you'll have - hopefully, if it's all gone well - a decent, no-fannying-about little boozer. Aye, you say dregs of humanity and slippery customers, but I prefer to think that it's just full of real people, or at least anyone who hasn't had an insulting niche bar tailored specifically for them. You thought this was going to be a panning, didn't you? Ridiculous notion.

For: Good for a post-work token visit, full of beans and looking on the bright side.
Against: I wouldn't fucking DARE go in later than half seven. Come on, man. It's a fucking loonies' bar.

Did someone mention sandwiching? The first two pubs on our punishing review schedule today were The Long Bar and here, and between them as you walk up Westgate Road is a well known sandwich outlet, whose unique boast at the time of writing this crap is that their products are 'hand cut'. Eh? Fair enough, I could understand that sort of boast from a diamond merchant or a one-man company making acoustic guitars using only traditional tools, but fucking hand cut butties? How can that be a luxury service?

Revolution
Collingwood Street, NE1 1JF
'Sticky crap for the kids'

Housed in an old bank and replacing the laughably short-lived wank-fest eatery that was Café Chinois - which you won't remember but I must keep on mentioning as a lesson to anyone with high-falutin' ideas for the catering trade - Revolution has been around longer than any chain bar has the right to be, probably because it's yet to even approach being truly shit. Typically - as part of the cod-Russian-themed chain - this place advertises itself as a vodka bar, and while their initial 90-distinct-types menu of traditional imported vodka has now been reduced to a glossy list of pop-flavoured sticky crap for the kids, there's still enough for alcohol snobs like me to be happily shafted for a shot of something unpronounceable. But, strangely for a bar, it's not the drink that's the main reason to come here, nor is it whatever bollocks the Revolution chain are claiming as their brand values this month. What I like most about it is the building itself. Serious money was obviously spent here on restoring the bank's old decor, with magnificent carved pillars, high, ornate ceilings and enough cold marble to rival Lenin's mausoleum (no, of course I haven't been, you daft bastard). And they've definitely been keeping on top of the spring cleaning, so it looks just as fancy now as it did when it first opened all those years ago, and that's not something you can say too often. The only differences I've really noticed over time are the plush new booth seats on the lower level, and the angled mirrors above the bar counter, the ones that let you see the pained, unserved expression on the face of whichever poor sod's been sent to get the round in. With the bar counter running virtually the entire length of the window wall, they never, ever seem to have enough of their snooty staff on to man it, and you find yourself thinking that a bit less of the cocktail-aerobics and posing, and a bit more speed on the service wouldn't go amiss. Plus, with that huge display of bottles in the window looking like an upmarket target for lob-the-beanbags at the fair, I wouldn't like to be around the next time Newcastle United lose a Cup Final. I imagine their lease will be up long before that happens again, though. Still - looking for positives - as well as the attention given to the decor here, Revolution's other plus point is its location; the sunlight blazing down Collingwood Street and through the huge windows makes it an absolute spunker of a bar for a spontaneous payday afternoon session, knocking off early and pissing your flexitime up the wall. Obviously, from my cantankerous point of view, the place becomes slightly less attractive when the pink ties and pin-stripes arrive once the sun's over the yard arm, and is a definite no-go zone when the fake tans start snaking round the block waiting for their eclectic beats. You might like all that stuff: I don't, but then you knew that already. On top of that, I'm deeply and sensibly suspicious of any bar that will grant admission to people who are prepared to queue up to get in. And I suppose that sort of sums up my attitude to the place; it's a fantastic-looking bar with decent beer at a manageable price, and it only has one major down side, namely the people - staff and customers - in it. Shame.

For: Afternoon, sunshine, nice pint, good company, half empty, no flaming DJ.
Against: All other times. And the over-attentive daytime table service gets on your bloody wick after a while.

For all the cheesy gimmickry inside, there's still been nothing to rival the bloody monstrosity of Westgate House next door, now mercifully long gone and demolished. That hideous office block captured the feel of the pre-Glasnost Soviet Union better than any carefully researched Russian theme bar ever could. Obviously, I know 1980s Vladivostok like the back of my hand.

The Sports Café
19-25 Grainger Street, NE1 5JG
'I'm mad, me'

The Sports Café is also in an old bank, the former TSB at the Station end of Grainger Street, the one that some bright spark knocked the wrong wall out of, almost sending the whole building sprawling all over the road. After spending years and a whole boatload of cash on doing it up, the building's present occupiers have produced, well, something that's a dead ringer for Sports Soccer on Eldon Square's Blackett Bridge. Even if you're not from Newcastle, there'll be one of those shops on your High Street, hawking cut-price training gear to lard arses who've never done an hour's exercise in their lives, except maybe the walk from the bus stop to the chip shop and up the road to the bar. This is the store that gives us proud Britons our national dress. The public wants what the public gets. And, if you take away the mountains of unsellable Donnay sweatshirts from those retail units and replace them with a few beer pumps and that, then you'll know, more or less, what the Sports Café looks like on the inside. Yeah, there's a few pool tables and some rubbish autographed gear in frames, but there's not a lot more. I had, I'll grant you, the most shocking hangover when I came to do the review, but it just seemed to me like staircase after staircase, leading to more and more laminate flooring, round and round and up and down; I got lost on the way out, for crying out loud. Look, I'll be honest with you: I'm sick of just slagging off bars willy-nilly, so I'm going to try to look for some good points here. Even though the Sports Café is part of a chain - and I fucking hate those on principle - I didn't mind the place when it was full before the match, with sports fans watching, like, sport. There: a positive comment. But I will never forgive them for the advert that some bored woman thrust into my hand the last time I was in, an ad for what they did at other times. Namely: The Sports Café Office Party, on Fridays where you 'drink, dance and flirt' and 'where office rules are made to be broken'. This, I assume, means the same gaggles of 'I'm mad, me' arsewits and blubbery brood-mares in hastily-applied slap squabbling and cackling about sweet fuck all over a sickly cocktail or a special offer bottle. Look at the plight of them, if you can bear it. One's crying; one's been sick down his shirt; he's trying to get in her pants; she's about to belt someone. All human life is here, stapling open the eyes of evolution and photocopying its face. And as ever, they're the only people in the entire bar who have yet to realise they have nothing whatsoever in common, besides utter despair. Saturday they'll be livid and thumbing out the poison texts, Sunday in a sulk, Monday looking daggers, Tuesday's a bit of a thaw, and come Friday they'll all be back here again, the same repression causing the same social disasters among the same otherwise-unemployables over and over again. It's a tragedy, it really is. And these jokers want to make a theme night out of it? It beggars belief, I tell you.

For: They've swiped that DJ from Idols and he's brought 'the fanny' - his words, not mine - with him.
Against: When is someone going to cotton on that poledancing podiums should be more than a foot off the ground? If I'm being deafened in a bar that advertises titties, then titties are what I want to see, not the back of some lanky twat's head.

That hangover I mentioned earlier? After an office night out, it was. Hence the bitterness about office workers, about institutionalised madness, and about my wasted life amongst fools. You think I just rant like I do to whack the beehive, do you? You think this is fiction? Write about what you know, they say. I've lived every fucking second of this nightmare and I'm whining about it as a warning, to you, because nobody else will.

The Star

79 Westgate Road, NE1 1SG
'A pig in shit, a sand boy, or even the proverbial Larry'

There's no point beating around the bush: The Star is as rough as fuck. On a match day, you can't move for screaming, scowling, glass-throwing headcases, pushing and shoving and daring you to say something. And that's just the bloody staff. The punters are the grimmest crowd you could ever imagine this side of the Grainger Market radgie bars, and would scare the living shite out of any stray tourist who got lost on his way from the Centre For Life to Eldon Square. And this, for reasons I'm far too innocent to comprehend, is a pub nicknamed the 'Shooting' Star. Still, at least all that gives me something worth criticising, rather than the complete mental vacuum caused by this place for the rest of the week. The Star between fixtures is an average, run of the mill, lowest-common-denominator, desperately dull, drab, gloomy little pub with absolutely no atmosphere at all, which means that I'm probably going to have to resort to character assassination just to pad this out a bit. Maybe it was because I was three days away from going on holiday when we visited, and was in the sort of mood where, if I'd seen a pig in shit, a sand boy, or even the proverbial Larry, I'd have told them all to cheer up, but I did get the impression that if the Samaritans did personal visits, they could do worse than start off in here. The punters in the front end seemed to be one step away from belting each other, while the back of the pub was full of people who looked like they wished they were dead. Fuck it, man, I wished they were dead myself. So, to sum up: The Star - you need it like you need a hole in the head.

For: If you're serious about topping yourself, rather than being in the middle of a drama queen sulk, then get yourself in here.

Against: Everything between entering and leaving.

Even being situated right across the road from the Academy won't do this place any favours, since your average gig-goer there is either posing in the hipster bars round the corner, or huffing and puffing at daddy for not being able to find a parking space quickly enough to allow them a sly underage swig of vodka from the hairspray bottle and a tweak of the eyeliner before the venue doors open.

The Telegraph
Orchard Street, NE1 3NZ
'Five quid a pint'

I'm going to give you an example of the sort of weak-willed, contrary prick I am. A few years ago the Telegraph had a refit, the type of makeover that I deplore on general principle since I regard all changes to everything, ever, as bad. Man, I hated it, and made a point out of telling anyone who would listen what a complete balls-up they'd made of one of my favourite boozers. But now the refurbishment looks just as shabby as the lovable dive it replaced, I'm going to do a complete U-turn and claim that I loved it all along. That's fashion for you. L-shaped, with stripped wood, retro-kitsch lighting, red and cream walls, and cosy booths, the Telegraph is clearly one of the best bars in Newcastle, and not, as I may have once erroneously implied (i.e. said outright), 'piss-poor', 'bowdlerised' or even 'unintentionally funny'. There's a range of original pictures on the walls brightening the place up with a contemporary touch, and while I was absolutely smashed the last time I was in so I didn't really notice, I'm fairly sure they've still got that one of a huge Elastoplast. The beer's always decent, the atmosphere's usually good, and as for the punters, it depends what time of day you go, really. It's postmen early afternoon; four bells onwards it's disgruntled office workers from whichever call centre in the area is counting down to overseas outsourcing and redundancy this week; and after that it's hipsters, heavy of spectacle frame and grating of voice. But at least you have to suffer neither track-suited scum nor moneyed fools who're unable to entertain the notion of a good time unless they've paid five quid a pint. Upstairs is the pub's major selling point, the fantastic rooftop beer garden where I've spent many hours watching the trains whilst pretending to listen to our lass wittering on about nowt. Well, I say many hours: all those hours were on the same night, on one of the rare occasions in this town when it actually stopped pissing down. And the Telegraph's upstairs room, if rain stops play, features bands (yay!) and DJs (take a wild guess!) throughout the week: check local press for details, and don't be asking me, cos I'm far too old and apathetic for that sort of thing. So, aye, The Tele needs a wipe-down every once in a while and, aye, there's always some cunt getting on your nerves, but it's certainly one of the top five in the city. Watch them ruin it again.

For: What they used to call a well-stocked jukebox, possibly the only one in the town that actually plays what I've paid for.
Against: Having to walk through that piss-stinking tunnel under the railway tracks to get there.

DJ rant #762. How come, when you see a promo poster these days for an evening's entertainment in a bar like this, the DJ - the bloke who plays records, lest we forget - now occupies top billing with his 'set', while the bands have to make do with a lowly spot further down the page in smaller font? When the fuck did that start happening?

Tilleys

105 Westgate Road, NE1 4AW
'Your average pitch black wankbar'

Now part of the sinister Head of Steam global conglomerate, Tilley's has been smartened up a bit from the stinking student ashtray it was before, and it's a damned sight better for it, too. Aye, the colours are pretty bloody awful - chocolate ceiling, mustard walls - but it still manages to be cool without being pretentious and buzzing without pummelling your bloody ear-drums. And any pub that has big windows so you at least know what time of day it is when you're there is good for me: try telling that to your average pitch black wankbar. And while it's probably expected in a pub review to talk about the stuff that goes on inside, the beer and chat (In a bar? Controversial, I know...) often takes a back seat to the life outside. Those windows are just the ticket for spying on the endless parade of parasites that seems to wander aimlessly up and down Westgate Road at all hours: there's nowt like seeing some pissed-up spotty oiks in Helly Hansen gear practically humping each other in a shop doorway at two in the afternoon to make you feel so much better about your own upbringing. And watching the police cracking down on the town's alkies over the road is always good for a grin. See the drunks wazzing away their dole money in the 'plaza' by the city walls, the one with the big fuck-off silver spike stuck in it. Laugh like a fart from a cyclist in the Tour de France home stretch as Plod pounces and pours away another two litres of economy lager before moving the miscreants along. And when your eyes return to the interior, instead of gazing dejectedly at the floor like some mopey-faced emo twat, why don't you glance up to the wall next to the window, where you'll see the big cartoon picture of Tara Palmer-Tomkinson looking foxy, demure and far more human than the appalling 'famous for what, exactly?' giggling nincompoop on the telly. Absolutely tremendous, that. So aye, I've seen a thousand refits, and they've all been far, far worse than this. From high street-standard dull-fest to stylish toss-free bar is no easy step to make, but I think they've done it. I suppose I'd better mention the customers, finally: they're more or less the same punters as the Head of Steam, The Forth and The Telegraph - it's all a bit bleeding incestuous if you ask me - but I'd still rather relax and sup with people who are just a bit dopey looking and/or snooty than sit shaking like a shitting dog among identikit Geordie Boys and Bacardi Bruisers looking to kick my fucking head in. For nowt.

For: Liefman's Kriek beer on draught. Oh, that sweet cherry poison.

Against: The sign above the door belongs outside a prissy hair-dressers and not a boozer.

I've always been quick to jump on the disadvantaged for their lack of standards, whilst ignoring the shortcomings of the more privileged classes. Not any more. A couple of female friends of mine once came back from the bogs here with reports of some strange - male - grunting sounds coming from one of the traps. Five minutes later, an extremely dissatisfied girl skulks out, followed by a smug and red-faced gentleman with an uncomfortable gait. Can you believe they then just sat there at the bar, like nothing had happened? (Probably true in her case, judging from the scowl on her mush.) And they were all rah-schtudent posh and everything. I still can't fathom it out. When money is no object, why the hell would you choose to rut not only in a public place, but in the toilets of Tilleys? Now, I've never been in the Ladies, so it could be palatial in there, but judging by the decrepit clip of the Gents, I think it's a little unlikely. What sort of human being could bear to fornicate in such hideous surroundings? What have the middle class baby-boomers been teaching their kids? I'd sooner take the dirtbag option and do it in the street. At least the council clean the fucking shop doorways occasionally.

Tokyo
17 Westgate Road, NE1 1SE
'Ever-spreading backsides'

Tokyo: formerly Po Na Na, Jakks, Berlin's, and always, always a bar for strokers. Let's see if this incarnation is any less annoying. Well, for a kick-off, having no names on the beer pumps may place them at the very forefront of bar design, but it can be a little irritating for the poor punter wondering what the hell he's going to get served. And it's alright forcing the bar staff to tell you what's on offer when it's quiet, but as soon as the inevitable beanie-hatted-goatee-bearded idiot turns up with his tunes it'll be a fucking nightmare. The bar started off being merely gloomy when we were in and then descended into pitch-blackness when some bright spark decided it was time to get a little moody, but I did at least have a chance to clock the decor before the eyestrain popped my lenses out. Curtains hanging from strange places, intimate booths along one wall, floor-to-ceiling mirrors along the other; all very tastefully done I agree, but I still couldn't help but feel like I was drinking in the Blackie Boy, and I'm sure that's the last thing the designers wanted. The call of nature forced me to check out the bogs: the usual expensive bar stuff, all polished wood and gleaming chrome, tragically offset by the beer belly-defying unpleasantness of having to piss into a hole in a cupboard, not to mention the indignity of hockling on your cock instead of in a trough. And it was only when I went for a slash - up the staircase that looks like my fucking bathroom did when I trusted the plasterers not to make a mess - that I came across this bar's real selling point: the beer garden. Enclosed by the neighbouring buildings on three sides, protected by a muckle sliding door on the other, and with fairy lights twinkling among the weeds, you can finally see the attraction of the place and maybe forgive them for their exorbitant prices. Slouching on the outdoor settees and ripping the piss out of the latest fashions as a cool breeze ruffles your hair is almost enough to make you forget that your bar bill has just sneaked in under an hour's pay for a pint and a half. To be honest, pretentious toss though it was, I didn't mind the bar itself. It was the punters who got on my tits; sour-faced office girls bemoaning their ever-spreading backsides over an expensive cocktail, and Celtic-tattooed chumps making the most of their footballer's mullets before the stranglehold of male-pattern baldness. Plus, if I'd just spent a fortune buying drink in a place like this, I'd at least try to make it look like I was enjoying myself. Miserable bastards.

For: I'm a sucker for beer gardens, so that's a definite 'For'.
Against: Oh, do cheer up, love, will you?

If you've ever wondered why it costs £50 for a solicitor to take a piece of paper from this pile, write their name on it, and then put it on that pile, then Tokyo's smug, corporate-laptop-bagged, expensively spectacled customers will provide your answer. Greedy, pen-pushing, arrogant, bullied-at-school, overbearing, PA-molesting, pin-striped needledicks, the lot of them.

Union Rooms

48 Westgate Road, NE1 1TT
'As bad as Peter Sutcliffe'

Thanks to the marvellous building in which it is housed, the Union Rooms is the least horrible of Newcastle's Wetherspoon pubs, even if that's tantamount to saying that Fred West wasn't quite as bad as Peter Sutcliffe or Dennis Nilsen on account of his terrific patio tiling skills. Once a jewel in the Wetherspoon crown, this bar has quietly frayed around the edges over the years and, despite occasional refits being thrown at it, now looks like a stately home gone to seed, or the sort of place Griff Rhys Jones would goggle his eyes about on that Jolly Middle-England begging show of his. I can see him now, leaping from room to room, bounding up the stairs, fixing his gaze upon the stained glass windows at the top of the staircase, and then falling flat on his extra-chinny face over the tatty carpet that lines the steps. That'll teach him. A haunt for students and paupers, tightwads and skivers, the Union Rooms serves up a reassuringly drab pint of bargain fizz to go with your something and chips, and provides ideal respite for punters who aren't necessarily out to enjoy themselves, a mindset I fully understand. On any afternoon you care to name, you can pull up a battered stool, have a window to yourself - there's enough to go round - and stare at your own personal rain. And if you're really lucky, you can treat yourself to the best graveyard view in the whole town. That, believe me, is its prime feature. I don't hate this place, though: it's not that bad, really. I just tend to view it as an acquaintance I don't see too often, one whose name crops up in conversation, but never provokes enough interest to have me reaching for the phone or digging out his e-mail address. He's fine as a memory or an entry on the Christmas card list, but by Christ is he boring if you actually meet him in the street.

For: Astonishingly, the first time I became aware of the pub's range of Polish lagers - Żywiec, Okocim and Tyskie - was the very day after I returned from a brief jaunt to Krakow.
Against: Oh Lord, not fucking Żywiec...

The Burglar's Dog guide to Krakow: Contrary to popular opinion, Poland is not permanently six inches deep in snow, nor is it in black and white. It is a country determined to throw off the shackles of its communist past and show its true colours alongside the greats of Europe. Here's my suggested itinerary for its historical showpiece, Krakow. Day 1. Morning: Wake with hangover. Spend five hours in 37-degree heat at Auschwitz-Birkenau. Fail to take bottled water. Or food. Afternoon: Travel on sweaty minibus to salt mines of Wieliczka. Queue in blazing sun for an hour. Let salty air of mines remove all healthy toxins from body. Evening: match usual Foster's consumption pint-for-pint with strong Polish beers, add celebratory cocktails and a splash of bison grass vodka. Collapse. Day 2: Stay in hotel toilet. Day 3: As day 2. Mind, those Poles don't half make you feel welcome. Not only do they know all the English phrases that could ever be needed in the service industry, but they were kind enough to offer to take me to hospital, too. Cultural ambassador? Me? Maybe if I got my fucking dribbling, weeping face off the pub doorstep, aye. What a mess.

Yates's

30 Grainger Street, NE1 5JG
'The finest bar Newcastle has ever seen'

If there was any justice in this world, then this would be the finest bar Newcastle has ever seen. Housed in a truly remarkable French Renaissance building built in 1886 by John Johnstone for the Newcastle and Gateshead Gas Corporation, one of the most impressive sites in an already astounding area of architectural excellence, this bar deserves to be nothing less than a sumptuous Grand Café to make it the envy of cultural cities the world over. Instead it's a Yates's chain bar. And it's bloody awful. From the problem-estate youth club colour scheme, to the sticky carpet remnants; from the stodgy nachos and burgers soaking up the average beer, to the dog-rough punters, you know exactly what you're going to get before you even walk through the door. I can safely say that this branch of Yates's is identical to the one in your town, except that this one has probably got a few more floors of mediocrity. You can't even make the most of the large screen TV, since Sky's afternoon matches are bleached out by the pub's only good point, the sun blazing through the windows for most of the day. An over-abundance of promo material advertises tacky theme nights throughout the year and highlights their seeming inability to use the word 'party' without sticking two exclamation marks beside it. And above the pool tables on the top floor, there's a patronising poster of beautiful people stand-ing, cue in hand and grin on immaculately painted face, helpfully showing the general gist of the game. Listen: I don't need to be told that a pool table is where you play pool, and I certainly don't need some fuckers telling me what sort of time to have. Simple rule of thumb: if they need to show you people (pretending they're) enjoying themselves, then it's a guarantee that you most definitely won't. This place is an absolute barrel of dross. How the hell has even one of these bars survived, let alone a nation-wide chain of the bastards? I promise you now: when my lottery numbers finally come up, I fully intend to give this building the pub it deserves. And you're all barred, the fucking lot of you.

For: Get a seat in the windows on a sunny day when you've got a thumping hangover and no real thirst for the drink, and it's just about bearable.

Against: They boast of being an 'unrivalled meeting place'. Fuck alone knows what that spurious claim is based on, but I'd sooner meet up at the bus stop outside, in the pissing rain if necessary, than ever set foot in here again.

Theme nights: the work of the devil. And no theme night could ever be worse than the humiliating spectacle of St Patrick's Day, whereupon the feckless, pissed-up inhabitants of this country attempt to compensate for their own lack of national pride by hijacking someone else's. I'm sorry, but you can't write off 364 days a year of jingoistic abuse simply by wearing a stupid leprechaun hat for the remaining 24 hours. St Paddy's Day should be exclusively for the Irish, and the rest of you sad twats can fuck the fuck off.

4

The Burglar's Dog UEFAEuro2008™ Special

Crikey O'Reilly: is it nearly that time already? Can it really have been almost two years since England's last major football tournament appearance? Why, it only seems like yesterday that Rooney and Ronaldo were squabbling like girls on the biggest stage in the world.

We imagine that by now you'll be making tentative plans for summer 2008's big games, plotting which bars will have the best atmosphere and the sweetest vantage points. And that's where The Burglar's Dog UEFAEuro2008™ Special comes in. We aim to give you the low-down on all the very best places to drink during the tournament with our in-depth guide to the continent's biggest sporting event. We'll tell you the places to go and the exclusive deals they're offering to help you make the most of this international celebration of football. Come on England! Come on England!

Our top tip for the perfect match-viewing experience is:

Stop in.

You might as well, for all the enjoyment you'll get out of going to the bar to watch it. Go on: lock yourself in the spare room with the portable, a few dozen cans and a pail to piss in. Avoid the pub at all costs. It'll be a disaster from start to finish. It doesn't matter what your gleefully optimistic arrangements are, you'll end up in the same fucking predicament as you do with every major tournament: either stuck in the queue for some shitey fun-bar, furiously poiking out the texts to your mates who've been in since opening time, or inside missing half the match thumb-bickering with the unfortunate queue-bound sods outside.

You can forget about the banter and the tactical insight. Your ears will be bleeding long before kick-off, thanks to the inane hollering of the fuckhead DJ, whipping up an atmosphere by pumping out Ibiza classics at illegal volumes. Think of the pushing and shoving, the infuriating service and the bar's insulting insinuation that this tournament - and every match ever - was their idea.

But the big screen!, we're hearing. What about the big screen?! Is that the screen that's so big it reaches down to the floor, so all anyone outside of the first three rows will see is the score along the top and the backs of every fucker else's head? Or is it the flapping, blurred, bleached-out sailcloth that's all but invisible unless you're rigidly perpendicular to it?

Everyone in the pub is an utter fool. When England lose, it'll be their fault. Let there be a by-law passed for each and every football event that forbids entry to the pissed-up meathead or the unctuous little cunt in the jester's hat. Enforce a minimum pint price, one that makes it less of a good idea to hoy it up, up and away at the first sight of a free kick on the edge of the D. And singing at the telly? Why?

Saints preserve us from the clueless, once-a-year England fanette, all tight replica shirt and billowing fat arse, yodelling her pig-ignorance of the beautiful game into the ear of whichever poor twat she's latched onto. Yeah, we know what you're thinking: you're thinking we're going to trot out some lazy, offensive clichés about women's understanding of the offside law. Balls, are we. But we are going to express despair that they've yet to grasp the 85-minute rule, which clearly states that, just because a deathly dull match is 0-0 in the dying stages, any man in her company is NOT automatically content just to have 'seen most of it', nor is he therefore likely to want to talk about work or soft bloody furnishings until the bastard in the yellow blows for full-time.

Forget what the telly has told you. Watching the match in the pub will NOT be like the adverts, not even the ones for some other fucking sport they call 'furtee'. There will be no dancing in the streets afterwards, no multiracial harmony and no beaming faces. There will be no stirring mix of heartfelt passion and respect for a game well played whatever the outcome. And there will be no blonde honeys in girly-fit England tops begging to swallow your muck just because you can name all of the '66 Final XI.

Instead there will be crushing disappointment at another premature exit. There will be a forlorn stream of spilt Foster's and broken glass. And there will be ugly scenes as we blow our collective gasket, releasing our pent-up fury on whatever comes to hand. The burger van will be in flames, roadsigns will be launched through the windscreen of the nearest foreign vehicle, and the Five-0 will be getting out the truncheons and the visors, ready to crack some fucking skulls.

Come on, the pricks in the Hackett tops will be saying: it's our national day. We need something to make up for the embar-rassment that is our St George's celebrations. In Ireland they have St Paddy's, in Brazil there's the Carnival, and even the bloody Latvians have their Day of Proclamation. This is what we do, this proud nation with so much cultural and historical impact on the four corners of the globe: each time we get - controver-sially, always controversially - knocked out of a major tourna-ment, we run fucking riot. After all, who won the bloody war anyway?

Look, we're never going to win a damn trophy, no matter what cobblers they trot out about team spirit and x-ty years of hurt. We're not even going to make the semis. That much is crystal clear, and you don't need us to spell out exactly why. Cometh the hour, cometh the farce. Take it from us, we'll fuck it up like we always do.

DON'T go to the pub to watch any of it. Stay at home and save yourself the heartache. Think of the whole extravaganza as being like Christmas, just with (marginally) better weather. By the time it kicks off for real, you'll already have had weeks of inescapable build-up, with every spiv and shyster trying to sell you shit you don't need on the back of some vague ideas of celebration. You'll have been bombarded with their lies about how you can't live without their cash-in clothing and their mile-wide twenty-grand tellies. The last thing you need is all that crap in the pub as well. Refuse to line their pockets. Tell them to shove it. Let them know what you know, that their fucking number is up. You'll thank us for it later.

Prediction:

Quarter Finals
EU Newcomer 2 – England 0
(Dubious penalty 36, Miles offside 72)

(Disclaimer: The Burglar's Dog Alternative Guide to Drinking in Newcastle was submitted for publication before the end of qualification for UEFAEuro2008™. Publishing's like that, you see. It takes time. If by any chance – and I only got odds of 5-to-2 at the bookies – McClaren or his panic appointment successor has fucked it right up and England have failed to make the finals, then don't come crying to us. And for fuck's sake, see if you can just sit in the house and twiddle your thumbs, or get out and do the gardening, or sign up as a crash-test dummy while the tournament is on. Do not let me catch you wearing a Guinness hat or pouting 'Ciao bella' or trying to get some mileage from the Barcelona top you bought on holiday. You're English and you're stuck with it, so don't be piggy-backing on some other nation's moment of glory.)

5

City Centre

'Described as the 'city of palaces' when completed in 1842, Grainger Town is the historic heart of Newcastle. Recent restoration projects mean that the elegant stylish Victorian and Georgian architecture can now be enjoyed to the full. The area takes in the magnificent classical Georgian buildings of Grey Street - including the famous Theatre Royal - Grey's Monument and the Edwardian Central Arcade, and leads to the city's main shopping thoroughfare of Northumberland Street, as well as the bustling Eldon Square centre. And Greggs.' - Norman Undercroft, Historian.

Adelphi
20 Shakespeare Street, NE1 6AQ
'Crocked and hopeless'

Newcastle's premier hooligan bar and helpfully just a bottle's throw from the cop shop, the Adelphi is the sort of place you admire from afar for its integrity, and then stay the hell away from for fear of a kicking. Me, I've never had any bother in here, but that's because I always wear my Toon top when I go, and because I try to swagger like I'm some sort of fucking hard case rather than the spineless little wanker I know myself to be. How man, I'm squit-shit scared of the puppet Gremlins out of the '80s films, never mind the human ones with the knock-off Burberry who reportedly get in here. There's not really much point in trying to have an in-depth discussion of the Adelphi's decor: there's the bar counter in the middle, a bog door through an arch somewhere at the back, a floor and a ceiling, and that's your lot. Every single other square millimetre of space has been covered by Newcastle United stuff. Photos, posters, mirrors, scarves, flayed tattooed skin; it's all there. From the dawn of time when we were a club that won things, to the charity fund for the crocked and hopeless we've been recently, there's a framed snap to celebrate it or make you cuss like a fucker. It truly is a remarkable display, comprehensive enough to feature the Judases and turncoats of Newcastle United history as well as the likes of Shearer and Milburn. Look, I don't often get in here, hence it'd be stupid to prattle on at length about the place, so I'll just tell you that, depending on your point of view and the colour of your shirt, it's either rough as fuck or a no-nonsense bar with cracking atmosphere. And because it's obviously not match day every day, what I'll say about the Adelphi for the rest of the time is this: if you want to spend time amongst weather-beaten codgers, harassed businessmen and slumming-it luvvies from the Theatre Royal, then this'll be right up your street. I'm a good few years too young to enjoy it now, but time stops for no man.

For: The opening hours, which, for as long as I can remember, have been whenever they fucking well feel like it.
Against: If you're ever charged with taking a photo of the Adelphi there's always some bugger parked outside, making it nigh-on impossible to get a decent clear shot of the place. Instead, you'll be reduced to standing with a massive zoom lens across the other side of Pilgrim Street, and made to feel like a junior Chronicle smudger covering an unsolvable hit-and-run case where the accused's family are hard as fucking nails.

Club v country: I can never get as fired up for England as I do when it's Newcastle United. Who does? Who would actually choose the national side over their own team, apart from club-hopping Cockneys or racist morons? Actually, I know fine well who does. It's the berks who believe that the more shitty merchandise you display, the more of an expert you are on the game. I dread the European Championships and the World Cup: every two years you get the same imbeciles who'd spit at you for the rest of time boring you to death with their borrowed platitudes and unrealistic expectations. And all this drivel about reclaiming the flag of St George? It was better when it was only the BNP who waved it: at least they have half an idea why I fucking hate them.

The Bacchus

34 High Bridge, NE1 6BX
'Mayhem and murder'

People keep telling me I'm too negative; in fact everyone I know has been saying that lately. So, just for a change, I'm going to try my hardest to give a positive review, despite the fact that the Bacchus is where I first met our lass, back in the days before decimalisation. If you haven't been in here for a while - and, believe me, I still see once-a-year punters spinning round and looking confused - then you'll notice a few changes from the old place. Firstly, and most importantly of all, it's a completely different pub. The old Bacchus was razed to the ground and the new one is essentially where that flaming rancid Goth shop Phaze used to be. Got that? Good. Now that we've established the basics, maybe you can stop waving your fucking arms about and smacking me in the teeth. Secondly, there's only one room now - if you don't count the little snug area off to the left where the grannies gather to plot mayhem and murder - with a huge bar slap-bang in the middle, a bar permanently encrusted with the fattest of fuckers in the sloppiest of suits. If there is one thing that remains from days gone by, then it's the emphasis on conversation and relaxation, with comfortable armchairs by the windows at the front, although I don't know why I bothered to mention them, since you'll never get to slump there. Take any lunchtime, any post-work swifty, or any evening session and see if I'm lying: there'll always be some gopper from a cosmetic counter sitting in one chair, with her shopping stuffed into another three. Her mouth will be Botoxed into a permanent pucker of rage and her habitual theft of her merchandise will leave her stinking like a whore's drawers. And you will never be brave enough to ask her to shift, no matter how many pints you've necked. Speaking of whores, my 'thirdly' is this: if the old Bacchus decor was what drew you in, making you feel like you were next in line in the brothel you'd never have the balls to visit, then I'm afraid all that's changed, too. Instead there's a vague cruise-liner theme - a bit like the Poseidon Adventure but, like, the right way up - with nautical photos all over the place and tons of fancy woodwork. Other notable decor items are the Burberry tartan carpet on the raised bit at the back and the massive wine glasses on the way to the bogs upstairs, though I must be going frigging blind 'cause I it took me three visits and someone saying, 'Up THERE, you moron' before I saw them. I could prattle on all day, to be honest, about this, that, and the other, but the overall impression is of a pub that purely wants to be just that: not a leisure venue, a 'luxebar', or a 24-hour party palace, complete with thumping four-to-the-floor when you're trying to eat your dinner. It's just a boozer, and a pretty smart-looking one at that, but it sure makes a change to have a quiet pint in here after putting up with the identikit bars that reared their coiffed heads in the time the Bacchus was in ruins. There. Is that positive enough for you?

For: If you're drunk enough, and you squint through the right bit of window, then the sign on Pani's Café over the road clearly says 'Penis Café'.

Against: During the Bacchus' eighteen month demolition-and-resurrection there was an internet newsgroup set up to cater for the people who were missing the place. The sad bastards. Who'd be tragic enough to go on the internet writing about pubs, like?

That Burberry carpet prompts me to give my bigoted two-

penn'orth on this matter: I saw an entire family - average age seventeen - of ne'er-do-wells in the town on the weekend of the review visit, clad top-to-toe in stolen designer sportswear, and pushing a pram up the Bigg Market. I failed to catch the name of the child for all the 'Heeyah man's and 'Y'daft cunt's, but following the pattern of the-posher-the-name-the-scummier-the-child, let's assume it was called Pronuptia Jade. And what was this future shoplifter travelling in? A fucking Burberry-effect pram, that's what. Why, it must've been the envy of the whole of the courthouse steps. Vermin.

Bar 42

16-18 Hood Street, NE1 6JQ
'Great meeting place'

I'm an early starter when it comes to the lash. And because I'm a lily-livered jessie, that also makes me an early finisher, tottering home having clearly had enough just as the rest of the town is getting warmed up. And that's how, from my bus-stop vantage point across the street, I've witnessed the bewildering spectacle of Bar 42. Countless are the times I've stood there in my big coat, cowering from the wind and snow battering down Pilgrim Street, and watched the procession of scowling, semi-naked trollops heading for this place. Time after time I've seen the endless queues of deep-frozen imbeciles in thermal chiffon, and been completely unable to fathom why such an awful bar is so bloody popular. It can't even lay claim to being a 'great meeting place', since once you enter you'll never, ever leave. And this is something I know to be true; Christ knows I endured it enough times before I put a blanket ban on work nights out. This is how it happens: 'Eeh, I'll meet you in 42 at 4.30. Hee hee, trebles! But Donna won't be there until 6, and Simon can't make it until half past. Me sister's not out 'til 8 and she's meeting her mates there at 8.30. And Linzi doesn't get off 'til...' So they stand in flaming 42 all night, waiting for fool after fool to arrive, none of them with the wit or intelligence to suggest that, just once in their lives, they might try somewhere else. Because that would be heresy: they go there because that's where they've always gone. Simple as. Night after night and year after year they waste their evenings in here, pretending to be happy. The music's crap, the atmosphere's terrible, the beer's over-priced piddle and the first thing any sensible person dragged in against their will would do is make a frantic search for the fire exits. Even the decor is depressing in that tatty, holes-in-the-carpet, grim late '80s way. But it doesn't matter what the management plan to do to it or how many refits they attempt, this place will always be the same: a dark, claustrophobic, low-ceilinged, punters-jammed-in sweatfest. And whether it's early doors or lasties, a lunchtime pint or an evening blow-out, if you drink in here you're an idiot. And you always will be.

For: The smoking ban means they've had to ditch the cats' litter tray at the bottom of the stairs.

Against: When I am king, closing down Bar 42 will be the second thing I do. The first of my regal decrees will be that there is a standardisation of the girl's name Lindsay. I mean it. And all the Lindseys, Linseys, Lyndsays, Lyndseys, Lynseys and especially the Linzis – with circles over each 'i' – who pack out this bar every night will have ONE WEEK to change their passports, their driving licences, their bank details and their e-mail accounts – 'let us no if u want the meal thanx linz xxx' – or they will be incarcerated. With no telly. And no legs.

'Why do you never come to office nights out any more?' they ask. Repeatedly. So I tell them, with as much patience as I can muster. 'It's because whenever I ask you a question at work about work, all you want to do is act the goat about how great Friday night will be. Yet when you actually hit the bar - to let your hair down, remember - all you can think to talk about is your damned spreadsheets and flexitime squabbles.' Got me, fuckhead?

Barluga

35 Grey Street, NE1 6EE
'Boxing Day sales'

Formerly The Metropolitan and still the lunch venue of choice for Grey Street's expense account business bores, the recently (well, since the last time I gave enough of a shit to go there) refurbished Barluga is still smarming away, turning its nose up at anyone with an ounce of sense. Incredibly, after all I've tried to teach them, this town is still burdened with the kind of fools who think sophistication is something to aspire to rather than justification for a public flogging, and all of them drink here. Please, for the love of the Lord, could you get this straight, all you giggling shop girls and balding bank clerks: sophistication can NOT be bought online. And drinking here does not make you a catwalk model or a style guru: it makes you skint. I don't go to Barluga very often, as I've said, but how come every time I go the bar staff always seem to have something more important to do than actually deign to serve me with my overpriced pint? Do I really look like I'm going to appreciate a nice straight line of serviettes when I'm choking for a beer? No. I just look like a very angry man, because that's what this place turns me into. I think the decor's changed a bit since the last time I looked; I'd guess that they've seen one too many Boxing Day sales adverts and they've decided that a hideous '70s revivalist colour scheme is the way to go. I don't remember the pretend snakeskin seats in the booths, but I definitely do recall the fucking beanbags upstairs: how the hell have they survived this long? And they're STILL - and I can only assume that they believe the constant mockery they receive is based on jealousy - trying to flog caviar at £45 a scoop, clearly in the hope that reviewers far more reputable and influential than The Burglar's Dog will mark it down under 'gastropubs'. Will you pack it in, man? Look, if I have to be fair about the place - I suppose it's in the contract, after all - I'd say alright, once in a while, for a single pint on a spontaneous afternoon session, it's tolerable. But if I'd come in here on a big night out expecting it to live up to its insupportable claims of greatness, and seen THIS,

I'd have to sup up, leave, head for the bus stop and go straight home. That's how depressing it is. And if you've ever been there and left without feeling slightly grubby, then you have no business reading this. Get yourself over to GQ, you fucking idiot. Barluga: truly a bar that only a complete scrotum could love.

For: In five years time this place will be long gone and you'll be able look back, with the sort of smirk normally reserved for the Sinclair C5 or Andreas Andersson, upon the stupidity that prompted someone to sell caviar in a fucking boozer. Alright, I might be being a bit optimistic on the timescale, but I'll dance on this place's grave if it's the last thing I do.
Against: I think they've even done away with the faux-naïf (translation: shite) paintings of naked ladies on the stairs. What a fucking gyp.

Chilled. If I see the word 'chilled' to describe a bar once more, I'm liable to stab some fucker in the neck. I can't think of a single thing that makes me feel less chilled than a manufactured 'chilled' atmosphere. Tell me, please, what the hell is chilled about beats too loud to talk, lights too low to see the spots on your dominoes, and a temperature so high you end up smelling like a cheese 'n' pickle sandwich before you've even got your (minimal) change back? Come on, TELL ME.

The Black Garter
31 Clayton Street, NE1 5PN
'Suck pint, suck face'

The Black Garter has a reputation, and it's one that produces heated debates and raging arguments over pints throughout the city. Is it the absolute rock bottom, the very nadir of radgiedom, or is it a down-to-earth, working class boozer popular with the employees and customers of the Grainger Market out the back? Sneaking in for a quick Friday pint on my way to somewhere much more snooty and expensive, I find that this place is now a far cry from the stinking, junkie-infested shit-tip it once was, the place that gave me a lifetime lip-on after some twat pinched my jacket. Recently closed for a week for a refit – I'm guessing it took a day to lay the new carpet, and the previous six to chisel the old one up – the Black Garter these days looks like your local used to before they panelled the damn place and stuck bits of trees and junk shop shite everywhere. And it is absolutely fucking heaving. I'm standing here, in the only available space, propping up the pillar overlooking the stage area, and it dawns on me where I've seen a pub like this before: it's just like the bar in *Star Wars 1* (if I hear you say 'Nyeurgh. It's *Episode IV*, actually...' I'm going to break your bastard nose), but without the tootling mutant jazz band or the rent boy under Alec Guinness's long brown cloak. This place is stuffed to the gills with the sort of characters that wouldn't even get in, never mind be thrown out of, every other bar in the town. Everywhere I look there's a Loony Toon or a stot-the-baal, a daytime drunk or a numpty. On the stool to my left are a couple of pensioners; she's on his knee, and he's clinging on to her for dear life. And they're snogging, noisily and passionately, like first date teens. It's suck pint, suck face, suck pint, suck face, and I can see our lass – who's always had a thing for geek love - thinking, Aw, bless them. I, meanwhile, am trying not to vurp into the back of my throat. There's a commotion behind us, and we turn to see what the script is: it's some old codger trying to sell us his worldly possessions from a black bin liner. Some of it, he tells us, still works. I'm not making this shit up, you know. I'll be honest with you: even though I know there've been no monsters in my neck of the woods since mediaeval times, I'm still too petrified to get the washing in when it's dark. Similarly, even though the Black Garter was the recent recipient of a Best Bar None Award, dished out for 're-sponsible management' and a 'safer, more welcoming drinking experience', it still scares the living fuck out of me. I don't know why that is: maybe I've become paranoid that the crazy eyebrows that make me look like a cunt also make people believe they can treat me like a cunt, shortly before dishing out yet another leathering. To be fair, nobody is giving me any grief, but I get this feeling that everyone's staring at me like I owe them money. But chicken-shit's my middle name, and I think you've probably realised by now that I see the world through bloodstained and shattered goggles. I'm not going to pretend this place is going to appear on tourist board fact sheets or in style mag 'musts' - no pub that has karaoke from four o'clock ever will – but its reputation is far, far worse than the reality. Who'd have thought it?

For: They call themselves a 'day bar', which means they open at 9.30am and shut up shop about 8 bells. And 8pm is the perfect time to quit drinking, as I'm sure anyone who's ever been left in the lurch when I've fucked off for chips before standing my round will tell you. Eventually.
Against: The posters – visible from outside and in – of legendary local drag artiste Miss Ophelia Balls. I suppose they'll keep the pigeons off the windowsills, if nowt else.

The Black Garter is an old-timers' bar, I think it's fair to say. Age is a strange thing, or at least your perception of your own age is: some days you feel nineteen and some days it's ninety-one. But there is one way of telling that you're approaching life's drinking-up time, and that's when you find Next clothes in your wardrobe. And when you wake up one morning – as I did today - and discover the bloody things actually fit you, then you know you're only three places from the front of the spiritual taxi queue. The next thing that will be 'just your size' will be a fucking plywood box. Jesus, where did it all go?

The Blackett Arms
11 Nelson Street, NE1 5AN
'Cleaning his ears with a beermat'

Following a recent refit, the Blackett Arms has combined a playful sense of chic with a traditional twist. Serving cocktails and cappuccino, and complimentary paninis with oils and balsamic, it's now become a serious rival for Café Royal across the road, and has got the fashionista crowd purring that it's this season's hottest venue. You weren't fooled by that cack for even a second, were you? Can't say I blame you. Take away every word except 'serious' from the first two sentences, and you'd have a more accurate description. In fact, if you just used the word 'sentences' and added 'to run concurrently', you might have a few of the punters summed up, too. Even though I've found this to be the least immediately ominous of the Grainger Market bars, walking in here I still feel like I've gatecrashed a gangland wake. Picture me staggering in bollock naked, booling our lass in the wheelbarrow position, with a flashing red nose, a pirate's hat and blowing on a party hooter, and then imagine the reaction of the kith and kin of Knuckles 'Knuckles' McKnuckles. That's how welcome I feel in here. The entire pub's clientele is gathered round one table in the room to the left and, foolishly, I catch the attention of the couple facing me; he's got his feet on the table and he's cleaning his ears with a beermat, and she's stuffed into her top like minced pig's knackers into sausage skin. And they're looking at us as if to say, 'Who are you and what the fuck are you doing in here?' Shit, man: Will this pint ever end? Even the bloke on the bandit doesn't like us; he's dropping his guts like a cornered skunk, probably to keep us far away in case we snaffle his sure-fire jackpot technique. Cowering nervously beside the doorway, I'm clinging on to the shelf to stop my knees from shaking and buckling under me. I'm laughing at the toothless gimp running the karaoke even though he's churning out stuff that would make the ghost of Bernard Manning wince with shame and still fucking up the punch lines. Did you just pour yours into mine, you get? Oh, Christ; now they're all crooning 'Happy Birthday' and we're singing along in fear, even though we haven't a clue whose big day it is. All the same, we're wishing dear Mumbles all the best for her mumbleth, swearing on our mothers' lives that she doesn't look a day over mumblesty. Seizing an opportunity, we sneak into the front room to sit down before we fall down, as some old crone butchers 'Tainted Love' on the stage next door and, glancing around us at the eviscerated seating, we're wondering what the fuck we ARE doing in here. This truly is a rough dive. But hey, this beer's not that bad, and at least we're safe from wankers whose latest haircut cost more than all the clothing in here put together. Another pint? Aye, go on then. Your round.

For: I like the way that the function room / venue upstairs - The Red Rooms - has a separate staircase to shield you from all the unpleasantness of the main bar.

Against: Just because I got out safely with my smart arse intact, doesn't mean you should try it.

At the time of writing, the Grainger Market is due for a massive refurbishment by the council, hopefully to make it - and its pubs - slightly less terrifying. They're planning cultural events and temporary art installations. They are, I shit you not. Maybe one day there really will be that playful sense of chic I mentioned earlier. Or, more likely, maybe it'll all KICK OFF, with pitched battles between the paintings. Who'd win: Perry with the palette knife, or Mackas with the machete? There's a Ladbrokes next door to the Blackett Arms if you fancy a flutter.

Boom!

14-16 Newgate Street, NE1 5RG

'Boom!'? More like...

WANK!

For: Well, come on: they have had a refit.

Against: I'd better explain. The review in the original edition of the Burglar's Dog consisted of one word, and that word was 'SHITE!' Pound for pound, all they deserve by way of a re-review is another single word dismissal, but I suppose I should attempt a few lines by way of an appraisal, even if it fucks with the formatting...

This'll be the proper review here, then. Now that we're limping towards the second decade of the millennium, I think it's time I finally acknowledge that the 1990s have gone. It's hard to do, believe me, but I'll give it a go. I have one or two good memories of the era tucked away to bring a smile to an overcast day. But I also have some dreadful memories, memories that flush me with deep, deep shame, and every last one of them is called to mind by this appalling '90s theme bar. With its shocking disco decor and its nasty collages of cheesy one-hit-wonders of the age, Boom! is the absolute pits of the city's drinking circuit. It simply doesn't get any worse than this. Whoever is responsible for this, whoever suggested doing the refit instead of taking a flamethrower to the entire building, foundations to chimney pots, should be bollocked with a banjo until the end of time. I only ever come here when it's completely empty before the match, squeezing in one more pint without having to jostle my way to the bar for a beer that some clumsy bastard is bound to spill anyway. I have no idea what Boom! is like in full flow, and a-fucking-men to that. But people with no brains and no shame tell me that this is the ultimate good time party bar. I'm not going to pretend to know what a good time is, but I'll hazard a guess at what it's not. It's not standing about like a lazy lob-on under mirror balls and searchlights. It's not drinking what could possibly be the worst beer in Newcastle, stuff that practically forms a crust of slurry on the top of your stomach. And it's not gawking at the posters they've done on the cheap, downloading tiny images from the 'net and zooming them up on the photocopier. They couldn't even be chewed to make them look artily pixellated, could they? Just press the green button and let the shitty resolution take the strain. But, desperate though they are, they're still left standing by the not-quite-in-breach-of-copyright tat for sale behind the bar, in a display that would make the wares of a barrow-lad look like Fenwick's window. Can't say it's Ali G? Fine, it's Herb Warrior. Crazy Frog is rights-managed? No problem: we'll just call it That Annoying Thing. Pin 'em all up, throw a few streamers at them and stick a glittery Stetson on the top. And the kids will lap it up, because – hee hee hee! – it's all a fucking big laugh, isn't it? There is one reason and one reason alone to come here, and that's to buy a pair of

Boom!-branded pointy foam hands, the ideal bran tub present for the colleague you despise. Parcel them up nicely, shove them under the Christmas tree with real care, and then watch in glee as they burst into tears when they open the wrapping. Their feelings of despair, disappointment, disgust and bafflement will be roughly on a par with what I am experiencing now.

Box

Swan House Roundabout, Pilgrim Street, NE1 6BL
'They'll need a fucking stepladder'

Coined by consultants in the 1980s and derived from a join-the-dots puzzle, the phrase 'thinking outside the box' is used to describe looking at a problem from a new perspective and without preconceptions. The trouble is, anyone still using that hoary old cliché in the 21st century is clearly so far inside the box, they'll need a fucking stepladder to get out of it. And so it is with this place. Formerly Bar 55°, the yawning designer pub built in the (reconstruction of the) old Royal Arcade, Box has revamped the premises, made it worse than it was before in every possible way, and then attempted to tart the whole sorry venture up with the piss-boilingly bad slogan... wait for it... 'Box: think outside it, drink inside it'. And in justifying their butchery, the owners clearly can't be bothered to fib in the time-honoured 'for your own good' business tradition, the one that once saw me presented with 'Bad news: we're making you redundant. Good news: think how much stronger the brand will be with the saving!' Instead, they've gone on record as saying, 'We aim to spend as little as possible, to make as much return as possible', and, feeling that the old arcade arches that gave the building its only character were, quote, 'not commercially viable in operating a bar or club', came up with the perfect solution: just block the bastards off. Deny their existence. Arches? What arches? Box is a bar by day and a Nite Club later on ('Nite' Club?! In this day and age?!). I can't and won't comment on the curtained-off club aspect of it, save to say that if you walk past the building – hurriedly – when it's in full swing, you'll see backlit exotic dancers gyrating on shelves in the window. I have no interest whatsoever in clubbing, and I'm well past the upper end of their target age range. But the pub bit, the part that's firmly within my jurisdiction, is fucking appalling. Despite the huge windows overlooking the roaring traffic and the cubist brutality of the All Saints office complex, Box is a dreary, blackened shell of a room, roughly on a par with the aftermath of a 3am settee blaze in a Fire Brigade video. It sucks light from the day, and with it my will to live. Orange disc lights hang from their ceiling gallows, red heart chairs await transplant to a more grateful recipient, and the balls skewered on the standard lamps in the windows pass silent comment on the drinks prices. The same geometric box pattern abuses the floor, the wallpaper and the mirrored pillars alike, while over on the black slate feature wall, Box TV pirouettes its CGI cubery to blanket indifference. Our drinks are served to us by the most uninterested barmaid we've ever seen, and we're treated to an unbroken conversation with her equally gleet-headed colleague that goes something like this: 'MySpace-fuck-jottermean? MySpace-fuck-jottermean?' Put a bloody sock in it and pay attention, you unprofessional fucking bint. And stop treating me – the paying customer, god damn you – as if I'm not there. This is awful. Look, I'll let you into a little secret here. In my guise as the Burglar's Dog I don't hate every bar in Newcastle, not even the ones I rip the piss out of. The general idea is that the reviews are all done from the point of view of a miserable old bastard, just so there's a consistent yardstick. Plus, bile is so much easier – and more entertaining – than praise. It is, trust me. But this fucking terrible bar deserves every single outpouring of spite and each flob of hockle that lands in its smug face. It has been openly commissioned by a self-confessed tightwad, designed with as much contempt as it was possible to show for its setting, staffed by reprehensible gobshites, and it's got the fucking gall to present itself as a luxury item. It is no such thing. Box is no more than an insulting recreation of the mortifying '80s drinking experience, shorn only of the mad hair and the slip-on shoes. And I know I've ended reviews with this word many times before, but this time I mean it: horrible.

For: How the hell can there be a plausible 'For' for a travesty like this? I thought we'd seen the last of the spirit of Dobsons when that place was forcibly shut, left abandoned, and finally demolished along with the Central Library. Obviously I was badly, sadly and fuck-me-Dadly wrong.

Against: They've got one of those bloody tax-loss bubble cars with their corporate logo on it parked on the terrace outside. And if that wasn't bad enough, go past on a night-time and there'll be a fucking mobile disco van pounding away on the roundabout chevrons, distracting the traffic and risking multiple pile-ups. Never mind the carnage, feel the profit margin.

In converting from bar to club, a triple layered Rockwool ceiling had to be installed to keep the noise to a minimum for the people in the apartments above. Really? Here's where I start thinking 'outside the box'. Surely it's not the racket from inside that will keep the residents awake; surely it's the fucking departing customers who'll be responsible for the disturbances. Anyone who's hoying beer down their necks at two in the morning is bound to be disappointed and obnoxious even when it's free entry, so what sort of fucking din are they likely to make when they've had to cough up club prices in the vain hope that someone will be drunk or desperate enough to fuck them? Mind you, I've got no sympathy for the tits in the flats above. It's the price you pay for hip city dwelling, after all. Me, I'll be sticking to my safe, suburban mediocrity. And getting some fucking kip.

Butlers

18 Nun Street, NE1 5AQ
'A cruel, cruel master'

If they're still calling this place Butlers Bistro, then it's about as far from the self-satisfied, arty-farty idea of traditional bistroland as you could possibly imagine. This is a bar where people drink when they're barred from the Clock. This is a bar where my so-called hard mates refuse to go. And, in spite of my concerns about the rest of the dumps surrounding the Grainger Market, this is the only bar where I've felt directly threatened rather than just worried by reputations. For years I didn't even realise that this was a pub; I just thought it was a greasy spoon café catering for the wall-to-wall pensioners who shuffle in through the day. I reviewed it half-heartedly a while back - just after one of the doormen got done for peddling smack, as I recall - and then spent every moment since steering well clear. They've had a bit of a refit recently but, tiptoeing in for a refresher, I find that it's still, even at five bells on a Friday, on payday, when the sun's out, rough as fucking fuck. At first glance this place is done up to look a bit like a hardware shop at Beamish, but instead of desperate parents dragging round kids who couldn't care less, Butlers is full of angry blokes in steel toecaps, and evil witches plotting hen night degradations. Strewn here and there are strings of Christmas lights, but I'd advise that you don't look at them when you're moving about: Butlers is so damned narrow that any distraction could be harmful, since if there's a four-foot arse wedged into a two-foot gap then you can't help but spill the owner's pint. The barmaid keeps mooching about, dutiful yet terrified, like the faithful hound of a cruel, cruel master. And whenever someone leaves, she's in like a shot, wedging the chairs back against the wall, as if the slightest discrepancy in their interlocking pattern would make it easier to yank them out and break them over heads when it all kicks off. Glancing away from the telly above the optics - the smallest big screen you could ever imagine - I see Father Jack Hackett worrying the bar, and next to him is the only reason this place is still standing: the clock. Set right in the middle of the bar top and visible from every point in the pub, this gilded, ormolu, Rococo timepiece is surely the work of a benevolent god, and its dazzling array of shapes, reflections and refractions are enough to calm the most furious soul. When tempers are frayed and voices are raised, they simply need to say, 'The clock, Billy. Look. At. The. Clock.' and all is well again. I just fear the day when someone nicks it.

For: Like eating chips from a sumo wrestler's nappy, it's an interesting experience, but not one you'd want to repeat.

Against: No matter how grim it gets inside, it's still better than the hideous breezeblock monstrosity of Wilkinsons across the alleyway.

Father Jack Hackett was, in case you'd forgotten, the drunken old bastard with the cataract in TV's Father Ted. People say it was a tragedy that Dermot Morgan - who played Ted Crilly - died in his prime, and brought a premature end to a fantastic show. They're right, but it was hardly the saddest comedian death in history. That award must surely go to Dustin Gee, showbiz partner of Les Dennis, who passed on just as they were about to make a name for themselves. See, if Dustin hadn't snuffed it, then Dennis wouldn't have been able to launch his fledgling career on the back of the 'Aw, the poor lad' sympathy vote, and we'd have been excused twenty years of his shoddy game shows and embarrassing impersonations that all sound exactly like Les fucking Dennis. Mind, that Ardal O'Hanlon isn't far behind. 'Ah, Ted. Why'd ye have te go and die, sure? Did ye see me in My Hero? I looked like a fecking eejit, so.'

The Charles Grey

118 Grey Street, NE1 6JG
'Arguably the best in Newcastle'

Let's be honest here. FMs - which The Charles Grey replaces - was an absolute disgrace. Imagine a poor man's Hard Rock Cafe, half-heartedly decorated with musical memorabilia of dubious provenance, serving up cooking lager and alcopops to a customer base of shoppers and tourists too scared to move more than ten feet away from the Monument. When I saw that the place was being refurbished, I harboured relatively high hopes that the bar on the site that is arguably the best in Newcastle would be overhauled to live up to its location. Imagine, then, my crushing disappointment in finding that the twin evils of apathy and corner-cutting have produced this, a Matalan version of the Bacchus down the road and round the corner, with a total refit budget of less than a ton. They've slapped fake brick cladding on the pillars, tied some twigs to the ceilings, and bunged a few pictures of historical characters - I suspect Earl Grey may be one of them, but I couldn't be arsed to work out which one - on the walls, but that's about it. It looks decent enough from the outside, but once you get through the doors you'll find the same old tatty carpet on the never-ending stairs leading to the same old mediocrity above. The whole place just seems so half-arsed, and even after racking my brains for an hour, the only things I can really remember are the chairs on the upstairs level that you need to stand on another chair to get onto. Look, this place isn't the biggest crime in history - the beer's decent enough, after all - but fuck, if they're going to occupy a prime slot you think they'd put some effort into it. The Charles Grey is like every other cynical tourist trap the world over, yet it could have been so much better with a bit more thought and a bit less transparent greed. What a wasted opportunity.

For: They're premise sharing with the Dobsons-replacing Basement Trebles Bar. I'm sure it's absolutely lovely down there...
Against: ...but since they've never, ever let me - or indeed anyone I know - in to see it, that's pure guesswork. The door staff tell me it's a bar exclusively for students, so if you don't look the part or haven't got an NUS card, you can't come in.

I will say this about the Basement, though: how fucking horrified am I to be told that I'm too OLD to get into a pub? What the fuck is the message there? 'This is a bar for shitfaced teenagers only. We don't want you coming in here and upsetting people with your good behaviour'?

Duke of Northumberland

18 Clayton Street, NE1 5PE
'An Oxfam version of Austin Powers'

If there was ever a bar to stop me bleating about the decline of the traditional pub and just start loving the deluxe lounge bar, then it's this one. I knew from reputation that this place was a bit rough, but I wasn't expecting it to be as harrowing as this. What a fucking dump. The Duke of Northumberland, aka The Clock, is not the sort of place you want to take your lass for a quiet pint, unless she's seventeen stone, lists her hobbies as 'pies' and likes headbutting total strangers. Don't come in with your mates; their cowardice in the face of terror will only disappoint you. And don't even come here with a fucking gila monster, unless you're absolutely sure it's packing a shooter. I am going to spell it out for you: there is no point in coming here at all. It's been done, and I did it, to stop you from being so stupid. Drinking in the Clock is like climbing Everest; unless you're the first, you're wasting your time. You get all the hardship, but you won't make the news. This bar doesn't have decor in the traditional sense. It has walls like the dirty protest of a prisoner in solitary confinement, plus scattered jumble sale pictures of the Duke himself that are probably only there to conceal weapons or a half-finished bag of pickled onion Walkers. I'm not saying they expect bother in here. But you see those mirrors, the ones you used to find on the stairs of double-decker buses? They've got them on the back wall so the bar staff can see it all kicking off in the doorways. In every corner and on every ripped seat sits a piss-soiled old bastard, either cursing his luck watching the racing, or staring into space and swearing at his demons. The gent to our left appears to have been clutching the same pint since 1973. I try looking down the back end of the room towards the dart-board. Bad idea. There's a bunch of scrawny whippet-boys sitting on a hair trigger. They're facing into the room and away from each other, like the only thing they have in common is their desire to see my teeth all over the floor. Fucking hell, man, it's only lunchtime. Hearing the smash of glass I turn round, expecting a jagged pint pot to be heading in my direction; it's just a clumsy barmaid, thank Christ. I laugh quietly and nervously, and pray my grundies can take the strain. And in the middle of all this, staggering about, is an Oxfam version of Austin Powers, oblivious to everything, including the dribble on his cravat. I toy with the idea of helping him out and explaining to him my fears for his safety. Then I think about it rationally and I leave him to it; anyone acting that much of a twat in a bar like this has got to be the simple kid brother of the hardest, angriest, least reasonable motherfucker in the whole town. Even catching his eye would mean the loss of one of mine. I'm sure of that. My pint finally drained, I head for the door and practically kick it open in my desire to get out into the street to mingle with the harmless nutters hanging around outside. And only in the fresh air do I realise this bar's one plus point: when the mallrat crowd around on Newgate Street tire of the protective bosom of The Gate, there's a chance that this will be the first bar they try in their search for authenticity, and it's possible they will finally get the hoofing they so richly deserve. Here, mate. I'll hold your coat.

For: Damn good beer. They wouldn't DARE water it down.
Against: Everything else. I'm not going to praise the place just because we got out in one piece.

I think I've worked out how we managed to stay alive. I thought we'd be killed for turning up with ties on, but as three of us were semi-smart with scruffy jackets and the other bloke was wearing a suit, we must have looked like we'd just avoided a two-stretch on a technicality and were going for a pint with our bent solicitor.

Duke of Wellington
High Bridge, NE1 1EN
'The same old deadbeats'

The Duke of Wellington was one of the first pubs I ever visited, and it's an absolute joy to report that it's still there, virtually unchanged bar a lick of paint and a re-hang of the picture gallery. Defiantly resisting the humiliating attempts at bouffantification of other similar bars in the town, the Duke remains a small, friendly pub with excellent beer and a good atmosphere. And, given its proximity to the piss-swimming butcher's shop that is the Bigg Market, you have to admit that's little short of miraculous. The decor looks, well, just like a pub - if you can remember what they were - with plenty of wood that's just on the right side of knackered, and blackboards that advertise not chemical-laden sodypops for drunken teens who don't like the taste of alcohol, but pints. Of beer. The only concession I've seen to the 21st century are a couple of new plasma tellies stuck in the corners that, incredibly, show Programmes That People Might Watch with the volume turned so you can hear what's going on. None of that vacuous Fashion TV shite here, or punters gawping at the screen because they've realised that once they've stopped talking about their haircut they've got fuck all left to say. So aye, it's a pub, like they used to be before the wankbars spread like a cancer through the town. Unpretentious is the word that would best sum the place up. And that's the way it should stay. You can say I'm a miserable old fucker for loving it and I won't care. You can ask where the sushi menu is and I'll laugh in your face. And you can stare aghast, wondering where the decks and the PA are, and I still won't give a shite. Screw you, I'd say. I like a bar that digs its heels in against so-called progress. I like being served my drink by human beings and not giggling jailbait. And I'm proud to say I'm one of the same old deadbeats who've been propping up the bar for the last twen... they've done what? They've got shot of the ancient wooden partitions and replaced the benches with comfortable seating? They've slapped up purple floral wallpaper? I bet I look a right fucking tit now.

For: Cracking little boozer at any time of day, except for...
Against: ...can you fuck get served on a match night for all the besuited pricks hogging the bar and pontificating over their halves of guest ale. MOVE, you fat oaf.

The same faces have been behind the bar of the Duke for absolutely ages, and I like that. I'd like to express my dismay at how, while European bar owners show a bit of pride in their work, landlords over here tend to be either truculent and grasping, or on the verge of a nervous breakdown, all thanks to the animals who make up their customers. On the continent (in cities at least) you can visit a bar at ten year intervals and you'll still see the same staff, happily chatting to their punters, safe in the knowledge that theirs is a respectable career in the public service. Over here, you're 'lucky' if a bar lasts a year before the next tacky refit and management reshuffle. And our beer's piss, too.

Enigma
Carliol Square, NE1 6UG
'The Ku Klux Klan'

As you may know, this book is the offshoot of the Burglar's Dog website. On that website there was once a low-quality feature called 'Burglar's Dog Design Solutions', a spoof guide to making a new or refurbished pub look identical to the tiniest degree to every other bar in the town. It was - and I felt certain that its farcical exaggeration was abundantly clear - supposed to be a bloody JOKE. However, a few short months after I cobbled it together and stuck it online, the Dog consultancy bore its first fruits in the shape of Enigma, a bar that followed the guide down to the last superfluous napkin. I didn't know whether to laugh, cry or torch the place. Let's be honest: I was never going to get nostalgic for Enigma's former incarnation of Wilders, middle-aged knocking shop that it was, but finding myself removed from the bewildered scum of my peer group and surrounded by a new breed of identikit punters was a little demoralising to say the least. I'm no drama queen, as I'm sure you realise, but I felt genuinely hurt, and sat in the corner with my head in my hands and caring arms around my shoulder blades, wondering, 'Don't they love me any more? Is my dress sense that poor? Is my danc-ing really so embarrassing?' Granted, they're a fair way off the beaten track, down the road alongside the abandoned fire station and around the corner from the ruins of the old bus terminus, so they had to try to appeal to as wide an audience as possible. And yes, their location directly across from the World Headquarters nightclub makes them a prime candidate for the 'official warm-up bar', whatever one of those is (I know as much about the Ku Klux Klan as I do about the clubbing scene). But was it really so necessary to go for the lowest common denominator in every single aspect? From the artwork that looks like something one of the 20th Century greats might have done shortly after being pepper sprayed in both eyes, a picture that commits the cardinal sin of being selected simply because it 'goes' with the furniture, to the reds and the creams of the colour scheme; from the subtle lighting to the flat screen TVs, it's all very tasteful in a style-bible sort of way, and very, very, very dull. Look, I know they've tried to bring in more of a local pub atmosphere over the years; I know they serve a decent enough pint with a smile and - fair's fair - it's a reasonable place for a quiet post-work whinge. I don't even mind the music shows on the telly, just so long as I'm spared the sound of the kids singing in that horrible accent they all seem to have adopted, one that's somewhere between east MySpace and south-west Starbucks (and not fucking Welwyn Garden City where they were brought up). They've even got a beer garden out the back, as long as you don't split hairs and argue that it's actually a beer bench at the quiet end of the municipal car park. But, fuck, there's nothing here that would ever make me choose it over a raft of other bars in the town. There's not even enough to compensate me for the struggle of having to go back uphill to civilisation once I've left. And which-ever way you look at it, Enigma's a shite name for a pub.

For: I'm being told there's a Bar Pukka in Ashington, so maybe Enigma isn't that bad a name after all.
Against: The poster in the bogs says that Monday night is busker night. My fragile, hungover brain can barely contemplate just how much misery that could inflict on the unsuspecting punter.

Buskers, though. Acoustic guitars. For years I've been nagging our lass to learn some chords on the guitar. But after watching a few of the 'North East's finest female singer-songwriters' yelling their way through dirges about their doomed love lives in a bar last weekend I had to tell her straight: touch my guitars and I'll break your wrist. You know why she's always refused to learn, though? Doesn't want to cut her fingernails. What is it with women and their nails? Have you ever heard a bloke go, 'Phwoar, looka the fingernails on hor!'?

Fitzgeralds

60 Grey Street, NE1 6AF
'Chocolate-box scenes your gran would love'

The author F Scott Fitzgerald is once said to have been chal-
lenged to write a story using as few words as possible. This is
what he wrote: 'For Sale. Baby's shoes. Never worn.' Except, he
didn't. Looking it up on the internet, I find that it was actually
Ernest Hemingway who penned that, which leaves me a) looking
pretty foolish and b) without a single noteworthy theme to base
the review on. I'm not going to slag this place off, though. Nor
am I going to throw some pummelling great tantrum. Fitzgeralds
is in no way unpleasant; it just bores the tits off me. And, much
as it shames me to say so, I'm probably just going to have to do
the review properly and make it factual, so you may want to skip
this one. Traditionally furnished with wooden panelling and
brown leather booths, and an ornate ceiling whose centrepiece is
a large, stained glass light reminiscent of a peacock's plumage,
Fitzgeralds combines racing green with muted shades of brown
and purple for a relaxed atmosphere. Fully carpeted throughout,
and with large doors looking out over the courtyard of the newly
built office block on the adjacent High Bridge, there's a spacious
feel enhanced by the extensive use of mirrors. As well as its
potential for relaxed business lunches, Fitzgeralds is also popular
with ladies of a certain age, and... this is making me feel ill.
Listen to me: 'Wah-wah-wah, ladies of a certain age.' Look,
they're ancient old biddies, and, from where I'm sitting holding
my nose, Fitzgeralds is just a couple of crossed't's away from a
lucrative sponsorship deal with leading fadge-mop product Tena
Lady. And it's dull: as dull as ditchwater, on a wet weekend, in
Torquay out of season, with John Motson, watching Bolton play a
friendly. And, as with its neighbour the Bacchus, it looks like a
fucking brothel. What the hell is all that stained glass supposed to
be? I don't know if they're trying for art nouveau or art deco, but
whichever it is, it always just says one thing to me, and that's Sir
John Fitzgerald Ltd, 1988. There's pretend books on pretend
cases, an inlaid clock above the bar that ticks off all the seconds

you'll never get back and, as well as the usual ad-hoc picture collection of chocolate-box scenes your gran would love, there's stuff by Toulouse-Lautrec, Rossetti and many others who'd be clawing their way out of their graves if they knew what their hard graft had amounted to. Yes, you get a decent pint here, and yes it's a million miles away from the snooty lounge or the sweltering theme pub, but I've continually bypassed this place over the years and, considering it's the style of pub I'm always hankering for, that's not much in the way of a recommendation, is it?

For: There's a verdigris peacock on a ledge just before you enter the bar's lower main area. I think it may well disappear just before the next Mother's Day. You'll not tell them, though, will you?

Against: Years and years ago, I was served a pint of line-cleaning fluid in here, an incident that has remained imprinted on my brain ever since. I still haven't forgiven them.

The missus pointed out that the walkway from the upper to the lower levels is like a catwalk. She's right. I sat facing out towards the door watching the semi-naked lasses strolling in - and scurrying back out again - while I made her look other way. 'Er, just keep looking at the decor, love, I really want this review to be accurate...' What a fucking rotter.

Fusion

31 New Bridge Street West, NE1 8AN
'Hypocritical wankers'

Formerly just a pointless little bar with delusions of grandeur, Fusion has recently been subjected to a refit that was not so much a makeover as a smackhead's apartment sale, with everything of value being flogged off to fund the habit. Well, maybe that's a bit harsh – this place hardly looks like Pete fucking Doherty's flat on a Sunday morning – but it would still be true to say that everything that once gave Fusion a modicum of character has disappeared, to be replaced by a whole lot of bugger all.

Gone is the painting just inside the doorway of a rather fetching young lady with make-up like our lass has when I make her cry for a laugh, pouting into a mirror in a way that suggested incestuous lesbian tendencies. And gone too is the painting on the toilet door of a golden geezer with a perm doing a move somewhere between the triple-jump and the runner-up manoeuvre in the finals of the Naked Arse-Kicking Championships. In their place is a forlorn stack of scuffed woodwork, battered leather and barren walls, held together by an air of resigned gloom. This is a bar in which to drown the sorrows. This bar is neutral territory for a post bust-up 'we need to talk'. And this bar is never going to make anyone's top ten. But I'm not totally averse to Fusion, and all its independent ways. I tend to view it like I view my local hardware store, where I nip in out of duty to buy a sheet of sandpaper or a clothes peg or a couple of nails, whine about the demise of the small local outlet, and then fuck off down the hypermarket with the rest of the hypocritical wankers. Every now and then I'll pull up a stool and sit in Fusion's front window in an altruistic attempt to make the place look busy, as behind me the hacked-off staff struggle to amuse their offspring with sock monkeys and lollipops and Auto-Tuned banshees on some poor man's MTV. And eventually my gaze will shift from the shining blue repairs in the now-grey Blue Carpet outside, and over to the courtship rituals of workers from the surrounding conglomerates. I'll watch in blank bewilderment as the office spod from the mailing room chances his arm with the company tease, and try to comprehend the bizarre two-step of love that each will perform, a bit like ex-Toon scapegoat Scotty Parker in a midfield tussle but with at least some sense of direction. He'll motion towards, she'll feint to the left, he'll beat a retreat, she'll beckon him closer. He'll chance a tap on her shoulder, she'll visibly flinch, he'll crumble in shame, she'll laugh her cruellest laugh. On and on it will go, until one of them smokes the only thing they have in common down to the filter and they'll part with a shrug, ready to 'accidentally' do it all again tomorrow. And I will perch there feeling all superior until it dawns on me that I'm sitting on my own, drinking dismal Foster's in a boring bar with no punters, and vowels will join consonants will form words will construct sentences in my mental suicide note. I've got to find a purpose in life before it's too late.

For: I'm particularly impressed with the way they have a massive bunch of twigs in a tottering vase placed precariously on the shelf in the window. 'You broke it: you bought it' is a fine way to supplement the income of an unpopular establishment.

Against: They're right on the toes of the Liquid nightclub next door, yet often remain empty while the club queue snakes round the block. Maybe they should get some dollybirds in roller-skates with usherette's trays full of beer out there instead of thrumming their fingers on the counter in here. I'll do it. What are the hours? I can't do Thursdays, mind.

The folly of public art known as the Blue Carpet is, let's face it, a pile of cack. And if it formed the C in my A-to-B, I'd do my best to ignore the fucker too. But I'd do it by focusing on a spot on the horizon and using that to guide me to safety. What I wouldn't do - unlike every single passer-by I've ever seen out there - is engross myself so completely in my mobile phone that if the second coming of Christ arrived butt-naked on a beach ball, it'd pass me right by. Mobile technology is spinning out of the control of its everyday users, and it's starting to worry me. 'Web & Walk'? Getting the bastards to fucking concentrate and walk would be a start.

Hoko-10

16 Dean Street, NE1 1PG
'Sleeping rough'

Once the city's latest razor-cut style venue, Hoko-10 used to pull off the trick of being so ridiculously over the top that it transcended its own wankiness. Now, despite still having the same pretensions, it looks like it's been found sleeping rough under a bridge and given a good fucking hiding. Hoko-10 is still a mix of split levels, dark browns, muted lighting and all the usual posh-bar bollocks, but you don't have to look too hard to see that this is scuffed, that's broken and there's a bit hanging off over there. I remember thinking when this place first opened that the cushion-stuffed wooden booths that you had to clamber into to get all, like, intimate with your companions were quite a nice, daft little touch. That was when the bar had only been open for a matter of days; I'd imagine they'll be somewhat less appealing these days, after years of being showered with eczema, broken glass and used condoms, and I'm certainly not prepared to hop in and check unless you're stumping up for protective clothing and extra-strength Marigolds. They've still got the tanks full of piranhas, all swimming about looking as fearsome as nature intended, but with an extra cockiness now that they've scared off the sushi chefs who used to stand next to them and pull 'you're next' faces through the sides of the tanks. Chefs? Fucking pussies. Anyone can be a tough guy when they've got a carving knife in their hand; try stripping a man's arm to the bone in under ten seconds and then you'll know tough, you pair of split-crotch panties. Attempting to flog sushi in a bar was a foolhardy plan anyway; it doesn't matter how elaborate the concept or how forcefully a bar rams a gimmick down the punters' throats, they all eventually realise that nobody in this town gives two feeble fucks about anything but getting ratted. And while it's clearly on the slide, I'm not going to pretend that this place has turned into the Blackett Arms. It's not a dump yet, by any means. But it's definitely a lesson in what happens when you allow drunken people anywhere near your fancy design statement.

For: Luxury roped-off VIP area.
Against: If you're stupid and insecure enough to spend a week's wages on a bottle of Krug to validate your social standing, then the rope needs to be there to keep you in, not us out.

Beer prices are a crime. But as long as one bar can make people pay them, then others will follow suit simply because they can, because that's the marketplace we're in. This is one of the few things I learned about business whilst working for a multinational company. You see when your joke managers are off to London for the day on 'business'? They're not building for the company's future. They're not strengthening the brand. They're not even arguing over how much money to piss away on IT systems that will never work. What they're doing is drawing lots to see which one of the greedy cunts will stand up and defend his 400% pay rise and buckshee share options, just so all the rest of the parasites can say 'Market forces. It's the going rate' when they get the same obscene deal three months later.

Idols

Newgate Shopping Centre, Newgate Street, NE1 5RS
'Honest incompetence in the act of love'

I'm getting old. There's no denying it. It's tricky enough these days to even get up the stairs at the match, never mind add any more unnecessary climbing to my Saturday afternoons. And it is for that reason, and that reason alone that I've been giving the subterranean Idols a wide berth for the past few years. But, y'know, to celebrate the back of another dismal football season, I thought I'd hobble down for a swift, raucous pint watching the strippers, and maybe write the review in the process. Ye bugger, this place has changed. Although the tatty stairwell remains the same, gone is the '80s throwback decor of industrial tat and springs and bits of tubas, and in their place is a minimal, empty shed so beloved of lazy bastard designers the nation over. And while they're still advertising exotic dancers, in their upmarket semi-refurbished state they actually mean dancing and nowt else. It's a tragedy to see the comedy strippers (two stone overweight, cellulite-ridden, knockers like beagles' lugs on my last visit) replaced by uninterested bunny girls and over-rehearsed, over-choreographed dancers in leg-warmers, especially when one of them is a fucking BLOKE. Dancing girls are really starting to lose their attraction these days, an' all. Bearing in mind that the inference of all the grinding and thrusting is the thought of what they'd do to you beneath the duvet, I just find your average under-dressed turn on the podium so utterly sexless; with all that left hand UP, swing hips ROUND, slap arse HERE business, it's all as regimented and as procedural as a fucking MOT-check. It's like in *The Man With Two Brains*, when Steve Martin finally gets to consummate his sham marriage to gold-digger Kathleen Turner and pronounces it 'so... so... professional'. What's wrong with a bit of honest incompetence in the act of love? Does there have to be a fucking British Standard for it? I've given too much away again, haven't I? Better get back to the review, by saying stuff like... And to make matters worse, it looks like when the previous DJ moved out, headhunted by the Sports Café round the corner, he not only took the strippers, the atmosphere and the legendary banter with him, but he even took his ladder, judging by the way some poor lass had to clamber up the optics and onto the shelf to do her act. Yeah, I know they're pumping out the dry ice for a bit of a showbiz feel, and bringing on fire jugglers to compensate for the lack of bristols, but it all seems a bit desperate and, more importantly, anything but a money-spinner. I only stood nursing my pint to see if the girl in the nylon mini-skirt with her hair all over the shop was actually going to set herself aflame; once she'd got to the end of the song with only a few soot marks and a splash of lighter fuel on her skimpy T-shirt, we were off, headed for somewhere more interesting.

For: The 'tits' will be back 'oot' sooner or later, you can guarantee it.

Against: Why can't toilet attendants just fuck off once and for all? Next time I see one, I'm going to cack in my hands, piss down my trousers, and puke all over my Toon shirt. Then I'm going to ask HIM, 'Alright, mate?' and see if he can work miracles with a bottle of Blue Stratos and a paper towel.

I've never understood the appeal of being a dancer. Fair enough, with all that exercise you get to be trim and toned and fit as fuck, even if you've got a face like a German helmet. But for the ratio of effort to reward, it's pretty depressing, if all your big break will ever amount to is being third grinning nobody from the left behind the latest clueless fuckpuppet RealityPop! winner. Still, it could be worse. They could spend every hungover Sunday morning hunched over a keyboard, hammering out witless pub reviews that nobody will ever even read, let alone enjoy. Now that would be a waste of a life.

The Lane

41-51 High Bridge, NE1 1NE
'Here, nar, here, nar man, fuck'n, here, nar'

Fashion is not made to last. It isn't just the passing whims dictating cuts, fabrics and colours that cause the sea changes in clothing, but the depressing lack of quality: if you bought a garment even a matter of months ago and washed it more than a couple of times, it won't just be out of style, it'll be starting to look a state. And if you multiply that out by a factor of years, you'll be left with a fucking dishrag with sleeves. Take, for instance, a bold, button-down YSL shirt and a pair of 501s: it probably looked the business in the mid '90s, but if you've seen someone wearing that ensemble lately, trying to get his money's worth, I'd wage billions against bollocks that he was clutching a can of Viborg and being thrown off public transport. That's the sort of thing that's happened here. Formerly Turks, then the Rat & Parrot for a while, and then Turks again, The Lane kitted itself up with a then-fashionable outfit a few years ago in an attempt to add a bit of respectability to its reputation, and has spent every day since in increasingly threadbare decay. And what was once a pleasant, sober, 'Good morning. How are you?' at the bus stop, has clearly spent all day on the drink and is now having its daily midnight brawl outside your front door. I know I'm always getting into bother for taking extremes as the norm, so I'm going to accept that what I saw on the review visit may not be typical. But I'm also obliged to say that, as well as being a right fucking dump these days, The Lane ticked off what my *I-Spy Book of Pubs* calls a 'shite bar Type 2', Type 1 being a bar that is shite, and Type 2 a bar FOR shite. Walking in for a post-work calmer I find myself barged against the doorframe by a scar-faced little cunt with a hooped sweatshirt and somewhere more pressing to be. Logic tells me he's been kicked out for acting the twat or smoking tack in the bogs, but thirty seconds into my pint, the little fucker is back in again, bending the barman's ear. I can't quite pick up the full gist of his conversation from my stool in the window, but it sounds to me a bit like, 'Here, nar, here, nar man, fuck'n, here, nar', and all the while the barman is looking at him with a pained smile and eyes that beg, 'Please. I'm off shift in an hour. Don't break anything.' The poor bloke shouldn't worry: this place has deteriorated so much since its plum and cream makeover that there's not really anything left to break, unless you count the original artwork in mixed media that proudly adorns the walls, 'Untitled #18' 2007, Xerox toner and Blu-Tack on A4 paper, being my current favourite. And thinking back, The Lane wasn't even much cop when they last had the decorators in: it was less a refurbishment than a case of 'Should we do it properly? Or should we just slap this paint on top of all the old crap and hope nobody notices?' And I reckon they've brought it on themselves: the price of the beer here would have rural Albanian peasants piling over for a cheap night out, and as well as being the main attraction, that's the one thing that is causing the problem as I see it, sneering over the top of my half-framed designer specs. Sales barely break-even, so no cash for fixtures and fittings, so the place looks a tip, so it only attracts idiots, so prices have to come down, so sales barely break-even, so no cash for fixtu... Rip it up and start again, I say. Bring in a pub chain. Charge a luxebar premium. Board the building up and leave it to rot like the rest of the street. Anything's got to be better than this.

For: At coppers a pint, I felt absolutely no remorse at leaving the bastard half drunk on the windowsill.
Against: I didn't even dare to see if they've finally cleaned up the permanent pool of piss on the toilet floor.

I hate being lied to by the council and the media. What the hell happened to the rumoured gentrification of High Bridge? We were promised a cafe society and a cosmopolitan buzz. They told us there'd be a mix of history and new business. And what did we get? Half a street of dereliction and a brand-new tattoo parlour. Is that what they meant?

The Living Room

12 Grey Street, NE1 6AE
'Swearing, nudity, incest'

Anyone remember Oliver's, the sandwich bar next to Burger King on Northumberland Street? The one that disappeared when Greggs decided to move in there and ensure a trail of pastry and litter from one end of the street to the other? Ah, it was grand; four quid for a sarnie - and that's when four quid was four quid - served on a paper plate with a few stale crisps and some 'luxury' coleslaw, sitting at a Formica table, watching yourself get onions all over your face in a hundred different mirrors. I'll tell you what, mind; I thought someone had been pissing about with my space/time continuum again, because the downstairs bar of the Living Room is exactly like that. *Exactly.* That's what happens when you go for a wazz as soon as you go in to a pub. The ground floor - the bit you'd come to first unless you were looking for a contrived intro to a review - is more full of creams and browns and exposed brickwork, all the usual stuff, and while the decor is par for the course for a bar these days, it did feel quite pleasant and bright. The whole wall of sepia prints of Christ-knows-who wasn't too much like an Athena closing down sale, I didn't instantly want to take a Stanley knife to the painting in the hallway, and the cocktail glasses with their wonky stems seemed well worth pinching. Top marks also for the coat hooks under the bar. It's the little things like that - the acknowledgment that some people in Newcastle do actually wear coats in January - that make an old bastard like me happy. Fair enough, the place is pricey, it's part of a chain, and there's a restaurant attached that just pouts, 'I'm too flashy for scum like you.' And who cares if the punters are a little on the mature side? What's wrong with happy couples out for a nice pint after shopping? And who but a curmudgeon would carp at a couple of well-spoken ladies chatting up the barman, getting off their Agent Provocateur-clad tits on expensive cocktails and bunging them on the plastic? That barman was a complete tosser, though. How come TV watchdogs waste all their time trying to ban swearing, nudity, incest and trivia like that, when they should really be clamping down on adverts for spirits? You know the ones I'm ranting about, the ones that try to portray bars as happy, exciting venues and not the centres for misery and sorrow-drowning that they so obviously are; the ones with bottle-spinning, shape-throwing, lime-kicking party scenes; the ones that give dickheads behind the bar the idea that it's perfectly acceptable to make me wait half an hour for my pint. I go to pubs to get drunk, and fast, and not to watch some grinning twat mucking about. And don't turn around to make wisecracks to your mate when I'm ordering, either, you berk.

For: It's actually alright, to be honest. Well, when it's quiet and you can feel a bit relaxed and decadent, anyway. Later on, when it's packed and people keep whacking into you, it's an overpriced pain in the arse.

Against: I can't believe some places are still doing this, but when I first tried to get in - the week it opened – I was knocked back for wearing trainers. What fucking difference does a pair of shoes make? What is it, a boozer or a bowling alley?

Cocktails on the plastic: a cautionary tale. The missus and I ran out of cash in one of Newcastle's flashier bars a while back. Normally when you run out of readies, you think, 'Hmm, time to go home.' Not us. No, we decided it'd be a wheeze to work our way through the cocktail menu and stick the bill on the credit card. Sitting on the bus on the way home, I turned back from gawping out of the window and thought, 'Wait a minute. I'm covered in puke.' Just like that. No warning, no squeaks or grunts or mm-mmnn-mms; she'd just opened her gob and fetched up her dinner in my lap. She's got the whole bus to aim at and I'm the one with a pocket full of mint leaves and olives? Disgraceful.

The Lodge

26 Mosley Street, NE1 1DE
'A terrible idea'

Despite the fact that loveable cheeky chappie TV presenters Ant & Dec had apparently ploughed quarter of a million quid into the refit and rename of the old Jonny Ringo's, and despite quite liking the previous incarnation of the place, the few times I'd been in since the change left me thoroughly nonplussed. In fact, I hated it. A magnet for stag parties, hen nights, and general arseheads, the place seemed to hold all my least favourite types of social groups, coupled with a dark, depressing atmosphere, with the overwhelming brownness of it being lifted only by spirit-strangling orange lighting. I went back again on a Saturday night to review it seriously and, sadly, found it just the same, only scruffier. Sat in one of the booths on the mezzanine level (the one with the broken telly, typically), I listened to a disembodied voice telling the punters how great the bar was and how the two-for-one offer was a bargain. What they're not telling you are the normal prices that, for a bar of this quality, are an absolute crime. This place has no business whatsoever charging three quid for a pint of cooking lager, unless Ant & Dec are trying to claw back some capital before bailing out of the whole sorry venture. Bloody Popolo doesn't even charge that much, man. The surroundings, the prices, the punters and the general unpleasantness of it all sapping my conversational abilities, I just had time to clock the massive light shades full of straws and cocktail stirrers and other amusing projectiles that people have launched from the balcony bar, before draining my pint and leaving, never to return. So why is it so damned popular, then? Is it the celebrity link, the vague hope of seeing the co-owners downing an off-duty Beck's between reality TV shows? Must be, but for all their 'proper Geordie, me' protestations, I don't think Ant & Dec would wipe their off-duty feet in the place, to be honest. Yeah, call me a sour bastard, and yeah, it's probably much nicer during the day with a bit of light coming in but, frankly, I'd sooner crap in my pants than even nip in to use their toilets. Horrific.

For: The fact that there's often a queue of one-born-every-minute fools lined up outside, making you much more likely to go somewhere else.

Against: If you have done any work - paid or unpaid - during in the last seven days, your colleagues will want you to drink in here on their big night out.

I'm a pedantic little fucker and I'm in a right bad mood, so I'm going to say this: the big, illuminated orange menu thing on the right-hand wall as you go in is littered with mistakes, most notably my favourite bugbear, the misused apostrophe. Fair enough, if it was handwritten on a blackboard by some divvy earning a quid an hour I could almost tolerate it, but this retina-ruining monstrosity was done by a professional. What the hell is the world coming to when 'experience of words' is not an essential qualification for a sign-writing position?

Market Lane
72 Pilgrim Street, NE1 6SG
'Smells all fishy and Dad-like'

Nobody refers to this pub as the Market Lane: it's always been known as the Monkey Bar, and here, just to prove I do things properly, is why. The blokes who built the Tyne Bridge, which starts just down the road, used to leave their hods, or 'monkeys', behind the bar in exchange for beer, and would only get them back after they'd settled their bar bills. So now you know. Lovingly restored outside and in, and extended across the derelict building next door – although it's a weeping shame they didn't take on the breezeblock eyesore adjoining that – this is a decent little pub with a bit of history, and provides a welcome antidote to the up-their-arse studied cool of Popolo on the other side of the alleyway. There's a right mix of punters, with old gadgies scanning the racing pages in one corner, ageing rockers in another, and an occasional office crowd in the no-man's land in between. And the beer's good. That's about it for the Monkey Bar, I suppose. It's a bit of an institution, and if the spruce-up has left you feeling a bit like your Mam has thrust a hanky that smells all fishy and Dad-like in your face and said Lick! then rest assured: while the wallpaper and the layout may change, it'll always end up with the same low-rent appeal. I cried salt tears the last time they gave it the once-over, back in the late '80s, but it soon regained its grotty charm so I'm not too worried about what they've done this time. Incidentally, and for the last flaming time, I'm going to spell this out for all you jellied eel-slurping, 4x4 driving, Bluewater-bound, M25-stuck Southern fools. It wasn't the Geordies who, in the 18th Century found a ship-wrecked monkey dressed in a captain's uniform and assumed that, because it couldn't speak English, it was a French spy and hanged it. That was the inbred bumpkins down the coast in Hartlepool, and it's a tale of which they're particularly proud. Better to be a monkey-hanger from Hartlepool than a sex case from Middlesbrough.

For: Cheese, nuts, pickled onions and crackers on the bar early evening. Perfect for a stomach liner, at least until the statistically proven 200 types of man-wee end up in the dishes.
Against: I am responsible for putting the wee there, thanks to the contents of my ever-present briefcase. Would you care to see a sample?

While I'm on the subject of regional stereotypes, people often ask why Newcastle and Sunderland hate each other. The simple answer is we don't: they hate us, but we just find them amusing. Have you ever witnessed such an embarrassing display of inferiority complex? We have a world-famous bridge; they get themselves a crappy fun-size version of it. We're a famous city - with the mandatory cathedral - so they mewl and whine their way to city status, whether they're entitled to it or not. Just the fact that it's Tyne and Wear and not the other way round is enough to turn them apoplectic, the poor, downtrodden, vowel-mangling oafs. And - despite the fact that we're geographically north of Wearside, you'll never hear of a mackem going UP to Newcastle - always 'through'. Or is that thrayeew? There is, however, one thing that Sunderland trumps Newcastle on, and that's the Air

Show. People from Newcastle go to the airport to see planes up close, and maybe even board them to destinations near and far. Sunderland inhabitants, meanwhile, gather on beaches and in fields to marvel at the displays above them. 'Lewk, Jewley! A big metal bird flying over thee 'ouse!' Fucking airshow. Only in Sunderland...

themushroom

82 Grainger Street, NE1 5JQ
'Nee knickaaaaaaz!'

Passing KFC at the top of the Bigg Market and heading along Grainger Street, I see a hen party dressed like Liquorice Allsorts coming the other way. I just know their destination – themushroom – is the same as mine, and sure enough I see them pile into the pub doorway. And I'm just about to lower any expectations I could have had for my pint when, incredibly, I see them all trooping back out again. Marvellous, I think: there's a decent door policy, and they've all been refused entry. Edging down the pitch-black stairway and into the basement I realise too late that no such thing has happened, and what I'm faced with now is a bar so bad that any self-respecting hen night would sack it off in disgust. Not too many of those around, mind. Squinting through the virtual darkness, I see a pub that manages to combine the very worst bits of Bar 42 and the city's most horrendous nightclub, the long-gone Madisons (ask your dad, if your mother's sobered up long enough to remember who he is). It's dark, dingy and depressing, and its feeble lighting that fades from pink to orange to purple is an insult to the optical nerves. Around me – I'd say sit, but it's more of a bounce – are fart-pissed Jocks in tam o'shanters trying their damnedest to cop off with the screeching gorgons in the rabbit ears. The bride-to-be is in the worst state of the lot of them: I find myself musing that, if all goes to evil plan, this foul-mouthed, cackling lush will be someone's mother this time next year, and I consider getting her phone number to give Social Services a head start. Our lass, meanwhile, is pulling on my shirt sleeve to draw my attention to some brassy bint at the bar who's got her thruppennies on show to deflect from the size of her arse: she's not so much Jordan as the entire fucking Middle East. Behind me and empty there's a curved dancefloor with barely enough room to swing a fat lass, and against the shelf at the back are a pair of right bloody tools. They're both busting a few moves to 'show off' and I can tell by their idiot leers that they're the sort of sickening jackals who use the word 'sex' as a verb. A couple of stray females join our table for protection but, I'm sorry, this just ain't our jurisdiction. Pints drained in one, we're off, getting the fuck out of Dodge like the yellow-bellied UN peacekeepers in '*Hotel Rwanda*', asserting that the impending massacre is someone else's responsibility. You're on your own there, pet. And whether through bad luck or poor timing, we end up stuck in a procession of kilts on the way back up the stairs, with another shovelful of shimmying shite coming in the opposite direction. 'Eeeeeeh!' screams the leader of the pack on seeing the traditional Scottish dress. 'Nee knickaaaaaaz!' We don't hang around to see the proof, and instead make a Herculean effort, throwing a few bodies around to escape the bar's microclimate and reach the open air. This has been one of the most unbelievably dire experiences of my life. So why am I laughing so much?

For: 'Basement cool... notoriously good craic staff... and top of the range local blart'. Not my words, but those of their sparkling website.
Against: Fuck. Me.

Hey, wait a minute. Maybe I'm having a pharmaceutical flashback, or something, but I've just remembered the last time I was in Madisons, in what must have been, like, 1989. All I can recall is a sense of really strong, pure, white light, and a feeling of real love and joy towards the people I was out with. Bearing in mind this is fucking Madisons we're talking about, and the crowd I was with were the cunt's cunts, I have this vague feeling that someone might have, you know, slipped me an E. Would anyone care to enlighten me?

Northumberland Arms

Prudhoe Chare, NE1 7AT
'Drunken, puking, disco dancing fools'

The Northumberland Arms has survived longer than any pub blighted by a shopping centre location deserves, mainly thanks to the delights of the bargain cruise break. Supping your pint in here on any given afternoon, you'd soon notice that this bar is part of some bizarre three-way European cultural exchange programme: Amsterdam gets our drunken, puking, disco dancing fools, and we get moustached shoppers hot off the Scandinavian ferries, all with matching carrier bags and a sense of deflation. And where do the Dutch go? I dunno, man. Do I sound to you like I've researched this crap? So aye, there's Helga and Sven, launching a couple of cheap Carlings after their citywide tour of the Baltic, the Sage, the bridges and Northumberland Street, proudly clutching their Marks & Spencer bags full of quality undergarments and easy-care suits before heading for the bus back to North Shields. Christ only knows why they end up in here, apart from the obvious proximity to M&S. Because this place, as any local will tell you, is a dump. Subterranean, down a flight of gloomy stairs, the Northumberland Arms is a relic from the days before it was realised that daylight is not a luxury extra in a non-haircut bar, and it's as grim as it's possible to be without crossing the line into menacing. As compensation for the basement setting, the lights in here are always too bright for my sensitive eyes, but I'm of the opinion that the billion watt bulbs and the strategically placed mirrors are there to stop any nefarious activities or sleights of hand. That's how suspicious I am. I can't even point to the food as a recommending factor, since it comes across like prison standard catering to me, ladled out with as much attention to presentation as you'd use to bin one of your dog's turds. I say the grub looks poor: you don't honestly expect me to have tasted it, do you? The sole logical conclusion I can come up with for this place's continued even-breaking is that, since this is the only 'public' bogs for miles around - despite the increasingly furious signs to the contrary on the toilet doors - people are guilt-tripped into buying a beer when they nip in for a slash, shortly before vowing never to return. That was certainly the case with me.

For: No kids allowed.
Against: Seeing people queuing up in an orderly fashion for their pints makes me think there's something shifty going on. And when I find out what it is, you'll be the first to know.

Stood watching the match on the Northy Arms' new plasma screen telly, I couldn't help but marvel at the advances in technology. HD, HHD, SuperHHD, the whole kit and caboodle. And maybe, in a few years' time, with the advent of AAAAA TV - that's Almost As Accurate As Analogue - we'll be able to see a striker bearing down on goal without his blur of a shirt trailing three seconds behind him. I'm being a little sarcastic, just in case you needed me to point it out. The great analogue switch-off? Why? To make way for something no better but expensive enough to line the pockets of industry, and foreign industry at that? Fucking disgraceful. Life's shit enough just following the route of birth, buy things, death, without being told that perfectly good stuff you've bought is now obsolete and has to be hoyed out on some greasy politician's say-so.

The Old George
Old George Yard, Cloth Market, NE1 1EE
'Like turds from a sewage outlet'

One of Newcastle's oldest drinking places, historically sited down a urine-drenched alley, the Old George is reputedly - and inevitably - haunted. Not by any restless spirit, you understand, but by buck-toothed, bearded, boring bastards on ghost hunting nights, pretending to search for spooks and spectres while trying to get their callused hands under the pullover of the nearest specky spinster. This is a dismal bar, I can tell you that for nothing. It's hardly surprising they're trying to pull in the sensible rainwear crowd, since if you're young and even half-alive, it's doubtful whether you'd make it fully through the doors without spinning on a sixpence and legging it. Here's the historical connection, as accurately as I can remember it. Way back in 1646, King Charles I was held captive in Newcastle by the Scots over some petty gripe or other. Being an affable race, they let him nip out for a round of golf in Shieldfield before the regally inbred goon scuppered it, whacking his monogrammed balls through the windows of the tower blocks of his subjects. And loyal as those subjects may have been, they certainly weren't loyal enough to hoy the fuckers back. To cheer the berk up, it seems they then allowed him to pop in the Old George for a swift pint and a Ginster's pasty from the hotplate behind the bar. And this landmark in history, this wondrous occasion, led to a room in the pub being named in his honour, with the chair in which he sat given pride of place and - clearly to retain some traces of regal DNA - the bogs where he shook his royal drops off remaining seemingly uncleaned ever since. That's how it happened. You see? I have been known to do my research, even if that amounts to no more than taking sneaky, blurred snaps of the pub's menu spiel so I can make asinine comments about it later. And if all that isn't enough to hammer home the historical notion, I can tell you that virtually every surface in here is stripped and stained wood, and the bits they couldn't be arsed to give what-for with the chemicals and sand-paper, they've just daubed in wood-effect paint. For fuck's sake, even the bloody radiators are 'antique pine'. They've got low ceilings with beams, creaky old furniture, an open fire and a whole host of stiffly grand settees upstairs, only one of which has anything even approaching a decent view of the big screen telly. It's not all clock-watchingly dull, though. For all that it gets the respectable, clean-living, courteous dickdrips from the Duke of Welly round the corner and the ghost hunters I invented earlier, the Bigg Market feeds straight into the other end of the alley, so at least you get the chance to ridicule and feel superior to the yobs bobbing around the doorway like turds from a sewage outlet. Aye, let's give the Old George their due: at least they're not pretending to be old and traditional, which in my book is a far greater crime than being merely dull. Be thankful it's not a King Charles I theme bar, with cardboard walls and plastic orna-ments, but instead is a genuine split-level mess of knocking through and adding on; nobody but a lunatic would build a bar like this nowadays. Which reminds me: I'd better warn you now that if nature comes a-calling, you'd be strongly advised to head for the toilets before you're bursting, or you'll piss your pants in the maze to get there. That's experience talking, an' all.

For: It's alright, man. Nowt to start throwing a tantrum over.
Against: I dare say it was a hell of a lot better when His Highness turned up for a half of Carling and a shot on the bandit.

When I was made redundant from my last job – on a Christmas Eve, charmingly enough – the room to the left of the main entrance looked just like Yuletide would have done in 1646 i.e. barren as fuck, with nary a sprig of holly or a shitwit in a Santa hat. Matched my mood perfectly, I'll tell you that much. I shall remember them in my will.

Popolo

82-84 Pilgrim Street, NE1 6SG
'Half a million to live above a roundabout'

Popolo is a bar that divides opinion. And, after changing my drinking habits and my laborious route round the town, I've discovered why. There seems to be a cut off point where the relaxed, airy café-bar that produces nothing more than those hitherto elusive chilled vibes becomes a thumping hellhole provoking blistering fury in normally placid individuals. So, to try and keep this balanced, I'm going to first review Popolo through the haze of a few late afternoon scoops, and then rant about what I've since found the night times to be like. Long ago this place was Don Vito's, a cheap, no-frills Italian restaurant. When the owner passed it on to his kids, they almost immediately closed it and turned it into a bar-lounge-kitchen, probably in anticipation of the wankers who'd be shelling out half a million to live above a roundabout when the Swan House office block was converted into flats. And while I wasn't exactly delighted, I didn't see that change as being the biggest crime in history, since

a) I'm clearly turning into a wanker myself, and b) Popolo looked just like the sort of place where I like to prop up the bar at last orders, albeit in somewhere like Paris or Berlin or wherever greasyJet are flying to this year. With crimson and pastel shades and clanking metal barstools, Popolo boasts the city's least irritating design-conscious interior, and has the added bonus of the front windows being tinted red to cut out the sight of the dereliction over the road. It's never heaving and never dead, and at least you get premium beer for the premium prices, unlike in some other bars with foreign names I could mention. And even though its original owners have sold up and moved next door, it hits the spot up until about half seven, the cut-off point I mentioned earlier. But when it starts filling up, everything goes to shit. It's easy to see how it happens. It doesn't matter how much effort you've put into your stupid outfit, or how much you blew at the hairdresser, if you're promised luxury and don't immediately get the service you think you're paying for, you're going to feel pissed off. Take, for example, the drinks menu – there's no denying that the cocktails in here are good, but I won't order them simply through deep shame at holding up the queue. The thing is, here I am definitely in the minority, since every other smug twat with the Aviator shades or elaborate ponytail seems to see it as a badge of honour that their drink is taking a fucking lifetime to mix. They had to wait, so other people can wait for them. Don't know about you, but I'd find it difficult to remain unflustered when there are a dozen people behind me wanting to knife me between the shoulder blades. Of course, when bars are getting busy and people are getting angry, they're going to need security, and it's no secret that Popolo's doorstaff make Tiger Tiger's look liberal, kicking off at the slightest indiscretion. I can remember seeing one old bloke being forcibly ejected, picked up by the arms and knees, carried out and thrown in the lane, obviously for not being pretty enough. And the poor old bastard was – to my eyes – the least offensive punter there. He was only having a bit of a nap, man. It was the rest of the cunts they should have turfed out. Look at them, preening and pouting and onding? Every statement? With a question mark? Those arseholes only came here because some style mag from That London told them to, like this is the only establishment worth bothering with in this shitty provincial town of ours. And, inevitably, they have to seen to be seen, even if it's only by jackasses as vacuous and stupid as they are.

For: Strictly no stag or hen nights.
Against: Simple undeniable fact – drink in Popolo and you will stink of grease for the rest of the night.

Popolo is Italian for 'people'. I've been thinking about the use of all things foreign as a marketing gimmick, and the idea that unfamiliar = exotic. I've often wondered if, deep in the foothills of Patagonia, there's a band of Geordie buskers playing execrable versions of The Blaydon Races and Home Newcastle ('Ye can keep ya London wine') as a payback for those fuckers with the panpipes on Grey's monument.

Rose & Crown
5-7 Newgate Street, NE1 5RE
'Badger's Arse of the Year Awards'

We at the Dog like a proper, down-to-earth boozer with a bit of history, and would cheerfully bypass any haircut bar you care to name for a portion of spit and sawdust. Oh, we like our old timers grumbling in the corner, our battered furniture and our authentic local grit, we do. Call us boring, call us inverted snobs, fit us with a frock and call us Fiona if you want, but that's just what we like to see in a town blighted by anonymous chain pubs and beige luxebars. But this place, it has to be said, is a fucking dump. With its prehistoric flock wallpaper, broken windows, tatty seating and general air of unpleasantness, the Rose & Crown would beat all comers in the Badger's Arse of the Year Awards and, to make it worse, it looks like it's doing it on purpose. This is where our Bill-tainted imaginations find city-drinking villains planning their blags; where they spend their time before they take one kicking too many off Plod and end up dribbling and confused and slumped over the Racing Post in the Clock round the corner. Spill their pint? I'd apologise and offer them a tenner and a free punch anywhere except my knackers if I so much as stepped on their shadow. And if you see a whole pub full of blokes with Phil Mitchell's head but wearing Noel Edmonds' shirt, are you going to take the piss out of them? Are you prepared to tell them their bar's a tip and that you'd prefer it if they didn't use the c-word in front of your lass? Like shite, are you. You're going to sup up quick, back the hell out and pretend you were never there. And if you have to change your name, your address and book yourself in for a session under the surgeon's knife, then that's just the price you'll have to pay.

For: The bay window at the front and its line-up of uglies guarantee that you'll never wander in by accident.
Against: It bathes the atrocious Boom! The '90s Bar over the road in a positive, glowing light.

Don't be giving me any crap about 'salt of the earth', either. You show me salt of the earth and I'll show you a string of convictions as long as my face. And posing for a picture with your bairns is no fucking let off. As if people are really going to see you in the Chronicle, complete with a babe in arms, and think, 'Aaah! He might have maimed three and slashed the throats of another two, but he loves his kiddies so he can't be all bad.'

Secco
86 Pilgrim Street, NE1 6SG
'And that's swearing'

Now extended from its original confines and given a ground floor frontage so people can actually find it, Secco has become the flagship of the De Giorgi family. For those who don't know, they're the micro-empire responsible for getting Popolo next door off the ground, sensibly bailing out and flogging it before it became overrun with wankers, as well as owning Intermezzo underneath the Tyneside Cinema until the Art Deco restoration project kicked them out. Now, you'll probably be expecting me to rip the arse out of Secco and all its European pretensions. But I'm not going to. And this is why. Because it's Friday afternoon, I've knocked off at half-three, and our lass has for once let me head straight to the bar instead of via the make-up department, the haberdashery and an inspection of every single fucking birthday card – twice – in both Fenwicks and WHSmith by way of a 'necessary' detour. The lads are at the bar – getting in some pay-day fruit beers instead of the Foster's I normally have to budget for – and the lasses are in the bogs discussing, no doubt, whether my lithium is really helping. I'm up on the clanking great mezzanine level, without a care in the world other than whether the structure can support my lardy frame, and I'm sitting here in my swivel chair, seeing the place as the designer's blueprint intended. I can appreciate the industrial vibe of all the metalwork and, as long as I'm not fucking insane enough to try to move them, I can bask in the warmth of the lamps, spending the evening in comfort rather than the burns unit of A&E. I've got coins in my pocket for the jukebox by the entrance and, if it wasn't for the fact that I can see that it's really powered by the iPod locked in the cage beside me, I'd be down there sorting out some tunes. From my vantage point I can see right over the bar, and over the threadbare bits in the poseur barman's pate that no amount of shockwax can hide from this height. And, best of all, I'm free to fiddle with workings of the DJ's decks, short circuiting the turntables to give extra 'spark' to his set later on when I'm long gone. The tin cans in frames aren't upsetting me too much, the fake-cracked tongue-and-groove will do for now, and the 7-inch Billy Bragg sleeve on the wall merely intrigues me as to what the Big-Nosed Bastard from Barking has got to do with contemporary drinking. Behind me is a table football game that mercifully has not a soul on it, let alone a bunch of hollering retards, and above that is a sign saying 'babyfut', the term by which Johnny Foreigner knows the game, comfortable with the pairing of children and recreation instead of looking to throw a fucking chair at somebody in the name of sporting passion. You know what? I might nip to the upstairs bar-café for a sandwich or some such later on and, if the bloody rain holds off for a while, mooch about on the terrace for a while before it gets dark. This is a strange sensation: I think it might be what they call 'enjoyment'. So what's to spoil it? Simple. When my own fantasy clientele – nobody, basically – is replaced by the trend-felching morons I suspect will form this bar's target market, all 'can I get?' and not 'could I have?' and asking for something called a 'lartay' instead of a pint. They'll be acting the twat – or worse – living out their own cosmopolitan fantasies, and they will make me want to scarper quicker than you can say, 'Like, ciao!' Pompinaio, every last one of them. And that's swearing.

For: No bar with a rooftop beer terrace can ever be shite, even if it overlooks the back of Grey Street, the unwiped bottom to the pretty made-up face of Grainger Town.
Against: They're making a big deal of the fact that the terrace is 'smoker friendly', which means that those dirty fuckers get all the views of the glowing embers of the western sky, while I'm stuck inside with DJ Flapz and the Pilgrim Street ruins leering through the windows.

Secco's ground floor extension took over the part of the building that was once a photocopying shop. All traces of the shop have been removed, which is a shame because I like to see features of the former occupancy incorporated in a new design. I've been to a few bars in Europe that have kept a teeny bit of their history as part of their decor, like a fruit 'n' veg shop in Germany and a pharmacy in Sweden. It's also ironic that a modern bar should replace a copier shop, because the area by the photocopier in my office is exactly like a modern bar, with people idly chit-chatting about last night's telly over a cool drink or four. That's when I get in early, though; during core hours it's like a barroom brawl in a Wild West saloon. And they wonder why we got a backdated fuck-all for a pay rise this year.

Trillians

Princess Square, NE1 6AQ
'Relentless, joyless, friendless'

It's not something I like to boast about, but I went to Trillians on its opening night, way, way back in the late eighties, when poodle metal was as popular with the kids on the street as smart-arse indie pop is now. A mirthsome mess of spandex and lace, and hair backtatted until it squealed, the bar resembled nothing so much as a no-budget Whitesnake video, one in which I was an all-too-willing extra. Man, I was a foxy fucker in them days. Nipping in for a re-review over 20 years later, pot-bellied and rapidly greying, it saddens me to report that the comedy flamboyance of Trillians has been toned down over the years, echoing in its own way the relentless, joyless, friendless grind of modern metal. Gone are most of the laughable devil masks, the knackered instruments, and cod-satanic paraphernalia, and in their place is a nasty collage of Kerrang!-approved rock heroes. And the beautiful people, those punters for whom every trip to get the round in was a sashay along Sunset Boulevard, are long departed; it's all grunting porkers with tribal tattoos and mini-Mohawks these days, each of them no doubt in a grindcore act that's as serious as testicular cancer. There's a gig-guide calendar above the bar, listing the attractions for the weeks ahead, although nothing for me will ever top the idea of a band called – and you need to adopt that rumbling movie-trailer voice to even utter their name – Nails of Christ playing on a, quote, 'Party Night'. I'll be chuckling 'til I'm dead in my grave about that one. I shouldn't take the piss, really; I'm sure their hearts are in the right place. Maybe I should just concentrate less on the sarcasm and more on Trillians' reputation for showcasing up-and-coming bands, as well as the next-stop-CIU-clubland balding former legends. It's not a bad venue, with a good view of the stage from most vantage points – if you dodge the pillars holding up the roof, that is – and if you're the sort of punter who can keep a straight face through the nightly dose of paddywack rock, then you'll be in your element here. Me, I could quite happily live the rest of my life without seeing another pair of knee-length black shorts or fuck-hard goatee. But overall, Trillians isn't all bad – in fact it's friendly enough, and the beer's alright – but, I'm sorry, I have to say I preferred it when it knew it was ridiculous.

For: The hand dryer in the bogs is absolutely roaring. Attach some wheels to it and you'd shatter the land speed record, no problem.
Against: Jeremy, take that eyeliner off and go and tidy your room.

Facial piercing: can there be a clearer signifier of self-esteem problems than an iron bar stuck through the forehead? It's tantamount to saying, 'Yes, I am pig ugly and I don't care who knows it. Dieting is for pussies. I am an individual and I am the truth. Now if you'll excuse me, I'm off for a cry and a wank.'

Vineyard
1 Grey Street, NE1 6EE
'Some daft bastard gets kneecapped'

I'll be honest here – I'd always purposely ignored the Vineyard, suspecting it to be just a poncy wine bar (maybe the words 'Wine Bar' above the door were a bit of a hint, though), but sheer boredom with the rest of the town's boozers prompted me to go and investigate properly. The good news is that, yes, it does serve beer. And the other good news – putting aside the obvious ruin of your wallet at seven quid a pair – is that it only serves Duvel. You've got to admire their bloody mindedness; not only serving just one beer, but having that one beer as the most deceptively lethal known to man. For the uninitiated, here's a brief guide to the Belgian elixir in the comedy glass: first one = 'Mmm, this is really tasty'. Fourth one = 'Oh, fuck, help me. I can't see properly'. As far as decor goes, the Vineyard is small and rustic looking, with all manner of clutter flicking the Vs in the general direction of the sleek minimalist bars in the surrounding area. There's plenty of designer dust and grime, knackered old marionettes (can't spell pupetts, me) strung up on hooks together with glittery stars hanging from the ceiling, and what looks like a grubby old basque draped over the wine barrels by the window. Top marks also for having the Christmas tree up all year round, too. From my vantage point I can see a full wine rack of empty bottles under the smashed-tile tables, and I'd like to think that some daft bastard gets kneecapped by the bottle ends at least once a night. Even the bogs show a bit of imagination: wandering down the rope-lit stairs and through the King and Queen playing card bog doors you'll find crazy-paved walls and lion's head fountains instead of taps. I must admit I wasn't really sure where the trough was, mind, so I just pissed in the nearest empty corner. Apologies to the poor sod who had to clean my mess up if that grating bit wasn't actually where I should have emptied my bladder. And I suppose that only leaves the customers to discuss. I have no idea what the typical Vineyard punter is like, mainly because we were the only ones in, but I can't imagine it being chock full of half-witted Geordie Boys at those prices. So, aye, if you've got money to burn and fancy a hangover the size of Brussels, I'd recommend it. I'm far too much of a miser to make it a regular haunt myself, like, but if you're buying...

For: In the age of the chain superpub and the associated misery that usually follows, being a tiny bar with a bit of character is a definite plus point in its favour.
Against: Constantly being told, 'You went to the Vineyard? You fucking wanker' takes its toll after a while.

Our lass, who's forever got her beak in those fancy, four-eyed reading books, says the whole bar is a bit like Miss Haversham's decaying wedding feast in Dickens' Great Expectations, only transferred to a Christmas bash in Newcastle. Our lass is a blithering idiot.

6

Hang The DJ

George Orwell once famously wrote that, 'If you want a vision of the future, imagine a boot stamping on a human face – forever.' Had he, however, been forced to suffer what passes for entertainment – and unsolicited entertainment at that – in your average city centre bar, then we're sure his pronouncements would have ended something like this:

'... imagine all human communication drowned out by some po-faced fuckwit behind a turntable.'

Now, before some cock whines at us for our blanket contempt for dance music and for being fifteen years behind the times with our griping, we'd like to set a few things straight from the outset.

First of all, we don't subscribe to the tedious notion that dance music is all theft and that anything that's not white boy whining over guitar, bass and drums is somehow invalid. Fuck knows we've endured far too many terrible bands in our time to support that laughable notion. Plus, any so-called muso who thinks their noodling is superior just because they've spent half a lifetime learning their craft is an arsehole. We all know that for a fact.

Secondly, we're not so bloody miserable that we want to rid the world of DJs full stop; we fully comprehend that people are so stressed by even the thought of getting on the bus in the morning – never mind doing a day's graft in some India-bound call centre – that they have an obvious human need to unwind. We understand that there is a place for clubbing. And while we'll never quite grasp how folk can escape from the nightmarish cacophony of endlessly ringing phones by listening to what sounds like a million of those same phones set to a thumping four-to-the-floor with some ickle gurl panting on about nowt, that's probably just down to our age, our hearing loss and our general resentment at our vanished youth. We'd never be so churlish as to deny the benefits of chucking yourself about and getting a few endorphins pumping through the system. Of course we wouldn't.

No, for us the culture of the DJ is fine in clubs, catering for people who've actively sought it out and who've paid for the (dubious) privilege. We really don't mind what goes on behind closed doors, as long as it doesn't involve children, livestock or poetry, but please, for the love of Jesus and all his little disciples, will someone please listen to us as we ask:

WHY THE FUCK DO WE HAVE TO SUFFER IT IN THE PUB TOO?

Why? Obviously the promises of untold riches and endless flap have left the market so crowded they're effectively trying to piss a pint into a pen top, plus the downturn in the popularity of clubs has left DJs seeking asylum in any place that'll have them. But why do we always get stuck with the really, really shit ones? Why should we be swamped by the bandwagon jumping scrotes? And why should we subsidise their poor investment in Technics separates?

Is their presence in the bar supposed to be a taster, a little dimebag intended to whet the appetite and make you want to schmoove on down to the nearest superclub queue to boost their flagging profits? Sod that. Being subjected to that incessant bollocks is no more likely to get us to move on to a club than an inbox full of Viagra spam is going to make us reach for the Visa card when we've got the droop. If we want something, we'll pester *them*, not the other way round.

It's really quite simple. Music in the pub should be background noise, pitched just above the air conditioning. Why can these idiots not hear what's happening? How man, fucko. Take off your cans and listen for once. You are not the most important sound in the building. If people are making more noise than your tunes, it's because they want to hear what is being said. It's because talking whilst drinking is what pubs are for. The fact that they are trying hear each other is not a valid reason for you to turn your shite up even further to compensate. The joint is not jumping, you prick; it's just plain fucking angry.

As we said earlier, we have no overbearing hatred of dance music; in the right hands, that is. What we find so abhorrent is the yawning chasm between the bar DJ's claims of 'cutting edge' and the formulaic slop that gets pumped in our ears when we're trying to have a pint and a natter. The sheer ineptitude of the average headphoned twat in the corner astounds us. If music is played at an inescapable volume, then surely it should emphasise the highs and lows, the dynamics and emotions. We're pretty certain that those qualities are something the original artist had in mind, at any rate. So how can some fucking arse be allowed to get away with half an evening's worth of musical murder, bludgeoning innocent 'choons' to death with impunity?

We wouldn't mind so much if there weren't so many outright lies printed on the promo materials. Maybe if they put as much effort into ideas for their acts as they do into their litany of mendacious adjectives, we'd feel a bit more appreciative. Uplifting, you're saying? Sexy? Joyous? Funny, 'cause all we can hear is the usual monotonous shite, with every tune at the same tempo to cover up a complete lack of mixing skill.

We really fail to see how these self-serving dicks can still consider themselves to be some kind of radical underground scene. After all, isn't there a maxim that states, if you can spot a movement, it's already dead? So where's the glory for these gravy train-chasing chumps who actively queue up to fuck its decaying corpse? If DJing got anymore mainstream you could sail a bloody yacht down it, man. Wasn't it Frosties who did that 'junior DJ kit' giveaway a few years back? How can something be rebellious and 'street' when it's been co-opted by The Man, tidied up, repackaged and sold back to you with your fucking breakfast cereal? When you've had the piss taken out of you to that extent then no amount of glossy flyers is going to give you back your credibility.

On top of that, the arrogance of these chumps is really shocking. 'Featuring DJ sets from...' say the posters. DJ set? A fucking SET? How pretentious can you get? How much of a 'performance' can there be - and it won't hurt to repeat this for the billionth time – in playing some other fucker's records in a pub? It's like a station announcer laying claim to a 'timetable recital' for crying out loud. And get a load of the witless 'star' pseudonyms of the ones who think they've tried, and the sheer lack of imagination of the ones who haven't bothered. 'Excuse me, is there already a DJ Decks? There is? Oh, I suppose I'd better stick with Dave Smith, then.' Christ, those aliases boil our piss. In the '70s they'd have been Donnie Spangle; in the '80s, Bolshoi Beneath; Snoozer in the '90s. That's about the stamp of your typical bar DJ. And why? Because they're all fucking cunts, that's why.

Where's the honesty with these arseholes? Why can't they spin some stuff they might actually LIKE instead of either studied cool or ironic cheesiness? For all their claims of musical freedom and barrier smashing, with their self-imposed boundaries and rigid format fitting they end up as evil as daytime radio. And where's the sense of joy? Why do we see them moping in, night after night, sullenly dragging their discs and equipment behind them? Cheer up, you knacker. Give us a fucking grin. Nobody forced you to pay £300 for that deleted 12-inch on eBay.

You know us, we hate to be negative. But we also hate anything that hints at the emperor's new clothes. We hate the hideous grasping of otherwise-decent bars, with their blind allegiance to this shite. 'Ooh, THAT bar's got a DJ, so we have to have one or we might lose a few quid.' Fuck off, will you? Ever thought you might actually get more punters if it wasn't for the nipple behind the decks? Christ knows, we'd certainly pay a bit extra if we could avoid feeling so beaten and depressed at the end of the night. 'Well, you could always drink elsewhere,' goes the tired argument. Yeah? Why should people who like to talk be forced to do so in shitty bars surrounded by shoplifters and heed-the-baals? Why does the ability to string a sentence together preclude a bit of decent decor? Why does the smell of fresh paint have to be accompanied by the din of utter cretins?

Look, we understand that everyone needs a hobby. We know that, to hit the heights in any sphere you care to name, you've got to practice, but is there just an inkling of a chance you could you do it elsewhere, eh? Look at us. We're on our creaking knees in desperation. We are literally at the end of our ropes. Please, could you do it in your bedrooms, do it in a rehearsal space, do it on the bloody moon if you must but, we're begging you, keep it the fuck out of the pub.

We'll buy you a pint if you do.

7

Haymarket & Gallowgate

'As well as being home to the whole city's administration at the Civic Centre, the Haymarket is the transport hub for its northern outskirts. Two excellent universities fill the streets with a colourful student population and the Northern Stage theatre has undergone extensive refurbishment and modernisation. Adjacent to the Haymarket area, the Gallowgate district houses Newcastle's Chinatown with its breathtaking arch, and of course the city's beloved underachieving football club, Newcastle United.' - Norman Undercroft, Historian.

As You Like It
Archbold Terrace, Jesmond, NE2 1DB
'Dumb as a box of cocks'

By rights I should hate this pub. For a start I should despise any bar that is either too pretentious or too under-prepared to have its bloody name on the outside of the building. I should mercilessly savage any boozer that bills itself as having a cosy, country pub atmosphere, yet comes across as the test-tube baby of a Calamity Jane saloon bar and a Munich beer hall built by the gayest man in all of Deutschland. And I should knock five flagons of fuck out of any place that has its sphincter so stretched by designer clutter, you could drive a jeep through it and still have room for a caravan with awning. Birdcages? Dried flower arrangements? A pommel horse? Bloody hell. Antlers on the walls? Elephants everywhere, including on the table legs so the tusks can skewer your knees? And sky-blue-silver wallpaper that would make a blind man barf? This is not fusion, this is What The Fuck? Wait: I'm not finished yet. Check out the painting opposite the bar, of the sour-faced naked woman with her hand suggestively on her bits to detract the viewer from her wonky eye? I'd tell you it was a bad copy of Manet's *Olympia* if I didn't think you'd see me as being somehow culpable. Outside to the east there's an open beer terrace, with superlative views over the Metro tracks and the depressing daily trundle of out-of-service carriages with their windows all smashed, while the western side overlooks the disaster of Archbold Terrace and some of the worst architecture ever inflicted on the civilised world. And it's in this end of the pub that my patience is really tested, since if there's one thing that should have me reaching for the Semtex, it's a fucking children's area, ostensibly designed for happy, responsible parents and their broods, but mostly just full to the brim with the childless and sad, and simmering with the stench of ovulation. With over-compensatory cackles and tearful eyes, tick-tock career women dive headlong into the Sticklebricks, while it dawns on their nervous men friends that tonight's the night when it's away with the anal tickle ring and it's out with the thermometer and the undies from the freezer. Look at the fucking children's menu; take a butcher's at the perennial kids' favourite, a 100% organic chilli with beef and smoked bacon, sweetened with mango chutney and served with rice. That'll have them rocking in their babygrows, won't it. Chilli Yum Yum, they're calling it? Whose turn is it at the nappy changing table tonight, darling? Not fucking mine, I'll tell you. And as for the rest of this bar's clientele, the ones for whom the breeding panic has yet to take hold, are they the sort of people whose company you'd want to keep after a stressful day at the madhouse? Let's look at the evidence: immaculately suited, impeccably coiffured and dumb as a box of cocks. They are getting on my fucking nerves, and it's only half four on a Friday afternoon. So aye, I should be panning this place, and fully intended to do so, since it is really, really fucking ridiculous. Its bar-cum-bistro-cum-supper-club-cum-cum-bucket ethos is guaranteed to leave the plebs of this city utterly bamboozled and, what's more, they're threatening to change all the furniture round every night to keep it 'fresh'. But none of that matters a jot. The main thing for me is that they promise – they've put it in writing – that there will be no DJs and no dance-floors, and since I've done nothing but whinge about all that shite for the past hundred years, that's certainly as I fucking well like it. Top work.

For: Plenty of live music, a decent range of beer, and hats off to a bar that refuses to debase itself with a bastard 'fun' element.
Against: The music's not permanently live, obviously. No problem there, but the last time I heard the fucking radio in a bar was in a communist throwback boozer in Hungary, back in the days when you had to make a serious effort to get there and not just pile onto easyJet with the rest of the piss-up pigs. I hated it then and I hate it now. Whether they're being satirical, knowing, or plain stupid in here by sticking ComaFM over the speaker system, I care not a fig. I just want it turned off. (And I DON'T want Corinne fucking Bailey fucking Rae in its place.)

It's said Mam Mam Mam that the most joyful moment in any human being's life is the first time their offspring utters a Mam Mam Mam word of parental recognition. Baby's eyes lock with mummy's, a tentative 'mama?' is gurgled out, and Mam Mam Mam the tears can't help but fall. Why is it, then, that the proud and recklessly Mam Mam Mam! optimistic parent subsequently becomes completely Mam! Mam! MAM! incapable of ever hearing the word again, unlike the poor MAM! MAM! MAM! bystanders who have their ears pummelled by the insistent din of the horrible little gits? At the bus stop, in the supermarket; in the street or down the pub: if you aren't MAM! MAM!! MAM!!! going to listen, then don't bloody procreate, you selfish fucking cunts. And that goes for you an' all, Daddy.

The Black Bull

Barrack Road, NE4 6BB
'What it's aaaaal aboot'

Do you yearn for the good old days of football, pre-Taylor Report, when the terraces were king, and tickets were four for a pound? When you were a supporter and not a consumer; when the stadium was a 'groond'; and where your biggest worry was finding a pocket in the next man's coat that was deep enough to piss in. Glory days, man. The Corner! The Corner! When the lack of a roof meant you'd end up drenched every single week, and not just on the trudge from the exit gates to the coach park after another showpiece semi-final defeat three hundred miles from home. East Stand! East Stand! Then – on a matchday - the timewarp Black Bull in the shadow of St James' Park could just be the place for you. There you can join the other misty-eyed interlopers trying desperately to blend in with the legendary Supporters' Club diehards. Can't make the newcomers out? Easy. They're the ones churning out cack like 'Whey aye, man. Proppa purb, y'knaa. This is what it's aaaaal aboot' in between reciting great chunks of that morning's Journal back page and claiming it as their own opinion. Go on: get amongst it. Stand with all the other emasculated losers acting the beery hard nut in a place they feel they 'belang' despite being too yellow to step in at any other time, and see them praying that none of the regulars asks them a difficult question or looks at them funny. And then witness the change in attitude when it's time to leave the raucous pub, and the creature comforts of the modern game hove into view. Tag along with them as they stroll peacefully to St James' without getting their fucking teeth kicked out. See their heads held high now there's no longer massive piles of police horse shit to soil their shoes. And see them gliding effortlessly through the turnstile and into their seats by five to three, ready to join the pie queue at ten past. Not so keen on the old paddocks now, are you, cocker? Or the open-air pissers. Not now you're sitting in pampered luxury, with the match commentary on the earphones and a steward to bitch to if it gets too rowdy. Must those lads on

Level 7 make so much noise? So, aye, come on: tell me again about your 'Ultra' status. Convince me that you're not Toon Army, you're Toon Barmy. I promise I won't try to reconcile it with your lack of singing, or clapping, or indeed showing any movement at all beyond fucking off fifteen minutes from the end to be first on the Metro platform. You, sir, are a hypocrite. You treat the Black Bull like a living museum, where you can get your hands mucky before tootling back to tree-lined suburbia. You eulogise the gritty authenticity of the tatty lino floor, the knack-ered seating and the old NUFC photos and stained glass crests, all of which look like someone's taken a shooter to them. You make twee little comments on the clock above the door that runs backwards, as if it's some sort of unique historical item when even Sgt bloody Pepper's has got one these days. And you bend my ear about rekindling the passion in the game, yet can barely muster a resigned grumble about the shortcomings of the current manager / squad / away strip / burgers / programme / mascots once you're in the ground. Piss off, will you? Stop trying to convince me that the Black Bull is anything other than what it is: a grubby little boozer on the edge of a drab housing estate, stowed off on matchdays and dead for the rest of the week, bar the odd numpty with a penchant for Bonnie Tyler Hour on the telly. You want a return to the Seventies, is that what you're saying? Short shorts and the magic sponge? Ronnie Radford and pitches like a swamp? Look, I know Gabby Logan's a bit ropey from the side, but I'm hardly likely to fall asleep watching Match of the Day and dream about knocking one out onto Jimmy Hill's chinny-chin-chin instead of hers, am I? Leave the past where it belongs and give your fucking head a shake, you berk. The Score-board! The Scoreboard!

For: The son of an ex-boss of mine was once refused service in here and despatched with the words, 'And you can fuck off an' all. Oot.' His crime? Being ginger. Excellent customer care skills there: straight out of the management handbook.

Against: Aye, you're right. I AM shit scared of giving the Black Bull a bad review, so that's why I've picked on the sad, fat, clueless stereotypes who pack it out before the match, and not the bar itself. It's bad enough hearing that the Adelphi want to lace me without getting this lot on my case.

Never, ever, even if you're desperate, get a coach to a major football match with the Burglar's Dog. Whether it's being driven all the way to Wembley at 3mph by the reincarnation of Albert Steptoe, or enduring a 'shortcut' that added another half a day to the journey, or getting wedged into a service station forecourt by the stupidest man ever to fluke a PSV licence, if it wasn't for fuck-my-luck I'd have no luck at all. And don't get me started on the post-Cardiff debacle, haring up the motorway with a blown-out tyre, flames shooting in all directions like it was the last Concorde out of Paris. Trust me; if you see me mooching up to your 'executive' vehicle, with a bag of miserable butties and an even more miserable face, seek alternative transport. Stump up for the train. Fly. Hitch. Go on a fucking Space Hopper if you have to, but mark my words: I'll curse you all.

The Carriage

Back Archbold Terrace, NE2 1DB
'It's free? Oh, super!'

Whose idiot idea was it for me to traipse over here to do this one? Formerly the old Jesmond train station and legendary for the adjacent railway carriage that isn't even theirs (it belongs to the Indian restaurant next door), the Carriage is another victim of Newcastle's twin university status. Once a quaint boozer by the Metro tracks, with stags' heads, ornate lampposts and a gentrified air, the Carriage now gives the impression of a country cottage long abandoned and infested by thirty generations of ever-breeding rodents. You break through the doors in your protective galoshes, and the rats fix you with a beady eye, staring at you, like, 'What? What's the problem?' And there's not a single one among them that will ever understand why you want to grab a copper pan from the fireplace and just run amok, bashing in heads and launching bodies through the stained-glass windows. Look, listen and fucking pay attention: student pubs should be stamped out. What sort of preparation for life can possibly be gained by huddling in a protective cocoon? When will students face up to the harsh realities of city drinking, where the queue-enraging scholastic habit of ordering drinks individually instead of in rounds is punishable by a ribcage shattered with a broken table leg? How long will it take these fuckers to realise that seats are for arses and not rucksacks of ringtones or whatever it is they spend all their cash on? Like a bitter ex-lover dumped for a younger man with a bigger wallet and a less floppy Johnson, this bar has become utterly hateful. Look at those fucking fairy lights on those twigs in that pot. They wish it could be Christmas every day, do they? Me too, but only because there's a better-than-average chance the clientele might have fucked off home to mummy and daddy for the festivities. Jesus, I'm angry, and not just because my crisps are stale. To be fair, though, I can't deny that the Carriage's customers are frightfully well spoken and polite, and I find that such social niceties are beginning to rub off on me. Spying an unoccupied stool, I saunter over and, with the spirit of the Empire etched on my face, I enquire as to its availability. 'It's free? Oh, super!' With a straight-backed, stiff upper-lipped posture I raise the stool to shoulder height, and with the full force of the Industrial Revolution, I bring it down, down, DOWN, smashing it to splinters over my interlocutor's skull. Put your fucking feet on THAT, 'yeah?', you Home Counties cunt.

For: This pub is where I draw the line. There will be no further forays into Jesmond, no matter how many NE2 dickheads get on at me with their badly typed whining.

Against: Even in a bar as grim as this, there has to be a basic level of competence. And even though she'll therefore doubtless be sacked fairly shortly, I feel I must highlight the service of the hopeless barmaid I got saddled with. It breaks my heart to report it, but - while she'd obviously had the brains to dress herself and stand upright - she needed to ask me for clarification three times on my order of two and a half pints of the same fucking lager. Come on, love: at least TRY to concentrate.

The current fashion amongst students - current since the early

'90s when the first sap did it in the first chain coffee shop - is to wear a scarf indoors, regardless of the weather outside or the ambient temperature within. Here's a question for you. If you were to sneak up behind and grab both ends of the woolly wank-wipe, pull them tight and set them on fire, what would the humanities-studying twat do first? Put the flames out, or try to breathe? And the answer, obviously, is neither; they'd just text their mates at the next table to complain and then turn up their fucking iPod to drown out the sound of their sizzling flesh.

Crow's Nest

137 Percy Street, NE1 7RY
'A blight on the Haymarket'

I walk past this place four times a day on my way to and from work, and it was only about three weeks after the refit that I even noticed that anything had changed. The Crow's Nest has quietly, and with the minimum of fuss, replaced the appalling Australian theme pub Bar Oz, and done away with the surfboards, the crocodiles and the rest of the woeful tat that has been a blight on the Haymarket for what seems like an eternity. In an attempt to recapture a bit of the building's original history (the sign above the door says 'Crow's Nest Hotel 1902'. That's as much research as I can be bothered to do) they've tried to make it look – and this'll kill ya – like a pub. Nowt flashy, no 'leisure experience', no shit-itching gimmicks, just a new carpet and a wipe down with a dishrag, something that Bar Oz needed for at least the last three years of its existence. The woodwork's all been buffed up and revarnished, the walls have been painted – badly, I'll grant you, as if under protest or a Community Service Order – in traditional pub shades of grubby red and burnt orange, and the emphasis seems to be, not on posing or networking or designing your next ridiculous haircut, but on beer and banter. It'll never catch on. They've even taken the trouble to sort out the basement area, with a new roll of wallpaper on the staircase and an attempt at basic hygiene, and if the bogs haven't been completely refurbished, they've at least been cleaned. There's still a stench of day-old mashed turnip down there, though, as a reminder of the bad old days. So aye, ale, chat, maybe a bit of no-nonsense grub and a gawp at the telly to see which calamity has befallen the Toon this week. That'll do me just fine. Like I say, there's nothing revolutionary, and nothing to make you shout from the rooftops, but there's nothing that demands that you pay through the nose for style mag wankery, and even if it still is and will always be full of fucking students, it's decent enough for a quiet afternoon pint. If I gave marks out of ten, I'd give it five, maybe six on a good day. High praise indeed.

For: One less theme bar is always a cause for a celebration.
Against: They've still got a DJ booth, which can only spell trouble.

Crow's Nest? I'm surprised such a thing exists. Crows really are the stupidest birds of all time. Even the fucking dodo had more gumption than those raaaacking little idiots. Look at them, bouncing along the side of the motorway, hunting for a bite to eat. 'Mmm,' they think, 'Roadkill. I wonder how that got there...' Next thing you hear? The thunderous roar of an eighteen-wheeler. And the next thing you see? A splatter of innards and feathers, with a shattered wing flapping forlornly in the back draft. Extinction's too good for the likes of them.

Fluid

17-25 Gallowgate, NE1 4SG
'File this one under M for mediocre'

I'm an arrogant, lazy and complacent little bastard. And those are my good points. I thought, for instance, that I had Fluid's card marked. Two floors of average wood and brick decor, the requisite sports bar quota of tellies, and twigs, branches and other design ideas they've pinched from elsewhere instead of thinking up their own. Add to that a reasonable pint, and a healthy cross-section of punters through the week giving way to a squeeze of fat Geordie blokes before the match. That'll do, I thought. Stick in a mention of the happy hours for the after-office crowd, maybe something about the food, and I'll be laughing. Nothing out of the ordinary to report; indeed the only thing that's even halfway unusual is something on the menu called a Fluid Burger, which sounds less like standard pub fare and more like something Marc Almond might have munched on. I'm just about to file this one under M for mediocre when I notice a poster behind me advertising Big Brother nights: watch all the evictions LIVE on Fluid's big screens. You have got to be fucking kidding me, right? Why, I ask you, when I spend eight hours a day toiling in a place full of attention-seeking idiots doing fuck-all while stuck in a building they can only escape from if they're kicked out, would I then go to the bar to watch more of the fucking same? Why would I encourage people to bore me to the noose with inane prattle about how it's 'so bad, it's brilliant', when all they really mean is, 'I am so alone in life's journey. Please don't leave me out of the conversation, regardless of what tedious, humiliating shite I have to pretend to like so we can have something in common'? You don't believe me about that poster? Look, I'm telling you it's true. And if you try to convince me that it was a one-off experiment, then tough tits. Since I certainly won't be coming back here again, in my eyes it will be forever thus. Let's face it: that sordid waste of airtime will NEVER go away, no matter how low they stoop. Even if the next series has live human sacrifice and transvestite giraffe fucking, there'll be no more serious repercussions than a couple of wafts of a child's slipper across the arse from the industry watchdogs, plus a few mock-contrite – and heavily sponsored - 'apologies', so it's unlikely the bar will pass up the chance to make a bit of moolah. You're not seriously telling me you're interested in turning up for the party, are you? Then you're a cunt. Don't argue: you are. And I am a bigger cunt for letting it get under my skin. Fucking hell, man. I am absolutely furious now. Look, I know the country's screwed, and when it comes to finding a solution, everybody and the boil on their bottom thinks they know best. I understand that the splintering of society and complete lack of empathy for one's fellow citizen might encourage certain groups to believe that voter power should be weighted in favour of some at the expense of others. A successful, Eton-educated entrepreneur might, for example, think he should command more clout than a single mother on benefits. Or, with current electorate apathy and the alarming rise of the BNP, the earnest young man on the street with the clipboard and loudhailer might believe that his passion should entitle him to more of a say. That is, of course, bollocks, and dangerous bollocks at that. One-person-one-vote is all it should ever be. However, I feel that to get this nation off its bloody knees, there should be a rigid choice: either you can have your say in the democratically elected government of our country, OR you can text 'Spazz' to Urr-Eight-Neyn-Fawa-Feyve. It's your future, fucko. What's it to be?

For: Fluid was designed by the company behind the Quilted Camel, Perdu, and Barluga, so you might expect so see a bit of glitzed-up glamour...

Against: ...when what you actually get is the Sunday morning, jogging pants, battered T-shirt, no make up, bad breath version of your Saturday night conquest. Great.

No, no, you're alright. I've calmed down now, enough to write something about pubs and not the shite on telly. I mentioned happy hours in passing in the review, just before I hit the fucking roof. Post-work happy hours break the spirit and crush the imagination. There's a clique in my office who, whenever there's a night out, stamp on the suggestion that there may be life in other parts of the city, and complain and wheedle their way into making everyone sit in the same dismal bar for half the night, just because a pint is 10p cheaper than up the road. And you can see that attitude creeping into the rest of their blinkered worldview. You could say to them, 'Right! We've won the lottery! Where shall we go? Pony trekking in Thailand? Surfing on Bondi Beach? Hang-gliding from the top of the Eiffel Tower?' The response? 'Wetherspoon's.'

The Goose

Eldon Garden, NE1 7RA
'A quality, traditional pub'

I believe that small is beautiful when it comes to pubs. It's a viewpoint that has held me in good stead over the years, and provides a yardstick with which to batter this gargantuan hellhole about the face and neck. Once the merely massive Filament & Firkin – a tacky chain bar that was good for watching sport, if nowt else – they then knocked through and annexed the smaller but no less grim Scruffy Murphy's next door to create this, the insufferable idiot's idea of a proper bar. Throughout all ten million cubic feet The Goose occupies, you'll find weak imitations of a quality, traditional pub, served up in that horrible ambience vacuum typical of Goose 'outlets' throughout the nation. You ask anyone, at least anyone with the tiniest bit of sense, and the best thing they could ever say about The Goose is that it's there, handy, by the bus station, and it's cheap. To be honest, the bus station has more atmosphere, and the beer is discounted so much it's suspicious, yet the damned place is still packed to the rafters night after night. Jesus, man, what the hell is wrong with people today? The berks who drink in The Goose are living, breathing, gibbering proof that you could sell people shit on a shovel and call it all-day breakfast if they thought they were getting a special offer. Everyone who comes in here out of choice - you're partway excused if you're heading to the match and you're only here because it's near the ground - should be locked away for their own safety. They are clearly not of sound mind. Students, dickheads, misers, psychopaths; they're all here. There's embarrassing Uncle Jimmy, and mad Auntie Joan, who's a lovely lady, at least until she starts twatting people after fifteen trebles and a Smirnoff Ice. And look at them over there: the pudgy, on-the-shelf moos drinking wine to show a bit of class, and then, after downing four cut-price bottles of Blossom Hill, they'll be wondering why, instead of in the arms of bliss, they're lying in the wet patch from some bloke they'll never see again. Oh, fuck it. I could sit and rant about the sort of knackers who are prepared to give this place the time of day until my spine fuses to the chair and my fingers are typed down to bloodied knuckles. But what good would it do? Pubs like this are successful because human beings are, by nature, thick as absolute fuck. I can count on the legs of the former Heather Mills-McCartney how many times I've been in this godawful place since it opened (a desperate pint at some fucker's retirement night out, and a swift leak-and-leave a few months later: I make that one and a half times). Take it from me; The Goose is a damned disgrace, a cavernous leather-bound shed, and a fool's paradise. And any so-called mate of yours who has the temerity to suggest you go there just to save themselves a couple of bob on their round should be ditched or beaten or thrown in the road. Hit 'em, and hit 'em hard. You know it makes sense.

For: Ample space to cram in the very worst of Newcastle's drinkers and keep them the hell away from us. Or so you'd think...
Against: ...since I've seen people actually lining up to get in. Where are these people coming from? Why has there not been a cull?

What the hell is the matter with bar chains? Why do they persist in wrecking everything they touch? You name any once-outstanding pub that's been bulldozed by corporate blandness and meal-deal homogeneity; name any innocent drinking venue that's been tricked and sullied, and you can bet your dimpled arse that a chain have had their dirty fingers in its crisp, white, schoolgirl panties somewhere down the fucking line.

The Hancock

Hancock Street, NE2 4PU
'Quietly, and with dignity'

The Hancock is a bar I absolutely despise. There. Got that out of the way. Why? I've got my reasons. Number one, I'm still sore that they did away with Bierrex, the relaxed European-style café bar with surprisingly few pretensions, and replaced it with this, a fucking Scream Fun Pub. You'd expect after all these years that I'd find some way to come to terms with it, but every sunny afternoon when I'm up near the Haymarket, I think of coming in here for one of the extensive range of comedy beers that Bierrex used to boast, and then remember there's now a choice of, like, one lager. But it isn't even the lack of variety that gets my goat. The real pisser for me is, number two, the students. Why do I hate students? Just look at them, man. Isn't that enough? No? Then picture them bouncing up to you on rag week, legs tied together and greasepaint all over their faces, shaking their fucking charity tins in your face like you haven't already - quietly, and with dignity - given enough. Imagine their braying, bucktoothed faces spouting their gobshite, over-rehearsed opinions on any topic they think they won't be pulled up on. Just listen to that berk over there, for instance. He thinks he's fucking Wittgenstein, bellowing his received wisdom and borrowed philosophy into that specky bint's lug. Why didn't the sexually over-exuberant tit just marker-pen it on his damn T-shirt? 'Ooh! Can I try my cock out on you, yeah?' Look, I understand that if a bar is near to the university, it's going to be full of academics. Hang on while I stop chuckling at the last word in the previous sentence. It's bound to attract students like dog's eggs attract dragonflies. But why this one? Why shun the bar on campus and then head straight for a pub that's little more than a college refectory, complete with a chip-strewn sticky floor? And it's not even as if the Hancock has the decency to simply wring its hands at the good fortune of just being in the way. This place is actively encouraging the loathsome little shites to part with their - or rather the taxpayers' - hard-earned cash with their patronising, 'it's your first time away from home kiddies, come and join in our wacky promotions' ethos. You'd think the future rocket scientists of our nation would be wise to it by now, but no. The irritating twats fall for it term after term, and sit there monopolising the beer garden - the one that's MINE by rights - whining on and on and on about having no money whilst scraping the scarf fluff off their £80 T-shirt with their platinum iPod Nano. And they've got the nerve to stare at me like I'M the cunt? Looks like Professors Fists and Toecaps will be taking the lectures next semester.

For: It's a joy to hear over-confident student wankers gawping at the Civic Centre across the car park and sneering about how they'd never end up there, safe in the knowledge that, in three years' time, with their useless degrees, the council is exactly who they'll be begging for some menial office job.
Against: Hancock's Half Hour? Fuck that. Nine and a half minutes of this place and we had to get the hell out.

When I was a kid the Jesmond area of Newcastle was a desirable place to live. Look at it now; with all its student boxrooms it's now nothing so much as a frigging ghetto. All the affluent locals have left, becoming ever richer by subdividing their subdivisions and hawking them out to gullible saps with far too much student loan money for their own good. I hate to break it to you, Ben or Tim or Jessica or Hannah, but when I worked for the leccy board, your fancy NE2 address was known to us as the fucking meter cupboard.

The Hotspur
103 Percy Street, NE1 7RY
'It doesn't take much to be knowledgeable about Foster's'

Situated in the middle of the Haymarket no-nonsense line of pubs, The Hotspur remains a proper boozer serving a proper pint to proper people who've got no time for any of that Tizer-flavoured fashion shite. What it has got? Frequent beer festivals, a healthy smattering of terrible beards, and big bastard bellies that'd stop you in your tracks. And what it hasn't: kids, expensive haircuts, and certainly no bloody DJ. Owned by one of the more respectful and least contemptible chains, T&J Bernard - whose values come from a time when 'chain pub' just meant creaming off the profits from an established boozer, and not destroying everything that was good about them in a desperate attempt to enforce the brand - The Hotspur is renowned for its choice of real ales, and also for being fucking heaving when there's a Toon match on telly. It's also notable for having an alley down the side that has seating, a telly and heaters, and for being down-to-earth enough to call it an alley and not a service pavilion, or some other such cobblers. I've never known the staff be anything but friendly, and while it doesn't take much to be knowledgeable about Foster's, they're always there with a smile and a word of advice for the discerning drinker, as opposed to the scowl and the dismissive shrug you get while the staff in more pretentious places piss about chopping up dandelions for £8 cocktails. I still recall the day when I witnessed a French lad in there who, when asking for 'blonde beer', was offered a sample from the pump to see if it was to his taste. If he'd tried that elsewhere, they'd have broken his fucking jaw. The punters, like the bar, are worn around the edges and comfortable with it, the music's palatable but not in the least bit trendy, and you're almost always guaranteed to get in a strange conversation with some lovable mentalist, whether you want to or not. Class. And if it wasn't for the students, it'd be perfect.

For: Beer, sport, conversation, atmosphere, staff. And the memory of the previous landlord, all three foot six of the lecherous little get.
Against: The bogs are rank, and I still haven't recovered from nearly standing in that discarded pair of heavily shat underpants three years back.

They say your best Christmases are when you're a kid. Bollocks, I say. Just before Christmas 2001 came a winter wonderland that'll stay with me forever. We arrived outside the Hotspur on a Saturday just before Final Score to find the inside absolutely jam-packed and the Leeds v Newcastle match on the big screen. We're standing out there in the freezing cold, wiping our breath off the windows with our cuffs so we can see the game, when it starts to snow; gently at first, then steadily, then a blizzard. There's snow on our heads, down our collars, in our pockets, and we're tapping on the glass like some Victorian urchins, with expectant faces that say, 'Please guv'nor, let us in by the fire.

It's perishing out here and no mistake.' And then, with the last kick of the match, Nobby cracks the winner in for 4-3 from the right. The bar erupts, we're dancing in the road, dodging the snow-blind traffic and, suddenly, finally, there's peace on Earth and goodwill to all men. Oh, man: what a moment. Our lass got me fuck all that year, by the way. And I've hated Christmas ever since.

Luckies

14 St Mary's Place, NE1 7PG
'Pasties with cack'

Newcastle City Council's environmental department have got some strange ideas about the upkeep of the town's streets. While I wholeheartedly encourage the bloke in the little muck-spreading van who drives up and down Northumberland Street every day, trailing a wash of filth behind him and spraying the kids' pasties with cack, I find it a little bit depressing that the pavements have gone to rack and ruin. Every time it rains you have to pretend you're Harrison Ford in *Indiana Jones and the Last Crusade* just to get from A to B without getting your trousers drenched by the puddles under the rickety flagstones: 'In Latin, Jehovah starts with an 'I''. Not Luckies' fault, I grant you, but it's enough to set me up for another round of tenuous linkage. Everyone's first choice bar for a guaranteed summer beers disappointment, this pub in the shadow of the Civic Centre has finally been refurbished after a geological age of neglect and rot. And some - The Chronicle probably, since they're always sticking the boot in - might say that the refit has been done to a standard that would make the Council proud. Undoubted vast expense has been frittered away with very little to show for it, as if they were so busy box-ticking and taking care not to offend anyone that the idea of producing anything of any merit has gone straight out of the window. So where there once was a determinedly scruffy little boozer with an American diner theme, the corridors of power and their unnecessary consultants have decided that this is what the public want; an eyesore of gift wrap wallpaper, beige ceilings and tasteful *objets d'art*, together with 'that' fucking shade of purple paint on any surface without an armed guard. Look over there; they've even got a terrible picture of the Civic Centre to reflect its lofty position looming over Luckies' corner location in a way that I would describe as Kafkaesque, if I'd ever been arsed to read any of his impenetrable, paranoid gobbledegook. The punters, as they've always been up this end of town, are students you can't help but detest, and office drones from the ten floors of '60s ugliness with the crown and seahorses on over the road. That's the indoor customers, at least. Outside you're stuck with anyone and everyone with a dead-eyed scowl and a rottweiler on a rope, whose sworn duty is just to ruin your alfresco pints. And that brings me finally to the bar's real pisser, the insulting, arcane policy of glass glasses inside but plastic pint pots out on the terrace, as if that's somehow safer and more civilised. I suspect the Council's licensing department to be behind that, too. I don't know about you, but being trusted so little that I have to drink out of a plastic glass would make me more violent, if anything. Aye, stupid beakers and breathing in bus fumes: guaranteed to turn you into a murderer.

For: Grabbing a seat on the terrace on a sunny day, leering at the student babes sashaying past on their way from their hour a week of hard study, safe in the knowledge that you'll never get or want the opportunity to talk to the tedious titwitches.
Against: Even if you camp out from seven in the morning, you will never get to grab that seat.

Second most depressing part of the student year: freshers' week, when fancy-dressed gimps hand out endless reams of bar adverts and drinks promotion leaflets, practically begging people to part with their cash in some shoddy fun pub. First most depressing? The way they look straight through me, as if I simply do not exist. Maybe my defeated, underpaid, style-free, hopeless, suicidal wage slave disguise is a little TOO good these days.

Mr Lynch
Archbold Terrace, Jesmond, NE2 1DB
'This year's must-have'

I hadn't been to the Archer in over a hundred years so when I heard that the place had suffered a refit I must admit I didn't have same sense of betrayal and dislocation as some of my mates. The scruffy-but-with-good-music dump has been replaced by a 'neighbourhood lounge bar', with more emphasis on DJ culture and all that depressing crap, and although they're plugging live music I have no fucking idea what 'too cool for school' entails. It sounds absolutely terrible. I really can't imagine the new layout being that popular with the bands who used to play here, what with the stage design being somewhere between bad cabaret and Punch & Judy, and the tacky audience area seating giving it that dreadful chicken in a basket atmosphere. When are designers going to understand that it's not necessary to be 'ironic' every hour of every day? As for the rest of the bar, they've tried hard with the deliberately awful '70s furniture, lamps, wall hangings and sit-in hairdryer, but I felt I was drinking in an installation at the Baltic rather than a relaxing bar. I dunno, maybe it's because I'm so ancient that I actually remember all that furniture from when I was a kid (golden rule of ironic kitsch: never get involved with anything you recall from the first time round), but it didn't make me smile knowingly; it just made me sad. Why? Perhaps in my mortgaged misery I don't like being reminded that this year's must-have is tomorrow's cheese. I saw no evidence of the advertised soul food when we were in, but you can bet your arse that they just mean the usual pub grub with a picture of some knacker with an afro on the menu instead of any rice & peas concoctions. And if you've seen any of their promotional stuff and are wondering what 'genuine people' they attract, it's this lot: uprooted ex-Archer indie kids, bored office workers from upstairs and tedious Jesmond fashionistas (that's Italian for wankers, by the way). Oh, and yes, yes, I understand the reasoning behind the pub's moniker, taken from the mysterious artist J H Lynch, copies of whose work adorn the walls, but it has to be said that Mr Lynch is a bloody dreadful name for a bar.

For: I hope to god that the presence of sockless haircut victims outside dribbling into their phones means you can't get a signal inside under all those tons of brutalist concrete.
Against: Although the happy hour beer is alright and reasonably priced, some fucker's got to pay for this hubris and you can safely say it'll be you.

No flashing machines or rigged shooting games for Mr Lynch's happy hours. Here you get a choice of Flip A Coin, Which Hand Is The Bottle Top In?, or Paper Scissors Stone. I, naturally, opted for the latter. The barmaid gave me stone; I gave her the finger and got charged double. Well, it seemed like a good idea at the time.

Madisons
Leazes Lane, NE1 4PF
'Weeping juveniles two-by-two'

I may live to regret saying this, but it looks as though this place has finally found a name and concept it likes, so hopefully there'll be no more pointless pissing about and rebranding every six months. It's been a bit of a struggle, I don't mind telling you. Over the years I've found myself racking my brains to come up with bitter satire on the grey desolation that was Bar 2XS (or Bar XS, or Bar XS2: I never did decide), only to be forced to do it all again when it morphed into the bizarre modern Indian eatery-stroke-drunken piggery hybrid of Sanctuary after that. Now it seems to be settled on the name of Madisons, my life should be a bit less of a chore. Ostensibly one of those fucking chilled vibe type of bars for young, successful adults, the Madisons I have come to know is either full to the brim with increasingly glum middle-aged faces after the match, or is peppered with under-dressed and over-cocky kids lurking in the corners. Now don't get me wrong. I'm not trying to suggest any negligence on the part of the door staff, and I might be getting older to the point where everyone under twenty-five is a child to me, but some of the shifty-looking customers here look suspiciously fresh-faced. I'd dearly love to know what the fucking rozzers make of it, or see them piling in and dragging out weeping juveniles two-by-two. It would at least lift some of the tedium from this dreary little bar, with its mandatory muted orange and murky purple colour scheme that looks like a well-kicked ribcage would by streetlight. Photos of jazz legends stare down from the walls, which is quite ironic since every time I've been in there's been zero in the way of Billie Holiday and an absolute fucking boatload of some dick with a turntable telling me how he's 'got so much love to give' over and over and over again. Why must bars persist in doing that, sticking up misrepresentative pictures to dupe the passing clientele? I'll tell you what I reckon: it's because, take away the opium and the exploitation and the lynching, the jazz scene had an enduring charm that a modern bar could never hope to match. DJ culture meanwhile is, from start to finish, a completely faceless nonentity and it's doubtful you'd even remember one of the fuckers if you'd woken up next to them this morning, tender-arsed and smiling. Go on; try it. See if I'm not right. Try to picture a superstar DJ's mugshot on a bar wall in seventy years' time in the same way that the glamorous past has been pillaged here. You just can't see it somehow, can you? There's not one of the cunts with even a smidgen of charisma. End up on the walls? They look more like they'll end up on some sort of sex offenders' register.

For: Subdued UV lighting in the bogs, so you can't see what you're wading about in. Sadly it also means you can't even spike a vein to relieve at least some of the misery.
Against: A word to the management: if you're thinking of ringing the changes once more, then please think again. I see enough expensive tinkering for tinkering's sake in my working life, so I really do not need to see it in the pub, too.

The original Madisons in Newcastle was a dire 'niteclub' over by New Bridge Street, the sort of moustache, tie and white socks establishment that gave Newcastle its grisly reputation. Fuck knows what's there now. I think it was a gym the last time I was brave enough to head that way, but I tend to avoid that area now it's become a training ground for serial killers and general dickheads who think it's only fair to slash the faces of total strangers and throw them on the central motorway just because they've wasted all their taxi money trying to pull some slobbering hound.

Newcastle Arms

57 St Andrews Street, NE1 5SF
'Faceless McLoungebar'

There's a bar that represents the absolute pinnacle of a pub designer's dreams, a bar they're sure that the whole wide world can't live without for another second. It combines the very latest in Contemporary Retro furniture with an air of sophistication, adding just a soupcon of chilled beats for that essential leisure experience. Thankfully, the Newcastle Arms isn't it. Traditional and historic, and looking like a proper boozer to boot, the (multiple) CAMRA award-winning Newcastle Arms is the complete opposite of the vapid, overpriced cackholes that are beginning to have a worrying stranglehold on the rest of the city. And considering it's on what is essentially the same block as the horrifying Gate complex, the fact that they've resisted the temptation to go for the big bucks and turn it into something that looks like a bloody furniture store deserves an award in itself. With a name that actually contains the town it's in, and pictures of Newcastle all over the walls, it makes a change to have a pub that underlines its own heritage and is not trying to hoodwink you into believing you're in some ambitiously faraway destination, or a faceless McLoungebar that could be anywhere and nowhere. The beer's tremendous, the staff treat you like a human being and not some fleeceable commodity, and even if it is a first pint pub for West End radgies hot off the bus at the Gallowgate, plus a claustrophobic push-and-shove fest on a match day, there's still more to recommend here than in a hundred haircut bars. What more could you want? A DJ? Hadaway and shite.

For: If I was ever put under house arrest, I'd like my house to be the sandwich shop between here and the no-frills Chinatown Express restaurant, with a sneaky side door into each. I'd back any tin pot military junta you care to name if there was so much as a whiff of that happening.

Against: Bloody global warming means I'll probably never get the chance to sit by the fire, warming my glass of port like a proper sad old bastard.

The Newcastle coat of arms is the one with the daft seahorses either side of a shield, with a lion atop a castle above that, and it's the one Newcastle United simplified for their club crest. How am I so sure about this? Because I had it on my living room wall when I was a kid. And why was it on the wall? Because my family are hereditary Freemen of the City. Oh yes; generation after generation of villains, lunatics, nursery school drop-outs and Chronicle salesmen, all charged with a musket in the defence of the City. And when I scrape together enough pennies for a silver coin for the investiture, I'll be on the list with them. The cows on the Town Moor won't know what's hit 'em.

Old Orleans
Haymarket, NE1 7PF
'Above sea-level'

Quietly choking in the fumes of the Haymarket bus station, Old Orleans has been providing an unnecessary Deep South theme bar for people with no imagination for a good while now. With mound upon mound of desperately poor tat, whether you're upstairs in the restaurant or downstairs in the bar, you're virtually guaranteed an astonishingly bad time. You could say that Old Orleans has become the baton-carrier for knackered trombones, Moon Over Bourbon Street signs and all-that-jazz since the Jerry-built 'New' version in the States blew over last time there was a bit of a light breeze. I suppose you could claim that the dreck in this bar can be considered 'new authentic' now that the genuine article is caked in mud and buried under an overturned station wagon. You could also point out that, if nothing else, someone at least had the wisdom to build this place above sea-level. But I think I'd rather have taken my chances with the looters and disease in Baton Rouge than have suffered the spectacle in here. Look, there's no point in sugaring the pill by telling you about when it's quiet; you need to get in at the critical moment and see it at its most potent, just to underline why you should never, ever be so stupid as to come in again. Best time? I'd say a Thursday evening, just after the offices kick out. See them waddle past the windows and through the doors, thirteen stone piglets with flabby arms aloft, in true dancing ant formation. 'Hee hee heeeee! Looka mee! Eeh Shelly, I'm ganna get pissed!' Watch in disgust as they order the most difficult-to-mix cocktails, with their hilarious, innuendo-ridden names. 'Can I have a Finger Up The Shitter With A Twist?' No, but you can have a smack in the fucking fat mouth if you want. Look at him, the contemptible prick behind the bar - yes, YOU, dickhead - shovelling in the ice with the ineptitude that shows why he failed the exam to shovel cowshit. Keep looking at him, since it'll be an eternity before he's ready to pour your pint. His sticky dreams of glamour are a distant memory and, because he simply can't be trusted in a decent bar, he's going to over-compensate by lobbing the bottles around in here, acting like Tom Cruise and that miscellaneous bloke out of *Cocktail*, even though it's been nigh on twenty years since anyone was even remotely impressed by such twattery. Did I say anyone? I meant except for the - and I hate to use the word - sluts at the bar, that is. With a chuck-chuck-chuck, a slop-slop-slop, a ho-ho-ladies and a tee-hee-hee; on and on it goes. The patter's getting filthier, while you're just getting thirstier. And angrier. You could piss off for a spacer to the Hotspur, or the Percy, or to fucking Azerbaijan if you wanted, and they'd still be there giggling when you got back. See when I finally get to Heaven? I'm having words with the Lord and I'm cleaning out His cloth ears. And the next time He's dishing out the hurricanes and the 'Acts of', He'll send them where I fucking well tell Him to, make no mistake.

For: The huge windows at the front open out on a sunny day, so if you grab the right seat you can howl with laughter as the bus station roof falls in. Again.

Against: They had better fucking NOT have 'live saxophone nights'.

I remember when they were building the extension to Marks & Spencer next door. Midway through the lunchtime nacho session, a whopping great rat came in from the site, did a soft shoe shuffle across the tiles and then fucked off back out again, to the shrieking, chair-mounting horror of the diners and shoppers. It made the front page, as I recall. Disgrace! Vermin! What About The Kiddies?! Me, I'd have had the cunt on Mastermind for having the sense to scarper before the happy hour.

Pacific Bar Café

12-22 Northumberland Road, NE1 8JF
'The socially inept and the recently divorced'

Pacific is a theme bar in denial. It likes to think of itself as a luxurious leisure venue catering to a discerning, upmarket clientele, but it's really just the worst kind of chrome and sparkle and desperation you could ever imagine. And I imagine a lot. This is an '80s bar that doesn't even realise it's an '80s bar. It's a relic rather than an ironic refit, and to step inside it's as if time has stood stubbornly still, with the same defeated customers from the same offices having the same conversations as they've done every night since 1985, with only bulging bellies and sagging scrota measuring out the years. How, though? The bloody bar's only been there for, like, half a dozen years: maybe they just built it around the punters. This is the sort of place the socially inept and the recently divorced from Sgt Pepper's go to when they really want to push the boat out. This is the bar where they still play Whitney Houston, for crying out loud. You get the same squealing and hollering as you've always done, the same boob tubes and spray on glitter, and the same insulting notion that horrific expense = good time. There's a coloured lamp to suit every bad mood, a pointless glittery artefact in every nook and cranny, and a whole host of soundless TVs to comfort the lonely and conversationless. The big staircase in the middle confirms that there's definitely two floors, maybe even three, but I don't think I could have got more than five steps up without bursting into tears at the wasted effort and absolute futility of it all. Oh, man: I'm so depressed. What a terrible, terrible bar this is. And even after all this time, I still fail to see how the fact that it cost £9 million to build can justify serving up rubbish beer at astronomical prices. For all the carping and pussy whining I've done about haircut bars, I'd still rather drink in Apartment than here, and that's tantamount to saying, 'Yes, I think I'd prefer babies for tea tonight.' You need this bar like you need an amputation.

For: Posh bogs.
Against: The mid-pub, mid-life crisis that prompted me to rant about the faults of the punters when I know in my heart that I'm really just describing my own decaying self.

Wait! Come back! In spite of what you heard about it biting the dust, Pacific Bar Café is very much alive. Yes, it may have had a few problems when its parent company died a death and yes, it might have lain there sad-eyed and gammy-legged and unloved in the cardboard box while all the rest of the litter found new owners, but now it's up on its feet again. Such a lovely story: I think I'm going to cry. Here's how the little scamp hopes to amuse you: with cartoon silhouette dirty dancers on the windows, and with some sort of mocked up raunch-cage high on the pillars. Has anyone got a sack and a large anvil?

Percy Arms

83 Percy Street, NE1 7RW
'A fitting tribute'

When I was a skinny little teenage twat with a studded belt that weighed more than I did, I used to drink in this bona fide, fuck-rough biker hang out, where the city's Mad Dogs, Spiders, Lone Wolves and Laurences gathered to compare sump oil stains before riding their hogs into the sunset and never lookin' back. Now it just looks as though it's been reduced to a biker apology pub, with an embarrassing plastic TT-bike stuck on the wall, a blinding Easy Rider sign above the bar, and not the least sign of WD40 let alone a Hell's Angel. There's plenty of pierced metal kids and old buzzards and tramps, but no real bikers to speak of. Even the die-hards with the Mam-bought Doors T-shirts under their leathers look like they need stabilisers to keep them upright, since they've clearly grown far Fonda (Christ!) of Burger King than the Lizard King over the years. What a tragedy. My disgust at the half-arsed theme tempts me to follow suit with this review; I can't be bothered to blather on about the beer (decent enough), the atmosphere (fine if you like a bit of Zeppelin) or the bogs (wait until you get home). What I will say is this: I was in the Percy on 27th April 2000 (photos from the night have the date on) and there was a bloke with a fucking huge Afro propping up the bar. Standing here at the back end of what I refuse to call the noughties, right in front of me I see that same bloke with that same Afro still propping up that same bar. Now I come to think of it, he was here when I was a nipper, too. Maybe he's just been waiting all these years for Bat Out Of Hell to finish; three more choruses and a couple of false endings and he'll have finally got his money's worth. That would make perfect sense to me. Take the singer out of the MC5, and take Columbian football legend Carlos Valderrama; add them together and square them, and you're still not even close. This man's 'fro is by far the most remarkable thing about the Percy, and when it all falls out they should glue it to a dummy and have it standing at the bar like that plastic cunt in the Drizabone who used to trip me up in Bar Oz along the road. That would be a fitting tribute to one of the town's last remaining characters. And it'd be the about the only real reason to come here again.

For: The biker motif means I can dedicate this review to the amusingly goateed little shit who used to get on my bus, complete with full regalia championing his Chapter, and wipe his oily kecks all over the seats. Being a tolerant sort of chap, I reasoned, hmm, takes all sorts; it was only after I'd got off I thought, 'Eh? If you're that much of a biker, what the hell are you doing on the

fucking bus, you odious turd?'
Against: Half a review on a bloke's haircut? That's just pathetic.

I feel I have to mention that the (possibly ex-) live-in manager of the Percy is a personal friend of Burglar's Dog 'Does what, exactly?' John Egdell. In the interests of anonymity and protecting the innocent, we'll call the unfortunate manager Derek, on account of it being his real name. Egdell likes to recount the tale of how Derek and the lads went off on a summer jaunt to, I dunno, fucking Torremolinos or some other place where daft lads go to get smashed and take photos of each other's nads. At the time, Derek (still his real name) was working in a bar in Gateshead. One morning that bar received a postcard from the lads on holiday. It had four words: 'Derek shat the bed'. Two days later came another postcard, this time less conversational than the first. This one said simply, 'Again'. Just try to remember that when you're in the Percy. And make sure you ask for a clean glass.

Rosie's

2 Stowell Street, NE1 4XQ
'Tattooed, pickled and rough as a nympho's knees'

Rosie's Bar is a Newcastle institution, and has long been regarded as the best place to kick off a night stuffing your face in Chinatown. Or at least it was, until the horrible, horrible Gate complex around the corner opened. But as long as The Gate continues to filter off all the fucking idiots wittering on about 'flied lice' then I'm a happy man. I can't imagine Rosie's giving a shit, like. It's not as if they're going to miss the trade: this place is busy at the best of times, and to describe it as even chock-a-block before the match would be to water down the truth for the faint of heart. If I had to pin a label on the customer base here, I'd say Rosie's probably attracts the crowd from the West End - tattooed, pickled and rough as a nympho's knees - especially now that the Newcastle Arms across the road has pulled its socks up. But I've never seen any trouble. In fact, some match days you get just as many away fans here as Toon ones, even if they are meek little real ale merchants following teams we expect to take a pasting. The decor in Rosie's is just the right side of tatty, with old sports equipment on the walls, a broken one-string guitar on the shelves and a clock that runs backwards behind one of the pillars. Anything you like as long as it's knackered and looks like it's been dredged up from the bottom of the Tyne seems to be the order of the day. And, above the bar, there's a row of dummy's heads with wigs on - Uncle Toboggan and Aunt Nebraska or whoever - that rotate and blink and tell you the tricky answers on the quiz machine. I think. Other than that, there's a ton of NUFC stuff on the walls - they could hardly not - plus massive windows with a head-on view of the Chinatown arch, and St James' Park framed beautifully through that. Of course, I'm just rambling and rambling about the decor to tease you, and make you wait for the best bit, which is – and this is no exaggeration – the pint prices that make you think you're in dreamland, or at least back in 1983. No shit. Sixteen pints and you still get change out of a fiver? No wonder I can't breathe before kick-off.

For: Dedicated customers, keeping the makeover mafia the hell away.
Against: The gents, and the door that opens up to give the far end of the bar a good view of things they'd probably rather not see. You might as well just lob your pecker out and walk through the pub for all the privacy you get in the bogs.

Those dummy's heads above the bar have given me a cracking idea. Why not use real severed heads, starting with those can-clutching scumbags who hang around Grey's Monument and harass you at the cash point? I'd pay over the odds to see their stupid fucking heads mounted on spikes, that's for certain.

Sgt Pepper's

Vine Lane, NE1 7PW
'Grim inevitability'

Sgt Pepper's is a '60s theme bar stuck firmly and inescapably in the 1980s. And it hasn't got a bloody clue. Call me a stickler, a pedant or an elongated teat, but it struck me as being a bit strange that, in a bar named after a Beatles album, there's a whopping great picture of Mick Jagger in a prime spot on the wall. Nice one. We arrived when the evening session was in full flow, which meant that we got to see first hand the stunning effect of the glitter balls and pathetic geezer-with-a-torch disco lighting, and to listen in astonishment to the Butlins Redcoat pretending to be a DJ. This bar is very popular with flabby blokes plagued by excess sweating and blubbery, sow-faced women, and while there was plenty of excited shrieking, the hacky looks being dished out between groups guarantee that one spilt drink would see lasses clubbing each other with their heels at eight o'clock at night. Sgt Pepper's, with a certain grim inevitability, is also a mandatory stop on the hen night tour for those too old and too crippled to make it down to the Quayside, so don't say you haven't been warned when you get molested. The speakers outside blaring shite like Dire Straits into the alleyway let you know before you enter what kind of music they play here; there's a constant barrage of late '80s golden oldies, giving the punters the chance to sing along to stuff before realising that they don't know more than the first line of a single bastard song. That's the night-time experience then; during the day you're stuck with the beer-stained Sgt Pepper's brand carpet and the gimme-two-glass-eyes-and-make-it-snappy tangerine and lime colour scheme. If you've ever wondered what the leisure centre bar in Hades is like, then wonder no more. This is it, and it wants you as a member.

For: The massive relief Union Jack design on the far wall must've kept some toerag on an Asbo occupied for at least a week. I hope to fuck they counted the damn woodwork tools afterwards, though.

Against: On account of the wizened old crones who make up my department at work, THIS is my office local. I'm ticking off the seconds until Thursday's Chronicle and the jobs pages. Have you got owt you want doing?

If you score in here you're in for a rude awakening the next day. Your conquest will be sporting a hairpiece, a corset and someone else's teeth, and will probably have gone to school with your dad. And humped him. You might as well top yourself to save the embarrassment of seeing them again. Go on. You know it makes sense.

Shearer's

St James' Park, NE1 4ST
'Insipid, gutless slop'

Opened at the arse end of 2004, Shearer's Sports Bar and Lounge underneath the Gallowgate End at St. James' Park quickly proved itself to be to Newcastle's drinking scene what Titus Bramble was to the team: huge, overpriced and utter, utter shite. But, while poor old Titus is long gone, thanks to the Shearer legend I fear this is a bar we're stuck with. If you've ever had the misfortune to attend a function in one of the many suites inside the ground, you'd know that Shearer's is more or less an extension of that depressing rat shit. And for those who've yet to witness the corridors of power, let's just put that the bar is on a par with, say, Chester-le-Street's third best nightclub. Why not pop along, dig deep in your pockets to buy an insultingly priced drink served on a stupid fucking club crest doily, and then try to find a spot to relax in the glorified hangar that is Newcastle's biggest bar? You won't, like, but at least you can feast your eyes on one of the many plasma screens showing DVDs of Newcastle's glory days i.e. when we still won fuck all, but at least it was entertaining to watch, unlike some of the insipid, gutless slop we've been served up since Shearer's opened. The blurb on the Toon's official site says something along the lines of the place being laid out in three distinct areas: ground floor, mezzanine and first floor. Fucking Homebase DIY on the Team Valley has much the same design, but it wouldn't entice me to part with my hard-earned, not even if they were showing Matchpot of the Day on the big screen. Shearer's apparently cost £2.5 million to build, which is roughly a quarter of what we'll end up paying the next panic-buy European import to fall over his own feet on the rare occasions he feels like being fit from now until the end of his contract. What a fucking waste of money. Ever the diplomat, Mr Shearer himself was asked on the opening night for a few words on the monstrosity that bears his name. 'It goes without saying I am very proud that part of St. James' Park will bear my name,' he said. At gunpoint. His then-chairman, thankfully, was unavailable for comment.

For: At least it makes the ground look finished.
Against: I have no problem with the angry youth of our city expressing themselves in biro on toilet cubicle walls, just as long as they make an effort to spell it correctly. I think you'll find it's 'Freddy ShepHERD is a cunt,' actually.

When European and domestic cup games are half full of miserable fuckers and burger-munching kids, when the atmosphere is like a mausoleum and all you see around you are once-a-season whingeing part-timers claiming to be the 'loyalest football supporters the wooooorld has ever had', what is the point of sticking the match on in the stadium bar as well? Where's the fucking sense in having an empty ground and a full boozer? (Penny drops: three pints in the bar costs about the same as a match ticket.)

The Strawberry
Strawberry Place, NE1 4SF
'Broken bones and asphyxiation'

Have you got the number 8 on the back of your Newcastle top with 'WE' above and 'MACKEMS' underneath? Do you queue all night outside the club shop to get your new replica shirt literally hours before the rest of the world? Do you have to be THERE, where it's AT? Are you, in short, a Toon lunatic? Then this is the bar for you. Get yourself along here on match days with all the other lovers of broken bones and asphyxiation who pack every square millimetre of available space, and you'll be laughing (as least as hard as your ribcage will allow). I've scratched my head for an hour and a half, but I still can't find a sensible reason for the match day popularity. What's the point in being in a bar a season ticket's throw from the ground if the crush means it takes you an hour and a half to get served? It's not like the club are going to present you with a bloody loyalty card if you risk life and limb squeezing in here, is it? Beats me. But here, don't get me wrong: this isn't going to end up as the usual Dog panning. In fact, there's absolutely nothing wrong with the bar itself, or the punters for that matter. It's just that it's always so jam-bastard-packed of a Saturday (or sodding pay-per-view Sunday) afternoon. If you go on non-match days, when there's space to breathe, you'll see it's a cracking traditional brown pub with a bit of history, awash with pictures of Toon legends new and old. You're guaranteed a good pint and friendly staff, there's a better-than-average chance of a nice bit of setting sun blazing through the windows - and the atmosphere is always relaxed; that's the old-time meaning of relaxed as opposed to fucking 'chilled'. But for the sake of the Lord, why the desperate squeeze on match days? Yes, it's a really good bar with a ton of Toon stuff and a raucous shouty atmosphere, but it's hardly the last lifeboat off the Titanic, is it?

For: I'd still sooner have the lifeblood pressed out of me in here than ever set foot in that bloody Shearer's over the road.
Against: Did I mention that it gets quite busy from time to time?

It's a good sign for a bar if all you can find to really gripe about is the hand dryers in the bogs. When are those bastards going to stop lying to us? How much longer are they going to insult us with their dynamic names like Cyclone and Jetstream and their promises of instant drying comfort? You whack them and you hoof them, you dance beside them like St Vitus, you turn their stupid nozzles until they come off in your hands, and what do you get, if you're lucky? Two seconds of freezing ferret fart, that's what.

The Tavern

10 Northumberland Rd, NE1 7RY
'A daring foray into the world of open-plan design'

This place has never really been somewhere I've given much thought to, and if I hadn't started working at the Haymarket end of town it's doubtful whether I would ever have noticed the latest alteration to the name. The pub has finally completed a full circle of name changes from the Tavern to Steppes to Huxters to Stepps (no second 'e') and back to the Tavern again, displaying a terrible dearth of imagination if nothing else. There's a sizeable chunk of me that thinks it'd be nice if I could apply this to my own life and get back the twenty years I've wasted in the meantime, especially all the time spent typing idiot reviews about dull little pubs like this. The name aside, there's been no real change to the inside of the bar, just the same old stuff painted milky-tea beige. If you liked it before - and I didn't, to be honest - you'll still like it now. I don't remember seeing the chessboards inlaid into the tables the last time I was in, so they might be part of the refit; then again, all I did the last time I was here was look at my watch, so I might be wrong. I don't really know why I'm not that keen. Maybe it's because the place always seems a bit grubby to me; the tables in the booths were covered with crumbs and salt and smears of ketchup, and that's no bloody good when you're out in your Saturday best. The sports bar idea looks to have survived the name change, with the huge screen upstairs still blaring out minority sports to over-enthusiastic knuckleheads, although the individual tellies in the booths have had their control panels boarded up behind a few tatty off-cuts. And that seems to be a bit of a theme running through the bar: if it's broke, just nail a plank over it and paint it brown. A final quick nip to the gents before moving on revealed a daring foray into the world of open-plan design, with an airy, taboo-busting approach to the toilet layout. Well, either that or some cunt had nicked the bog door.

For: I had my first ever city pint in the original Tavern, bright-eyed, slim, and clearly underage. I remember it like it was yesterday...

Against: ...and could probably do a more accurate review of that incarnation than I ever could of the new one. It should be illegal to try to trade on former glories: this bar is no more the Tavern than a Whitley Bay sandcastle is Krakatoa.

That missing bog door could just be the thin end of the wedge. As if to underline the transient nature of the drinking world and how much of a fucking pain in the arse it is to keep this Burglar's Dog carry on up-to-date, I'm hearing that the Tavern's days are already numbered. It seems that there are plans to turn this place into – and bear in mind that even the eastern Europeans are starting to ditch theirs for being old hat – an Irish theme bar called Shamrox. Yes, that's the spelling they've got in mind. And I fully intend to raise an objection, in the highest court in the land if necessary. They're not getting away with it.

Three Bulls Heads

57 Percy Street, NE1 7RN
'Something sticky underfoot'

Apart from the fact that the Three Bulls Heads could do with a bit of a spring clean, there's really bugger all to say about the place. It remains a typical city centre bar - well, what typical city centre bars used to be before they all became pitch-black luxury establishments - and it could really do with a lick of paint, or at least someone with a bucket of paste to clag the wallpaper back up. It's not that it's a complete dive, or anything, but there always seems to be something sticky underfoot on the rare occasions I go in these days. The decor, like you care, consists mostly of old pictures of the town and the Toon, with plenty of big mirrors and tellies and what have you to brighten the place up. No problem with that, I say. And it's always useful in a pub like this that's a million miles past heaving on match days to have the bar in the middle, making it a bit easier to get served without any of that hey-man-how-man pushing and shoving. Match days are when you'd probably feel safest here: on non-match days, it just tends to be populated by punters who just don't give a fuck any more. Unless you're starting, like, ye twat. I've personally never had any bother here; it's a place that's good for a few afternoon pints talking bollocks about nothing, and then leaving before the hardcore radgies turn up. But aye, overall, I suppose it's the sort of boozer that I tell people is fantastic without ever bothering to go there myself. Just goes to prove what a whingey little cunt I am.

For: Sensible prices and no bloody kids allowed.
Against: Over to the wife: 'Girls! There's a bin for your used sanitary products! Try using it instead of the frigging floor.'

I've already confessed to being a metaller when I was a kid. One of the places you were duty-bound to loiter in and get mugged by glue-sniffing skins back then was the old Handyside Arcade. The Handyside, in roughly the area where the Three Bulls is now just in case you don't remember it, was a run-down Victorian shopping arcade full of period charm, and was exactly the sort of place that the Council (and shitehawks like Starbucks) are begging to redevelop and preserve. What's there now? Eldon Garden - yet to see its 500th shopper after ten years of business - and a half-arsed, in-name-only recreation of the original Three Bulls Heads. All this forces me to muse on what exactly it is about human nature that leads people to adopt the mentality of 'MUST. DESTROY.' only to end up a few years later trying vainly to recreate what was there in the first place. Everyone does it, sure as eggs is eggs. Trouble is, if you stick your paw up and say, 'Excuse me; this is alright, this here. Can we keep it?' people look at you like you're having a wank at a wedding. Makes no sense to me.

The Trent House

1-2 Leazes Lane, NE1 4QT
'The first sign of dickdom'

The Trent House is, if not actually as World Famous as they claim, definitely a Newcastle institution. In a poky little building off the beaten track up by the RVI, The Trent has miraculously survived the appalling makeover craze that has swamped virtually every other bar in the city, and yet is still free of squalor or psychos. In fact, they have a cast-iron policy of refusing to serve any sort of scumbag. Class. This place is a Soul Bar, a description that makes you fear the worst, but here it's one that's evolved naturally rather than fallen out of a crate like the abortions I could mention by using the words Mr and Lynch. It's a little bit tatty, but in a good way. Yes, they do refits every now and then, but they do them like you'd do up your own place - change a few colours, move this here and that there, maybe throw up a few new pictures - and they always manage to keep some semblance of their personality instead of desperately grasping at a fashionable, shop-bought identity. After all this time they've still got the foreign currency pasted on the walls, and the African masks and that, but there's not a whiff of tackiness, not even in the prophylactic - that's blobs to you - display cabinet. Actually, I don't remember seeing that the last time I was in, but that's just because I was so busy gawping at the original table-height Space Invaders or, to be more exact, down the top of the lass playing on it. There's two floors, with the upstairs room usually full of squabbling students hogging the pool table - in a laid-back way, obviously - and while you'll have to juggle your pints up the stairs until the upper bar opens, it's a good place to just slump yourself down and listen to the fantastic free jukebox, the one that's never yet played what I told it to. Now I'm not saying The Trent is without its faults; constantly claiming to be cool is the first sign of dickdom, and for all that their promo stuff boasts of a twat-free environment, using the expression 'v' popular (my quotation marks) does let the side down a little. Still, for every negative there's a positive and a half, and even if the wall of the down-

213

stairs bar heralds the embarrassing slogan 'drink beer be sincere', there's always the tremendous 'be nice to people, don't be a twat' halfway up the stairs: that's long been the mantra at the Dog, as any fucker will tell you. So aÿe, they can be a bit up themselves, and they attract a lot of idiots, but they can't really be held responsible for this term's intake, and I'd still rather be irked by a bit of individuality than be numbed by any more chain bar mush.

For: I once got indirectly barred from here despite being out of the country at the time, thanks to a dispute between the management and one of their former staff and the subsequent banning of 'everyone you know'.
Against: Comic Sans. On every bit of tabletop blurb. Simply unforgivable.

Alongside the toy farmyard animals that sit behind the optics on a little ledge behind the bar, is a half empty tube of KY and six packets of Extra Strong Durex - I stayed seated.

8

Ouseburn & City East

'Learning from the mistakes of the past whilst both embracing sympathetic redevelopment and retaining history, the Ouseburn and east of the city are home to Newcastle's art spaces and its emerging music venues, as well as its educational city farm and stables. Funny we should mention stables, because I feel like I'm flogging a dead horse with this introductory banter. Are we done yet?' – Norman Undercroft, Historian.

The Cluny
36 Lime Street, Ouseburn, NE1 2PQ
'The usual vulgarity'

This is going to be a bit tricky for me. It's not very often that I come to review a boozer that I actually really like, so the chances of this being full of the usual vulgarity are looking pretty slim. Let's see how I get on. I am, by all accounts, a bit of a tosser and a stuck-up twat. I'd say I can't help it, but the truth is I do it on purpose just to get on people's tits. I also have a reputation for spending more on a holiday than most sensible people would spend on a trip to the moon, and when I'm off on one of my la-di-dah European capital jaunts, this is exactly the sort of bar I seem to end up in. It's in an old whisky bottling plant and still has an industrial look about it. It's huge and bright, has a band on every other night, and it even has an art gallery on the upstairs level. The beer's decent and varied enough, they've got a better range of spirits than the secret mini-bar under my desk at work, and our lass, who's a right bloody whinger when it comes to food, says the grub is pretty good. Alright, fair enough, I might have spent half the night after eating in here puking thick, brown vomit up my bathroom walls, but I blame that on the dodgy pint I had in my local afterwards. Putting aside the minor quibble about the pub being an absolute bugger to get to, and conveniently ignoring the fact that ninety percent of the punters whenever you go are manbag-swinging knobheads, I'd go so far as to say that this place deserves the near-legendary status it seems to have in every two-bit 'alternative' style mag you pick up. I love it, but then it's not every boozer where you get to sit out in a beer garden between a big chimneystack and derelict warehouses; if they'd put a few more seats out there I'd be in heaven. Oh dear. This is becoming rather dry, isn't it? Shit. Piss. Arse. Nipples. There: that's much better.

For: They've finally sorted out the pillars in the venue bit, so you get to see the bands for your £12.50, and not the bloody speaker stacks.
Against: To paraphrase Mark E Smith from The Fall, people from Byker are alright; it's the people IN Byker who are twats.

I take back what I said about the food. I'm no Ainsley Harriott: any old junk will do me when it comes to soaking up the ale. But even I know that it's not on to charge a fiver for nachos and then serve up fucking cheesy Doritos, you robbing bastards.

The Cumberland Arms
Ouseburn, Byker, NE6 1LD
'No talent required'

According to the pub's own website, the Cumberland Arms,

'established in the 1850s, is truly traditional, with real ale, folk sessions, live music, storytelling...' Normally I'd rip the piss something rotten out of stuff like that, shatter a few illusions and generally stick the boot in, but after trying to rewrite the same slagging a hundred times for all the identikit designer bars in the town, it fills me with joy to see a place as unique as this. It really is as good as they say. Notable as a live music venue, eclectic doesn't even begin to describe the range of acts they have on upstairs. For every sonic laptop terrorist there's a round of lavenders-blue-dilly-dilly on a homemade banjo; and for each fey, shy indie strummer there's some over-confident loon who thinks reciting his wince-inducing poetry constitutes entertainment. And that's just for the paying customer; if you're crackers enough to favour a more hands-on approach, then I can guarantee you'll be up for the 'sessions', where every bearded deviant for miles around comes to throttle the bejesus out of his comedy instrument, blocking the sitting room and playing a G chord nonstop for three and a half hours. No talent required, just a nine-pint grin and an alarming sweater. Still not enough for you? How about cookery classes? Humorous improv? A sewing circle, then? Maybe you just want to relax with a pint, or sup as much mead as you can neck before the hypoglycaemic coma kicks in. Or perhaps you're after a bench outside with views over the Ouseburn Valley right the way over to Dallas Carpets and the Gateshead tower blocks in the distance. It doesn't really matter what fondles your nadbag; if you're the sort of lunkhead who thinks any bar without a thirty grand paint job (beige and purple, naturally) is beneath you then you won't even have got this far down the page. But if you're prepared to unleash the inner honey nut loop then rub some Lurpak in your hair, grab a paperback or an old compendium of games to swap for beer, stick on your favourite anorak and get yourself along.

For: I think this is the first review ever by the Dog that's been entirely based on FACTS and not the usual space-filling nonsense. Blimey.

Against: If you're coming from the top (i.e. non-Cluny) end, getting off the bus at the arse end of Shields Road, I'd advise that you carry a spare pair of shoes to replace the ones that'll be robbed before you even hit the roundabout.

If the Cumberland does have a downside, it's their traditional outdoor-but-indoor bogs, with what look like bullet holes for ventilation and bare brick walls. And that's brick walls where the plaster has fallen off through centuries of neglect and widdle fumes, and not some New York loft space design statement. Nobody's going to mind slumming it when they're wazzing out the odd jar, but if you're planning on hunkering down for a fireside winter pint marathon then it could get to be a bit off-putting. Just saying, like.

Free Trade Inn
St Lawrence Road, Byker, NE6 1AP
'Sleek contemporary design classic'

Two things that will strike you when you go to the Free Trade Inn: 1) It's an absolute dump, and 2) it's fantastic. Struggling along the nettle-strewn path up from Quayside, you find that what looks from a distance to have been derelict for thirty years is actually one of the best, scruffiest bars in the town. From the dirty brown walls with huge holes in the plaster to the boarded up fireplaces, there's been no attempt made whatsoever to smarten the place up or to impose any sort of diabolical theme. In the age of the sleek contemporary design classic and polished stone furniture, it's good to still be able to spot a few Formica tables with S&N Breweries blue star in them, an' all. There's not really much in the way of decor to speak of: just art-for-sale and gig adverts on the walls. And I like that approach. Even the punters seem like a friendly bunch, with barely a trace of Bigg Market idiots or lounge bar style-victims, though what I will have to point out is that the Free Trade attracts a lot of students; the pricks who scribble borrowed quotes from the latest TV alterna-fave on the otherwise magnificently vandalised bog walls should be barred for life. Get your own personality, you sad twats. The standard of the pint's good, and there's a choice of two beer gardens - one overlooking the Tyne (both the river and the pub of that name) - to park your arse in and watch stray dogs chomping on wine corks and gravel. Fuck it, man: what's not to like about the place? Especially since its very existence is one in the eye for all the greedy developers who want to stick another unoccupied office block right in front of the bar and ruin the view. There's always some battle or other with skyscraper-obsessed fools, and it'll be a sorry day if those wankers finally come up with a big enough backhander to get the go-ahead. Whoever coined the phrase 'the banality of evil' clearly had the gentrification of the east quayside in mind. Clearly.

For: I've been on to UNESCO and they're quite happy for the Free Trade Inn to go on their list of protected World Heritage Sites. Well, maybe not.
Against: It's always pathetically understaffed when I go.

Guinness drinkers: what is their fucking problem? How come I always seem to get stuck at the bar behind the sort of dickhead who orders his mate's Foster's in an Australian accent (it's brewed in Manchester, you tit) and then waits until the very end of his massive round order to say, after a lengthy dramatic pause, '...and a pint of Guinness'? It takes about a month to pour, and you KNOW that, you obnoxious shites. Stop making such a fucking spectacle of your tastes, stop making me wait forever for my pint and start ordering the damned tarmac at the beginning in future. Jesus, man.

Logic

Argyle Street, NE1 6PN
'A throat cut from ear to ear'

The Quay Point development to the east of Newcastle is a triumph of low-rent box room flats with inadequate soundproofing, and looks specifically designed to deprive its student tenants of any sleep for the entire duration of their course, turning them into the nippy little Nazis their business management qualifications require them to be. Located at the western end of this lab-rat maze is Logic, or Bar Logic, or Logic Bar, a potluck lounge pub with an ersatz Moroccan theme tacked onto it. (Ersatz is a great word for shitty sham; I wish I'd looked it up earlier). The wooden slatted exterior hides a scatter cushioned boothfest, with garish flock wallpaper reflected in whole walls of mirrors, and lamps from a junior school version of Ali Baba casting greens and yellows and blues on the ceiling. And, once again, the sinister emulsion brotherhood has offered the choice of their purple paint or a throat cut from ear to ear. There's wickerwork bar stools, wooden blinds and a full range of exotic potions behind the bar, like Carling. And Stones. And the ingredients for a cocktail called a Wibble. I see there's also an upstairs bar, with more of the same, but locked away from my prying late afternoon eyes. I have no idea how long Logic has been here: it looks new enough to still be full of its own self importance, but old enough for every single item of table-top promotional literature to have been through the boil wash. Twice. I'm not going to pan Logic today, mainly because I don't care enough about it. But I won't be back unless I really want to waste a companion's time and leave them as unimpressed as I was. This is a student bar, pure and simple, with all the ignoramuses that go with it. If that's what pokes your prostate, then good luck to you. It looks alright at the minute but it WILL be wrecked in the near future, and there's no point in pretending otherwise. Why? The evidence is on the toilet walls, where the bogey retrospective exhibition is already being installed. And who's responsible? It has to be him, the prick in the corner in the festival T-shirt, since anyone prepared to root about for a weekend in mud and shit in a hole in the ground can't possibly be bothered about hygiene. It's the fucking logistics of the wiping that confuse me, though. You need one hand to keep your flies from mangling your chopper, and the other hand to point it in the right direction. How the hell can you get a finger up your sneck, too?

For: The fun-size plasma screens, taking you right back to when a 14-inch portable was big enough for an average bedroom, instead of the mile-wide bastard no one can be without these days.

Against: Widescreen. Wide. WIDE. W-I-D-E. See the next development in TV technology? Tallscreen, the revolutionary 'new' system that restores the picture to the proportions it had before Sony convinced you to part with three grand for the lopsided shit you've got now.

The small print at the bottom of the menus says that the photos are for guidance only and should not be taken as a literal representation of the food advertised thereupon. Too true. It's like that when you see protesters outside McDonald's, with their placards showing a crudely drawn sketch of a cow in a bun, all sad eyes and blood-dripping limbs. The fucking burgers NEVER look as good as that when you get them. And do animal rights activists never stop to think they might be taken more seriously if they didn't look quite so much like animal rights activists? Put it this way: I'm a vegetarian and I still hate the scruffy cunts.

Moot

132-140 New Bridge Street, NE1 2SZ
'Yeah, I quite like it'

Some events and some thoughts have the power to shape your personality and even to alter your life. You'll be wanting a for-instance, I assume. It was a fair few years ago when it happened, but some woman came into my office at work and tried to flog a load of fake watches; Gucci, I think they were. And, you know, it being just after payday and everything, I handled the goods and mulled over a purchase for maybe five seconds, or at least until realisation came and punched me in the eye socket. What I realised was this: if you're even prepared to entertain the notion of status symbols then you're a cunt, and if you get a fake one on the cheap then you're a double cunt. I give daily thanks for the lessons life has taught me. And this bar, this Moot place, is to an authentic, chilled luxebar what a dodgy timepiece bought on holiday, from a blanket, at midnight, while pissed, outside a Chinese restaurant, with glass tanks in the windows, containing crabs, with all their wee claws taped up, for, um, example, is to a 32 diamond Tag Heuer. Like the appreciative noises in that office way-back-when, on throwing Moot open to the group I'm hearing stuff like, 'It's not that bad, this' and 'Yeah, I quite like it,' and I'm thinking, hang on, this isn't fucking right. Call yourselves mates? What we have here is a bar with the pretensions of Perdu but done on the budget of Boom! Will you look at the state of that wallpaper: hand-made luxury print? No. Durable blown vinyl? Uh-uh. Ironic retro flock? Not exactly. Half a dozen rolls of silvery Christmas wrapping from Everything's A Pound? Now you're talking. And take a squint at that big box thing in the window; imagine seeing THAT under the tree on December 25th. You'd be expecting the best present ever but, when you'd peeled the paper off one end as they've done in Moot, your Yuletide would be in ruins. As usual. Quietly, so as to keep the peace, you'd mutter, 'Oh, right... you got me a DJ booth. Cheers.' and then come midnight, when there's only you and your benefactor in the room, sticky-eyed on gift-grade whisky and full-to-puking on Pringles, you'd wrestle the fucker to the floor to get the receipt to take it back. This bar is not my idea of anything approaching luxury. Pictures of Marilyn Monroe are not my idea of glamour, since Marilyn Monroe is car boot sale glamour, glamour for simpletons and turdwads. And this decor is not my idea of a design statement; not when this sofa is only three-nine-nine in the winter sale, must end Saturday. What sort of a name is Moot for a bar, anyway? Picked by a text-in competition, apparently. How the fuck did anyone capable of wiping their own arse sanction that from the list of entries? Was it the only one? There's a Moot Hall in Newcastle, sometimes used as a law court, so it might be a reference to that. Some twat needs hauling before the judge for coming up with Moot, I'll tell you what. There's also the possibility that they're going for the 'moot point' angle: the debate, the heated discussion. Sod that: I'll be debating where else to go, me. A decent boozer, for a start. The whole thing is just wrong, and from my viewpoint - at home, in a bad, bad mood - this place is destined for failure, mainly through trying to cater for all and pleasing none. Moot is nowhere near pompous enough for the moneyed haircut bar clientele it wants to attract, and the students they'll end up getting won't be happy until they've trashed it like they do with everything else they touch. And Moot have only got themselves to blame: if all they can see is the wave they're chasing, then they can't come running to me when they sever both legs on a rusty Stella can.

For: Anything that detracts the attention from that repulsive university building over the road – a big, upturned Dyson, more or less – has got to be a plus.
Against: Saying 'Fuck this: I Moot of here' only works when you say it out loud and not in print.

Went down to the basement area last time I was in. Less of a cesspit than it used to be, they had some idiot DJ plying his trade to literally nobody. A billion decibels, an unbearable riot of flashing lights and a dry ice machine on full; I tell you, it was Dresden, Hiroshima and the 'collapse' of the Twin Towers combined. Bollocks to that, I said. Sitting back upstairs, though, an almighty siren goes off and the management leg it down the dancers to see what the score is. The tool had only set the smoke detectors off with his tomfoolery. I half expected the daft cunt to wander up with one hand wiping the soot from his face and the other clinging to a 12-inch for dear life, like it's Carry On Up Yer Ronson. Fucking amateur.

New Bridge Inn

2 Argyle Street, NE1 6PF
'Saggy tattooed tits'

The New Bridge is owned by the Sir John Fitzgerald chain and, if the night I finally got round to doing the review was anything to go by, is populated with the exact post-work crowd that used to monopolise the pubs around Grey Street in the centre of town. That's really the best way to describe it: from the cracked coving down to the tatty carpet, it's along the same lines as Fitzgeralds (visits in the last three years: one) and the pre-rebuild-masquerading-under-legend Bacchus, and is another one of those bars I used to gripe about as being bog standard but now, in my stubborn, nostalgic way, worship, revere and avoid at all costs. Why? Because nowt pleases me more than being deliberately miserable. There are wooden booths with leather seating. They've got old pictures and books, and ceiling lights shaped like saggy tattooed tits. There's endless nooks and crannies in which to sip your half of Dogslobber (ABV 1.2%) or your glass of medium dry white, plus chest high dividers at the back that are just crying out for a game of bar volleyball. And if the telly's boring, you can always take your life in your hands and stare at the odd indigenous grumpy geezer in the corner who is wondering where the fuck all these wankers have come from. It's a fine old bar, with a relaxed atmosphere and a place that I really should get to more often, if only in the hopes that I might wake up there and realise the last twenty years have just been a bad, bad dream. Finally, in the interests of common sense and word count, I'd like to pose an open question to the clientele based on prejudice, bitterness and a seven-pint-slanted viewpoint. If, as you claim, you're high-powered, super-intelligent executives making decisions for the good of the people then how come a) you're always leaving your coats and baggage all over the place so nobody else can sit down and b) you're then genuinely startled to find your laptop missing and your briefcase covered in hockle?

For: I'd highly recommend this place...
Against: ...if it wasn't for the soul-sapping, fearful trudge across the motorway bridge that divides New Bridge Street, not to mention the Manors Metro smackheads

I've got a bad feeling about bars along this way and the sort of punters they're beginning to chase. The Cluny: exclusively for hipsters. The Ship: desecrated and wine-listed. Tanners: DJ-courting. I blame all the new, expensive, shoebox apartments springing up all along the banks of the Tyne. You know, the ones with the commanding views of all the other new, expensive, shoebox apartments springing up all along the banks of the Tyne.

The Ship Inn

Stepney Bank, NE1 2PW
'Whey, boss, ah knew it was a 'pa...' word'

Dating back to the early 1800s and once one of the city's most fascinatingly historical alehouses, The Ship suffered a brutal refit sometime in 2006 when some complete clown threw away most of the period detail and tried to revamp the pub as a fucking wine bar. Out went all the stuff from its last makeover – I'd say circa 1921 – and in came a cack-handed attempt at smooth city drinking, which, to be fair, had its own place on the timeline: the last time I saw something as abysmal as that was in the dark days of the Joe Robertson empire, back in the mid-to-late eighties. It wasn't just that the new look was shit, but that it was unfathomably shit; clearly they'd called in at the timber yard when the illiterate bloke was behind the sales desk. How else could they have ended up with scratty fucking warehouse pallets nailed to the walls where their planned designer panels should have been? Whey, boss, ah knew it was a 'pa...' word. Look closely under the drinks posters and the endless reams of indie-cinema flyers, and every fourth plank has THIS WAY UP branded onto it. I remember being perched on a chrome stool by the window just after the refit, trying to read the wine list by the light through the Venetian blinds, and being on the verge of tears, knowing full well that the place could never again be historic, only historically themed. Thankfully, though, the punters have been having none of it, and any pretensions the pub might have had towards an upmarket clientele from the Ouseburn's burgeoning creative scene have long since evaporated. In their place is a comforting mix of bone-idle students, mangy dogs, flustered businessmen, and boiler suits and hobnail boots, together with what appears to be a nun – please, Lord, say it's a nun – getting gently hammered on sunshine Hoegaarden. Common sense has stuck ice cubes down the pub's collective trolleys about what an utter fucking disaster the refit was, and the staff now greet all-comers with a thin smile and an 'I know, I know' shrug, looking upon the surroundings as they would on a regrettable tattoo. The idiosyncratic nicknacks seem to be making a comeback, sticking cocktail jazz on the jukebox would guarantee you a good howking, and overall it's a vast improvement from the horror show that greeted me the last time I was here. But I don't care how much of the clutter they put back in, or how much they scuff it up: until they accept that those bloody awful pallets have got to go and start setting about the fuckers with the crowbar and the claw hammer, it'll never be a patch on what it once was. After all – and as I say to the women in my office as they're poring over the catalogue pages on their daily Avon skive – it doesn't matter how expensive your paints are, you can't make a masterpiece when all you have to paint on is a knackered old sack.

For: The old leather bench, once part of the pub's interior, too cumbersome to be lobbed into the refit skip, and now wedged against the wall on the exterior terrace.
Against: The gentleman slumped on it appears to have soiled himself.

The building faces due south, so at any time on a summer's day you get the full benefit of that sunny terrace. And – despite the pub's location in a regenerated former industrial area - you can still feel close to nature. Downwind of the horseshit from the stables up the hill, or choking on goat piss fumes from the farm at the bottom: every breath is a meal in itself.

Six

2-4 Howard Street, NE1 2LF
'$[x-\Delta] + \Sigma/z$ = Clean that fucking mess up'

I don't suppose it's any great secret that I'm not the man I used to be. Call me henpecked, browbeaten or just plain pussy-whipped, but each and every weekend these days is spent either up a ladder with a paint roller, or clutching a glossy catalogue in some DIY megamart. And it's with a sense of almost heartbreak-ing irony that, on the one Sunday I'm allowed to escape from the ball-crushing tedium of the home furnishing circuit, I find myself in here, looking at what amounts to the cut-price 'casualty' department of one of those selfsame gigastores. Take a look at this pitiful, limping excuse for a boozer. It's like someone went out and bought a pub kit at an amazing discount, then once they'd got it home they realised exactly why it was so cheap. Both literally and figuratively – are you calling me a liar? – there's a castor missing from that, an integral shelf gone astray from over there and that defiantly non-generic spanner is nowhere to be seen. And all the bits they have got left, they've lost the bloody instructions for. What a fucking shambles of a bar this really is. Every single thing in here looks like it was bought on a whim and then thrown in the garage for a rainy day, and not in a good way, either. Hanging from the ceiling is a tragic display of low-cost white cloth, like the train of a bride who's been regally shafted by the dress shop, the cruel shysters scarpering with her dreams and her loot the week before the big day. And between those drapes are unsavoury lamps, clearly made from balls of pubes raked out from amongst the dirty dishes and crusty Kleenex under your average student's divan. The seats are fake purple snakeskin, and the picture of an exotic island to my right seems on closer inspection to be a shower curtain Sellotaped to the wall. Behind my head is an unlikely dictionary definition of the word Six, and over the way, past where the barmen are trying to remove laptop viruses in lieu of serving punters, there's a big equation in a frame. I'm imagining – because I'm piss bored – that it's there to tempt the odd passing maths genius to tax his grey matter, like a saggy-arsed Good Will Hunting. But my only solution is $[x-\Delta] + \Sigma/z =$ Clean that fucking mess up, man. Many years ago, when I used to ride shotgun with a TV repair company – ostensibly for security and training, but in reality so the family dogs could shag me senseless while the engineers got on with fixing the tellies – I remember thinking this place was an average housing estate boozer, but now it seems to have firmly established itself in the eyes of the city's drinkers as 'just another one of them shit student bars ower Byker way'. I wouldn't care if it was just quietly catering to the student pandemic, but these berks are actively marketing their common room vibe, where you'd get all the stuff you'd find in halls without the stinking kitchen or the tiny box rooms. Strangely, though, they've missed off the only benefit I can see: if the ignorant little bastards have to leave their hovels and step outside for a beer, then there's a far greater chance of the remaining locals being able to pick them off with a rifle from the rooftops.

For: I like the discrepancy between their claims of 'comfy, clean, cool' and the arse-aching, grubby tip we found. With a capacity for lying like that, they'll sail through their finals and rise to the pinnacle of their destined call centre career within a matter of decades.

Against: If it's pin-drop quiet on, say, a Sunday afternoon, and you go for, say, a massive, massive shite, the entire bar can hear your brown trout thrashing about.

Shoehorned a bridal reference in there earlier, just so I can say: Guys! Are you constantly bombarded in your workplace by the incessant interrogations from your female colleagues about when you're going to get married?! Does your day amount to 'Tie the knot!' and 'Do the decent thing!' or 'Make an honest woman of her, tee hee hee!'? Do you want to put an end to the cackling round the cauldron once and for all?! Then why not do what I did? Ask them, at five-minute intervals, for a solid week, if they've given their other half his brown wings yet. 'Kicked your back doors in, eh? EH?! Let him in the tradesman's, have you?! Eeh, why not?! Go on! It'll be l-o-v-e-l-y!' Believe me, it works a treat! My disciplinary's next Thursday, by the way. Wish me luck.

Stepney's

3 Bridge View, Stepney Lane, NE1 6PN
'I was THIS fucking close'

I've got a bee in my bonnet about the typeface known as Comic Sans. I may have mentioned it. I hate it and everything it says about the institutionalised morons who use it to display their wackiness. In my working life I am constantly subjected to its amusing curves and its 'baby on board' lines, and I have reached the point where I simply refuse to deal with it any longer. Any documents in it passed my way go straight in the bin, and e-mails - especially the ones saying 'Fwd: Fwd: Fwd: Fwd: Try this. It really works!' - are deleted immediately. I'd go so far as to say that if I was presented with a cheque for a million quid written in Comic Sans, I'd burn it - uncashed - rather than stand and look at it while I was doing the paying-in slip at the bank. I tell you, having seen advance pictures of the front of Stepney's, I was THIS fucking close to just ranting for an entire review about Comic Sans instead of writing a review. I'd even printed off the pub's name - double sided to save paper, naturally - in several mixed cases just to make sure. It turns out that the Stepney's sign is in some other font, one that's as close as it's possible to be to Comic Sans without actually making me boil with fury, so I suppose I'll have to do a proper review. Situated in a warehouse unit between those hideous Quay Point flats and the thundering Metro line, Stepney's ticks all the boxes a student could ever want, with cheap beer, floppy striped seating and a pool table that's virtually impossible to use unless you angle your cue down from chin height. It's got the usual pale stone, bad carpet and shipwreck wood, plus a line of what look from here to be orange pastel pictures of naked blokes. They have a trusting bring-one-take-one book swap shelf in the corner; me, I'd ditch that straightaway, since your average little cunt from Yoo-neh can't even be trusted to do a simple thesis without stealing it from the internet and claiming it as their own graft. They also do a 'Sing for your Supper' night, which is essentially an open mic for aspiring musicians, poets, performers and jackasses who think they're comedians to make a tit of themselves and get paid in roast dinners. That's what I've been told, anyway. Bearing in mind I go on holiday more times than I wander down these back streets, I feel almost as if this bar is in someone else's town, a town that can do its own raging about pubs. I just remain indifferent to the whole lot; I don't like it much, but I can't be arsed to pan it. I'm fairly sure that if I took the trouble to make it one of my regular bars I'd have a different student wanker pissing me off for a different reason every single night of the year, but for one-off review purposes I have no complaints. That's almost a complaint in itself.

For: Pubs in warehouse units: not a bad idea. At least I'd be able to say, 'Aye, love, whatever you want' when our lass is dragging me round carpet stores, and nip next door for a jar while she's filling in the paperwork.

Against: I complained about the students pinching all their stuff from the internet, then did exactly the same myself for the factual stuff in the review. But it's not like I'll ever tell anyone.

Call it coincidence, synchronicity, kismet or fluke, but the day we came to do the review and saw Stephen Hawking's A Brief History of Time on the bring-one-take-one shelf was the exact same day as I had Hawking on the phone to me at work. I swear it was him. Certainly sounded like the fucker, anyway. I could hear all this whirring and clacking and I'm thinking, 'Eh? Is this a prank call? Hello?' Eventually his computerised patter comes out, and it's in the most miserable, monotonous voice I've ever heard. Friday afternoon, an' all; you'd think he could have cracked a smile. And he's banging on and on and on, never once sounding remotely interested. I said to him, 'Don't you fucking adopt that tone with me...'

Tanners

1 Byker Bridge, NE1 2SW
'Frothy piss'

Sometimes being well off the beaten track can be a blessing for a bar. Practically in Byker, and therefore outside the hideous grasp of today's bar designers - who, let's face it, would have chris-tened it t@nners, blacked out all the windows, and dished out branded miners' helmets at the door - Tanners has been given a bit of a refit recently, and a refit like they used to be, where they keep the same name, the same character, and just give the place a fresh lick of paint. And it's class. The beer's good, the atmosphere's not far behind, and the punters are a mix of growl-ing old timers - always a plus point in my book - and younger folk who look like they might actually have something to talk about other than their phones. Y'know, the sort of people that you used to see in bars before they became catwalk dressing rooms or playpens for overgrown kids. The refit, for the record, has gone as far as some tasteful green paint, a few candles on the way to the bogs and a lick and a promise on the outside walls, and most of the decor is provided by art-for-sale: I wouldn't buy the damned stuff, like, but that's because I'm a tight-fisted wee shite and not any reflection on the quality. And even if they are advertising bloody DJ nights, at least they've had the decency to keep the live bands on too, even going so far as to remove at least one of the panels obscuring the performance area. It'd be nice if they got shot of the other one an' all, but I suppose I'm not that desperate to see the bloody bassist's feet tapping away. The only problem that I'm having, to tell the truth, is trying to pad this review out. It's a piece of frothy piss to give a bar a deserved savaging, but not so simple to wax lyrical on somewhere halfway decent. So, aye, I liked it a lot, and even though at five bells on a sunny Friday night I'd enjoy a pint in Baghdad, I'm prepared to stick my neck out and recommend it. Watch it be a bucket of toss when you go, though.

For: Decent surroundings and no bloody wankers.
Against: I'm frightened of Byker.

Of course, all this lavish praise might just be the usual blinkered nonsense, coupling nostalgia with half a dozen post-work pints and no tea. If you've been sworn at, kicked, punched or gouged in the Tanners long after I've skipped off merrily into the sunset, then don't blame me.

The Tyne
1 Maling Street, NE6 1LP
'The Burglar's Dog's shite'

This is weird. At least half a dozen times we'd wandered right along the east Quayside trying to find this legendary 'Tyne' boozer without once coming anywhere near it. And then, one Sunday afternoon, it appeared before us like some low-budget Brigadoon, and our prayers were answered. Thank Christ we persevered. A quick history lesson: many years ago, the owners of The Tyne were turfed out of the Barley Mow on City Road by that awful Firkin chain, so they basically took everything from the old pub - the management, the atmosphere, even the bloody pub sign - and lugged it lock, stock and barrel along the river to what used to be the Ship Tavern under Glasshouse Bridge. And there it remains today. The thing is, there's very little in the way of a tacky '80s 'theme' here, some criminal mullets notwithstanding. It's not so much that time has stood still, more that it's proof that pubs can thrive and have a bit of character without being subjected to the whims of arsehole developers every few years. In case you're worried, though, I swear I'm not going to start telling you that this is some sort of primitive dive that I'm praising to the skies on account of its embarrassingly Luddite quirks. They know their way around the wonders of technology, alright; at least enough to have that rarest of things, a website that's updated with upcoming events when they're upcoming, and not when their techie consultants get round to changing the site. Have a look at www.thetyne.com, and you'll see for yourself. It's obviously not fit to pick the sweetcorn out of the Burglar's Dog's shite, but it's worth a visit nonetheless. Even the stuff on the free jukebox is bang up to date, though you have to be an expert in gynaecology to fiddle with the insides and get the damn thing working. The decor's nowt to write home about - some Gaudi-style bust crockery on one wall, a church pew outside, a big sunflower mural in the beer garden under the bridge, band posters everywhere else, but none of it seems forced in the way that your average refit does. I'll reserve judgment on the live music in the beer garden, since I've got no idea what playing under a bridge does for the acoustics, but 10/10 for effort regardless. All this, and the beer's spot on, too. And just to show you how good this place made me feel, I didn't even mind seeing bairns in here, since they looked more like hippified children of the revolution than the usual pre-teen pickpockets trying to nick your wallet. If only I wasn't such a bone-idle bastard I'd be along here every week.

For: This place just underlines what a complete cock-up the Firkin chain made when they gutted the Barley Mow. They wrecked a perfectly good boozer with their laughable dreams of the future, and then bailed out when they got bored, leaving it free for the debacle of Stereo.

Against: Do not, under any circumstances, use the hot tap in the Gents. You will lose your skin, your bones and possibly your life. You have been warned.

This pub's previous incarnation, The Ship Tavern, was apparently a whorehouse long, long ago. A brothel? On the edge of Byker? Jesus, how low would you have to stoop to satisfy your urges there? Have people never heard of the chopped-liver-in-a-jam-jar trick? Though, on reflection, the liver probably cost more.

9

The Dog In The Bog

MAXIMISE YOUR BAR'S EARNING POTENTIAL! ENFORCE THE BLAD-DER TAX!

Landlords! Do you feel that your licensed premises are not being utilised to their fullest? Are you convinced that your customers' disposable income would be better off in your pockets rather than those of the next sucker on the vine? Do you - quite rightly - despise your paying public? You should. After all, the ungrateful bastards are wiping their expensively shod muddy feet all over your floors and are clearly making no contribution to the thruppence a week it costs you to power your state-of-the-art lighting system. True, you've already forced these vermin to pay over the odds for your vile, gassy lager, but what about when they feel the urge to answer nature's call? Are there no further opportunities for money grabbing? Can you be sure that the potential for ripping the piss out of your clientele until they squeak is maximised? The Dog in the Bog has the answer.

We firmly believe that the average customer is completely incapable of even the rudiments of cleanliness, and requires assistance, guidance and necessary force to wash, dry, buff, scent and massage their hands, body and face to your exacting standards before re-entering your drinking area. We will not hear of the lower orders of society spreading harmful bacteria throughout your lavish establishment, of these heathens traipsing through your corridors unfragranced, or of their having passed water without experiencing the wildest of beatings with a scrubbing brush.

With The Dog in the Bog, you can be sure that your tipsy and bewildered customers will be so intimidated by the over-attentive, leering, presumptuous berks we will subcontract to pounce on them the very second they've shaken the drops off, that they'll willingly part with their hard-earned cash simply to avoid further embarrassment. Allow us to carefully select your perfect toilet attendant from our register of lapsed-conviction offenders, with the guarantee that all will be proficient in both the half- and full-Nelson. Why not sign up for our obligation-free demonstration and watch amazed as our representatives indiscriminately splash around the very latest genuine fragrances - like Brut, Kouros, Denim and Creosote - purchased fresh from the Quayside market each Sunday morning and forced upon your resentful customers before the hooky labels peel off. Marvel at just how much pointless shite and how many half-empty bottles of dubious content can be unloaded from a single tatty Head bag and spread along your designer fittings.

All our agents receive special training in financial processing, and are willing to accept most recognised forms of payment for their unsolicited manhandling, such as cash, cheque, Visa, and punch in the fucking mouth. We guarantee that our employees have zero understanding of the word 'no', and will have the agility to trap even the most determined of dodgers. Their knowledge of perfumery will know no beginning, and their reluctance to get out of the bloody way will remain unsurpassed in the industry. And for that extra-personal touch, every day each of our attendants will lovingly attach a fresh, hand-picked pubic hair to the nasty white soap of your choosing for no extra charge.

Contact us now for your free* quotation.
Tel: 08457 5554716211
E-mail: thedoginthebog@theburglarsdog.co.uk

The Dog in the Bog is a subsidiary of Burglar's Dog Racketeering Services Plc.

Should you wish not to utilise our services at this point then don't worry: we will simply send some div along to set up shop in your crappers regardless. Take your cut or fuck right off: there's money to be made and dignity, privacy and human rights mean nothing to us. Oh, and we don't do cleaning, so you'd better get some fucking old wifey in to sort that. You think we're going to mop up piss and go hunting for bog roll on your say-so, you joker? What the hell do you think this is?

*An administrative charge of £19.50 is payable, to be offset against your first purchase of suspect Paco Rabanne.

Gay Scene

'Based around the Centre for Life scientific museum and the Times Square plaza, this area is home to winter events such as skating on the outdoor ice rink, and summer celebrations like the huge TV screens erected for the major football events. That's about it, really. There's a what? A thriving gay scene, with numerous cafés, pubs and clubs? You're shitting me, right? Really? You want me to say a few words about them, I take it. And you're saying you'll dock my fee if I use the word 'sodomite'? Get me my agent, will you?' – Norman Undercroft, Historian.

@NE

1 Marlborough Crescent, NE1 4EE
'Wait-for-me'

Situated at the very heart of Newcastle's gay scene, @ne (At One) has a uniquely chilled atmosphere that's buzzing with happy funky house anthems, live vocalists, musicians and free internet access. Well, that's the official line, anyway. What it actually is - from where I'm sitting, at least - is a bog standard, wait-for-me! lounge bar, only one with an eye on the pink pound. From the embarrassing use of the @ sign - now as fashionable as your dad in Evisu jeans - to the grand piano and bongos on the stage area, this shameless cash-in is a welcome as Marmite in the Vaseline. A limping excuse of exposed brickwork, red chairs, parquet flooring and the usual twig-in-a-pot crap, @ne is no more and no less a haven for the gay equivalent of the rent-a-cunt punters who give that fucking abominable Perdu a reason to open its doors. The minimal and tasteful decor runs as far as huge '60s chandeliers, fuck-me wallpaper as artwork - that's fuck-me as in gorblimey, as in trousers, rather than any sort of invitation - and a big red painting of a bovine-looking eye, one that's crying out for a razor blade through it in the manner of Buñuel's *Un Chien Andalou*. And you don't need me to tell you there's also a DJ, plus the ubiquitous Ophelia Balls drag act wheeled out one more time. Look, I'm sorry if this isn't what you expected to read; trust me, there's no homophobia involved in the dismissal of this place, just a contempt for the insipidness of today's lucky dip bars. And this is alphabetically first on the trawl to the 'other side'? I fear the worst.

For: If you set your stall out to be fashionable, you've got to keep on changing or suffer the consequences. Roll on the next style mag issue date.
Against: I dread to think what's next.

Whether you're gay, straight, or just not fussy when you're sozzled, bars that strew around tea lights in arty little glass jars are an absolute nightmare. And this is why: imagine it's nearing the end of the night and you're a bit the worse for drink. You're not mortal by any means, but you've switched from the lager to the spirits, if only to stop yourself from bursting for the bogs. You're gassing to someone you really fancy across your designer bar table, and you're maintaining eye contact, imagining yourself to be charming, debonair and intimidatingly handsome. Still with that penetrating gaze, you reach down for your tumbler of single malt or imported vodka, raise it to your lips... and singe the end of your fucking hooter on the damned candle you've picked up by mistake. It hurts like hell, take it from me.

Baron & Baroness

Times Square, NE1 4EP
'Burning poo'

Our lass is mental. She looks at the 17th Century roof beams in the Baron & Baroness, then looks at me and says, 'Do you think they're the originals?' Sorry to report, dear, that this bar has been here for, like, a month, and the building itself less than ten years, so it's a little unlikely that that condescending git off Grand Designs will be tugging himself into a frenzy at the sight of these heritage features. Dopey mare. I never thought I'd use this expression in a review, but the Baron & Baroness is like a poor man's Gotham Town. Yes, really. Chandeliers, pulpit, ornate carvings, you name it, it's all large as life and twice as cheesy. Obviously I'm not that much of an arse that I'd complain about the lack of authenticity of the place, but I still can't say I'm a fan of this bar, or, for that matter, any of the other bars in the Centre for Life development. Having them all crammed together in adjoining units makes the place feel like the Mediterranean Village at the Metro Centre at best; at worst it's like a row of Butlins chalets, and the crap they were playing on the jukebox would certainly be more suited to some dispiriting seaside holiday camp. The Baron & Baroness is right in the middle of the gay village, but as it was practically empty when we were in - hardly surprising at six bells on a Saturday night - I can't really tell you about the state of the punters. There were a couple of podgy dykes looking pretty pissed off in one of the nooks upstairs, if that's any help. We left after a solitary pint to escape from the geezer standing outside who seemed to be burning poo and wafting the stench into the bar; the sign next to his performance said 'Barbecue', but I remain unconvinced. I can't really stick the boot into the pub, though, since I know I'll never drink there again, but I'll end by saying that if a place like this opened on my usual drinking route, there'd be merry hell on.

For: They served the best pint we'd had all night.
Against: Some old doll sitting outside looked and sounded exactly

like my drunken former next-door neighbour. Just for a second, mind, but long enough to have me hunting in the haversack for the claw hammer.

It's not exclusively a gay phenomenon, I grant you, but I saw it here and I'm stuck for a wildcard so I'm going to whinge about it now. I want to ask, What the FUCK is wrong with mobile phone users today? Are none of them educated enough to realise that a mobile is a device you talk into and through which - via the miracle of science - your voice is transmitted over the airwaves? It is NOT something you place beside your head while you fucking SHOUT in the vague direction of your mate in the next town. Man, I hope those mutation scare-stories are true.

Camp David
8-10 Westmorland Road, NE1 4EJ
'Irrational hatred'

With the Burglar's Dog only being a bit bi-bar-curious after eight pints, and my hastily typed post-visit notes containing just the lines 'said a thoutasbaNSD TIEMS begf0perfe' and 'blankdf is blanbd nowe mytatter wherre it loveces a bvit cock', I think we can safely say this review will be a struggle. But here goes. Run by the people behind North along the road, Camp David aims to combine beautiful decor with an exquisite cocktail list. With a newly refurbished bar and staff with a great attitude, a mixed clientele of straights and gays are guaranteed to want to return again and again. Camp David has a superb music policy and the nicest spiral staircase ever... You can tell I'm cribbing this, can't you? Ah, sod it. This is impossible. I've even tried plodging through the internet to find some other reviews of the place to plagiarise and they're all saying the same thing: it's quite nice but it's nothing special. It's almost like it's been designed to be piss-take proof. Even the simple facts are a bit hazy, and bearing in mind it's never a good idea to have a crateful of beer instead of your tea, these are the things I can recall: it's a sock-shaped room with lots of exposed brickwork; there are pretty natty cross-shaped lights above the bar; at the arse end of the room they've got some soft, squishy and positively hazardous stools. That's it. That's the sum total of my recollection. No grumbling about the beer quality, no irrational hatred of the bar staff, no ridiculing of the toilet facilities. And I can't even remember any punters at all, let alone anyone to make low-quality stereotypical quips about, so that's that line of mockery screwed, too. Buggery buggery bollocks, this is hopeless. Oh, I know: Camp David is really expensive, apparently. I could gripe about that, but since it wasn't my round I neither know nor care whether that's true, and I'd feel like an utter fraud and an ungrateful little twat if I started complaining. Forget it. Christ, I was smashed. There's a lesson to be learned somewhere.

For: Watching some daft cunt trying to sit on those marshmallow stools and falling arse over tit onto the floor with their pint all over them. Twice.
Against: When that daft cunt is me.

It says here that Camp David have had Scissor Sisters Tour DJ Sammy Jo gracing their decks. Don't know about you, but my idea of heaven is to have just one day where I don't have to hear the bloody Scissor Sisters. And the same goes for Shakira, Rihanna and all the other bearable-once-but-not-all-flaming-day merchants. It's not so much their songs I object to, but the fact that the fucking wankers in charge of radio playlists seem to pull their heads out of the charlie dish on a Monday morning, say 'Bollocks to the 200 new singles out this week, let's just stick the same old stuff on hour after hour because it fits the format'. Bone idle bastards.

The Dog

5 Marlborough Crescent, NE1 4EE
'Sugar my arsehole and call it a doughnut'

Imagine the lesbian bar of your dreams. Picture trim, toned, beautiful girls sipping superlative cocktails on leather sofas, and exchanging meaningful glances by flickering candlelight. And conjure up the mental image of soft girl-on-girl smooching giving way to full-on Sapphic lust in a secluded back room. In my pathetic, dim-witted, misogynistic way, I like to imagine something along those lines. Do anything for you, too? Yes? Sorry to plop on your pizza here, but this place is nothing like that, nothing whatsoever. What The Dog, the scene's most prominent lesbian pub, actually has, is a ghastly crowd of bootfaced dykes scrumming and mauling amongst decor to shame the very worst of the Bigg Market. I'd stick with the fantasy if I were you. Formerly known as the Barking Dog, this bar was where I cut my gay review teeth, and where I was convinced some bloke was trying to tap me up. Well sugar my arsehole and call it a doughnut, but maybe it was only my paranoia that made me think the cunt was after me; perhaps our lass was the real prize and he was just breaking the ice for his charming, buzzcut lady friends. I'm sure she would have loved to take a trip upstairs with them to The Dog's legendary how-how-hoooowlingly bad karaoke, where the horridest, squattest, punchingest lezzas take a real delight in a bit of tuneless bellowing, like doomed Friesians in an abattoir. She'd have been right up for hoying herself around to cheesy '80s hits spun with no real care by a school disco DJ. You'd have been in your element, wouldn't you, love? No? Ah, she's just being shy. Wait a minute; dirt-cheap beer, you're saying? Get yourself in, pet.

For: Proper plug-ugly, humourless, militant, angry stereotypes.
I've never been convinced by the we-do-naughty-things-together posing of her with the tits and her mate - with the tits - in the Daily Star.
Against: And just to underline the mirth-free approach, I've heard a whisper of an insinuation of a rumour that they once threatened legal action against a website that slagged them off. Maybe I ought to tell them: you can't sue people just because they don't like you. If you could, I'd be fucking rolling in it.

This pub is called the Dog; we are often referred to as the Dog. Potential for confusion, huh? Not, however, as much confusion as when I once wanted to know the football scores from the Chronicle's internet-usurped sports offshoot and asked the geezer in the newsagents over the road for a copy of The Pink Paper. Hmm. You can tell I made this bit up, can't you? There's no fooling you.

The Eagle

42 Scotswood Road, NE4 7JE
'The return of capital punishment'

Every genre of pub and its associated demographic has its archetype, its epitome, its handy hook for lazy fuckers to hang their prejudices on. If you hate giggling checkout girls running wild, then a trip to Buffalo Joe's will reinforce every stereotype you could ever have; if you've got a grudge against shoplifters, a swift pint in one of the radgie bars will have you campaigning for the return of capital punishment. And if butch, leather-clad queers writhing about in the darkness turn your sensitive stomach, you'd be advised to stay well clear of The Eagle. Even their website tells you to keep the hell out of it if easily offended. The Eagle is, almost down to the last dotted i, the gay bar of your very worst nightmare, only with more of an intimidating industrial vibe. And when even the bar's biggest champions warn you it's not recommended for anyone who is weak of body, mind or spirit - that's me on all three counts - you know it's not exactly the venue for tea and scones. Factually speaking, The Eagle plays host to regular live entertainment including top male strippers, and the basement area of the building is billed as being men only at all times, including, I would suppose, the jizzmoppers. Christ, I thought my job was bad. Go on, amuse yourself; try to imagine my face on the review visit. Think of my expression, my jaw-dropping, pint-slopping, eye-popping astonishment, followed by my hasty retreat and subsequent therapy. And then whack yourself upside the fucking head for imagining that I'd even go there in the first place. What the fuck do you take me for? Duty only goes so far you know.

For: The reflex action and involuntary movement that lifts my hands to squeeze my head to prevent me from even picturing it. Ugh.

Against: If a straight bar carried on like this, how long do you think it would last? Serious question.

Hang on. This all seems far too ridiculous to be true. I suspect that it's all just a great prank, and that the basement bar is full of nothing so much as the gay scene's chin-stroking intellectuals, having a quiet pint and a bash at the crossword, safely cocooned behind their elaborate subterfuge. Or maybe it's the hideout for the world's most wanted terrorists, luxuriating in upholstered comfort and having a good old chuckle to themselves as the world screams coming-ready-or-not. I'm not planning to test any of this out, like.

Eclipse

48 Clayton Street West, NE1 4EX
'Fat, stupid, paranoid'

'No more heroes anymore', sang that grizzly twat out of The Stranglers when I was kid, back in the days when you could have a face like a turd and still get on Top Of The Pops. I can't recall him being as overjoyed as I was when I found out what had happened here, though. A nation celebrated and called for a public holiday when Eclipse took over, gutted, and completely refurbished what was the shittiest bar the city has ever known, the dog's toilet that was Heroes. In terms of comparison with its predecessor, Eclipse could hardly fail to impress but, set against all the other modern bars in the town... well, that's the problem: it's virtually identical to all the other modern bars in the town, albeit firmly aimed at the gay community. We only witnessed the downstairs area: lots of wood, lots of blinds, lots of tellies, but very few things that struck me as being out of the ordinary. The punters seemed friendly enough, especially when it dawned on me that the bull-dykes at the bar were staring, not at me, but at the screen above my fat, stupid, paranoid head. As for the beer, I didn't notice gay Foster's tasting any worse than straight Foster's, but we'd been out for hours by this point so I can't be absolutely certain. And that's about all I can remember, to be honest: can't say I'll ever go back, but that's only because it's a gay bar, and not because it's in any way unpleasant.

For: The demise of Heroes had at least a dozen other pubs in the town shitting themselves for fear of being labelled the new Newcastle's Worst Bar. And rightly so.

Against: I'm sure there'll be some arsewit who'll bemoan the disappearance of another traditional bar. Listen: getting nostalgic over Heroes is like getting nostalgic over the time you stood in dog shit.

I took it as a measure of how placid and tolerant I've become lately that, even in my twitching, uneasy, homophobic state, I still managed to maintain more dignity than the complete arseholes that were gathered outside at the time of the review visit. There were half a dozen idiots in full Rockport regalia leering through the windows and trying to look menacing, like in Assault on Precinct 13. What the fuck for? Did they take it as a personal insult that these 'porvorts' could set up another bar? Or were they just wrestling with the uncomfortable fact that they really fancied a piece of the 'action' themselves? I wish they'd kicked off, though. It'd have been hilarious to watch them getting stomped by a handful of nancy boys.

The End

78 Scotswood Road, NE4 7JH
'The witness-protection scheme'

I've hit a bit of a stumbling block with this one. There's this song that some weirdo at my school used to sing, and that has stayed with me ever since, tattooed indelibly on my juvenile, snickering brain. It goes a little something like this: 'Oh Rocky, stick your cocky next to mi-ine'. And even though the gay bar that was Rockies has had, not so much a makeover as the full effects of the witness-protection scheme, and is now called The End, I just KNOW that if I went in to try to do a serious review, that that song, egged on by the nine pints of Dutch courage I'd need beforehand, would come tumbling out at the most inopportune moment, and would guarantee me the biggest fucking kicking the world has ever seen. So that's why I'm going to do some proper research and put this review together with hard, concrete FACTS instead of the usual bollocks, prejudice and supposition. Let's see how far I get... Once a riot of sound and spectacle, The End has ditched Rockies' kitsch for the feel of a homely lounge, where mocha leather sofas surround low level occasional tables and cube stools, and where soft warm lights and colours surround your senses. With an eclectic mix of everything from soulful jazz to the very best in vocal house, this bar promises something a little different from the hedonistic overkill of its previous incarnation. A vast array of cocktails is available for you to sip while you relax and unwind with the 'Sunday Night Live' sessions, featuring guest DJs and Sinatra tribute acts. And the customers? Well, as my gay mate so succinctly put it, it's full of fucking puffs. Ha ha ha! So near, yet so far...

For: Free wi-fi internet access all week long, if that means anything to you.
Against: Come on, it's a designer-haircut-luxebar-lounge. And as such it can fuck off.

I still can't remember the name of that kid who sang that damn 'Rocky' song. I tried looking it up on that Friends Reunited site, but gave up in disgust when I saw the patter of some of the morons I used to go to school with. They're either shambling mammy's boy cretins or the sort of wankers who've just gone on to brag about how they're 'pulling down' forty-five 'K' a year and have a personalised reg-plate (one that reads KN03 HED, if there's any justice). Ever wonder WHY people lost touch with you, you tedious fucking cunts? See if you can work it out.

Gossip

7 Westmorland Road, NE1 4EQ

'Why is Graham Norton always on my television?'

No. No. NO. I don't care what you say, or how much you pay me; I will not drink in a bar called Gossip. I cannot bring myself to enter a place whose very name conjures up images of that fucking Scrubbers Talking Shite thing that's on ITV on weekday lunchtimes, bringing dried-up, menopausal bitterness into our living rooms. I will not cross the threshold of a boozer that invokes a show so bad that, if a Flymo accident had left me limbless and the telly was mounted high on the wall, I would throw myself on the floor and gnaw through the flex rather than endure another second of some over-opinionated gasbag with fuck all else to do with her time. And that's the heterosexual option; THIS Gossip here is a gay bar, so not only would it be Talking Shite, it would be Talking Shite with Graham Norton. I'm struggling to think of anything worse. Why is Graham Norton always on my television? Why must we suffer his endless Saturday night inanities? Surely it would be far simpler to line up all the Desperate Darrens on his search-for-a-star programmes, ask them to fellate him one-by-one for marks out of ten and a shot at the prize, and get the BBC to stick on repeats of Dad's Army instead of wasting the nation's precious time. So for this one, I'm not even going to pretend I've been in and sampled the beer and atmosphere like I did for some of (or most of... alright, ALL) the other bars in the rest of the gay scene. I don't care about the darkened windows and subdued chandelier lighting I've read about. I have no interest in the winding staircase or the cosy alcoves. I refuse to do much more than acknowledge their DJs and plasma screens and, for all I care, their pool tables can go and fuck themselves; although how they'll physically achieve that, I wouldn't like to speculate. I think it's enough for me to point out that this bar is there, chuck in a few token obscenities, provide a certifiable audit trail that the Equal Opportunities Policy has been applied, and move on to the next one. There can't be many more to do, can there?

For: Hang on. I suppose I could always link this place to THE Gossip, the American band fronted by fat-lass style icon and in-your-face lesbian Beth Ditto.

Against: Did you see Ditto posing naked on the front of the NME? I'm sure she'll be absolutely gutted to hear, but when it comes to the indie-rock honey hierarchy, I don't think I'd climb over Charlotte Hatherley to get to her. Fucking hell, man: I wouldn't even climb over charlotte potatoes.

I could never work in recruitment. No fucker would ever get the job if I did. But I've got a mate down south who does, and he's only too familiar with the mechanisms of Equal Opportunities policies, designed to ensure that nobody is treated unfairly because of their race, age, sexuality and so on. In an attempt to do this, companies are apparently now asking increasingly detailed and ever more invasive questions of their applicants. Gay, straight, bi. Heterosexual, metrosexual, retrosexual. My mate assures me that, if you're filling in your form and agonising over whether to tell future employers what you haven't yet told your closest friends then the boxes you tick serve no other purpose than titillating the office drone who's inputting the statistics. So it was with one application that passed before his gimlet eyes. The candidate, whether confused by the various terms, or reluctant to state his preference, or simply in no mood for red tape, scanned all the available options and then drew his own box at the bottom. And what were the words he wrote so carefully beside it? NORMAL MAN, that's what. That's the fucking spirit.

Switch

4-10 Scotswood Road, NE4 7JB
'Extortionate ponce-bar'

Regardless of the sexual persuasion of its clientele, the thought of spending time and money in any boozer describing itself as Newcastle's trendiest bar is about as appealing to me as a night on the hoy with the catchiest leper. Fair enough, with its big red sign and its windows that open onto the street, Switch looks alright from across the street, but that's only if you're on the way to somewhere else, in a hurry, with no intention of stopping. When you get closer to Switch, however, you'll see the reality, which is a shuddering fun pub priding itself on hardcore cheese and head-splitting DJ sounds. Catering for the repugnant young-and-noisy crowd, Switch is run by Pure Leisure and, because they also own The Bank next door and luxe club The Loft upstairs, I'm excused from doing anything more by way of a review of those places than acknowledging their existence. Switch has a curved bar and a floor that's partly carpeted, wooden and tiled - no bet-hedging there, then - and they've got custom-made carpets, which is no sign of greatness, as anyone who's ever endured Sgt Pepper's will tell you. The paintjob features everyone's favourite pairing of mustard and maroon, and I suppose makes the place sort of like a gay Tilleys, but with shit, shit, shitty shit music, of the type that only a 'lively disco bar' could tolerate. Switch's standing as the official warm up bar for Shag Tag! (their exclama-tion mark: it's certainly not mine) means absolutely nothing to me, but it sounds appalling. If, however, you have a burning desire to go and see the Shag Tag Queen and get your sticker, then step the fuck up: I'm sure you'll get exactly what you deserve. Let me get this straight: they're actively encouraging the worst sort of Bank Holiday seaside tackiness, yet they've still got the nerve to charge extortionate ponce-bar prices for the drinks? I'd like to think there's a gay equivalent of the Burglar's Dog somewhere, sitting in the corner and becoming more and more furious that every fucking bar is pandering to the biggest imbecile in it. Surely there's someone whose heart sinks like jism down the pan at the thought of yet another cabaret night, and who finds the idea of 'fun' with Miss Thunder Pussy as wearisome as weeding. Is there nobody who'll say, Listen for once: what if I don't fucking WANT to get in the party mood in every single pub I go to? Come on man, make yourself known. Quit letting these fuckers tell you what you enjoy. You plucked up the courage to tell your folks when you came out, so you could at least have the bottle to let these cunts know that their number is up.

For: I'm a massive fan of typos, so the unintentional honesty and simplicity of their website's 'Why not take a look at our oneline menu?' question makes me a happy man.

Against: You're still smarting about the way that I've lumped the Bank and the Loft in with Switch, aren't you? I am not doing them, and that's final. Put it this way: if you went to the estate agents and someone was selling a house with an attic and a garage, would you demand a separate print out for each? No, you wouldn't, so quit whingeing.

I'd be surprised if I'm the first fool to pose this question, but I haven't yet so much as eavesdropped on a satisfactory answer, so I'm going to ask it here: why are all the gay bars traditionally down this end of town? Is it because the Blaydon Races 'gan along the Scotswood Road' and right past all the pubs' doors and windows? I'm asking because the night of the review visit was the same night that the Bigg Market was stowed off with people in running gear, what with it being the 9th of June and everything. Is that the reason for the location, though? Is it so the punters can lean out or stand on the steps and yell, 'Yoo hoo!' at all the participants, before marvelling at the athleticism and the flolloping cocks? Bearing in mind that researching this chapter has ticked off every possible gay stereotype (I made a list), I'm going to say it here and you can quote me: Yes, THAT is the reason.

Twist
Times Square, NE1 4EP
'Endless to-do'

It's time to face the fact that I'm getting old, and that my memory is not quite what it used to be. It's now, what, the dog days of summer, and it was only when I was on my way to the Arena to embarrass myself in the name of rock watching some band I'm too ashamed to mention that I remembered that, far from Twist being just a name on the endless to-do list, I actually had a few unseasonably alfresco beers there earlier this year. Stupid bastard. I wasn't even drunk that day, either. Playing Tetris with my recollections, I've come up with a picture of having an average pint in a boxed-in beer terrace amongst foul-mouthed, hissing shitwits; the gay counterparts of the Bigg Market's 'tits oot' squad. Other than that, I'm screwed. And, because I'm a closet homophobe with the emphasis on the phobia part, a second visit is out of the question, so the rest of this review will have to be full of the usual waffle and space filling. But what I can tell you, from the one and only sideways glance I made when I was getting served, is that this place looked exactly like the Jolly Miller in Gateshead's Low Fell - along from the Angel of the North, and passed by many / visited by few - so I'm just going to describe that and pray that nobody can spot the join. It's a huge place with no pretensions of cosiness, with drab green walls and job-lot furniture, the odd bandit and even odder punters. In one corner sits a tapioca-faced youth in a Bench hoody; in another sits your gran, wondering where that smell is coming from. Outside are a few tables, and you're asking yourself, are these people the bar's typical radgies, or are they just passing through? And why does it have to be Carling every frigging time? I think what I'm trying to get at is this; for all the flashing lights and the regeneration-area location, this place feels like the sort of housing estate hellhole I fear I'm going to end up wasting my twilight years in. And I doubt they'd thank me for saying so.

For: The ice rink outside the Centre for Life from mid-November onwards.
Against: Never mind the chicken and the egg. Which of these comes first: the gay act or the gay voice? Is it the love that dare not speak its name, or is it hissssing your essssses through your bottom teeth like a poor man's Lily Savage? Somebody must know.

Gay blokes do get an unnecessarily hard time, though. I once went to see the stationery lads at work to scrounge a box of A4 paper. 'Alreet mate? Got a big job on, then?' they said. But when I mentioned that a gay colleague was involved then it turned into, 'WHAT? He wants to stick the fucking paper up his ARSE, does he? EH?' Funnily enough, he did, too.

The Yard
2 Scotswood Road, NE4 7JB
'Popular with coffin-dodgers'

Never let it be said that we don't personally visit every bar in the town, even if it was just once, for one pint, in 1989, when it was called something else. On the, ahem, review visit this place looked exactly like *'Moulin Rouge'* at its campest with what research tells me was the performers from Greta the barmaid's drag show milling about. I couldn't help but stare: not out of freak-show value, but since I thought I was Robert Smith out of The Cure at the time, I was only jealous that the geezers in there had better makeup than me. Old queens, as I believe I can get away with calling them without a hoof in the nads, will remember this place as the dark and depressing Courtyard, which was so popular with coffin-dodgers that it had the nickname The Grave-yard, but a revamp has transformed it into a cosmopolitan bar complete with street tables in summer. All ages converge on what is now a very open and airy bar, with plenty of pastel shades and stone flooring; it's good to see that the gay commu-nity has to suffer the same shite as the straight. There is also a... oh look, fuck this. Let's just report the trials and tribulations of our old friend Allan Weir of the excellent pubsnewcastle.co.uk site, who does this pub review lark properly instead of pissing about like we do. Even he, stout of constitution and open of mind, clearly looked at the promo flyers on the windows, peered round the door to clock the decor, and then ran like the fucking wind as far as his little legs would carry him. You bottled it too then, Al?

For: This space is intentionally blank.
Against: Why do ninety percent of internet forums - like the one I rifled for research for this - seem to be directed at some bloke called Lol, as in 'I shud of getting banned I was pissed and fell

over, lol xxx'? Who the fuck is Lol, and why is he so interested in all that crap?

In desperation, I lifted the facts for this so-called review from a well-informed gay website called JH's Homo Pages. In it, JH gets in a tizz about the punctuation in the phrase 'Newcastles Premier Gay Bar (sic)'. I know how he feels. It gets on my floppy tits the way that there are about eight people left in this country who know how to use apostrophes properly. You see when I die? Some dunce stonemason will take one look at my surname, see there's an 's' on the end, and decide it needs an apostrophe in there. 'Here lies Mark Jone's...' That'll be me: trapped for all eternity beneath a punctuation error. You think I should just go and shoot the fucker now?

11

The Gate

'Opened in November 2002 after three years of construction work, The Gate leisure complex has expanded rapidly, and now boasts fourteen venues, among them a cinema, a casino and numerous restaur... are you sure this isn't the last one? Are we talking about that glass monstrosity here? The one that's infested with kids? The one whose beer 'gardens' are under a mall roof? Can't I just write something about the escalators? I LIKE escalators...' – Norman Undercroft, Historian.

Bar Bannatyne

The Gate, NE1 1UN
'God's gift to comedy'

I came in here with a couple of mates before the match, hoping for a perspective other than the 'this is shite' one I normally get from our lass. 'It's just like *Cheers* in here,' they said. Hmmm. Let's weigh up the evidence, shall we? How about we start with the things from the long running TV sitcom that this bar lacks? One: the stairs. Two: The warm, friendly, everyone-knows-your-name greeting. Three: the characters, unless you count a whole host of pissed-off Geordies getting angrier by the minute at the hopeless, no-eye-contact service and the hundred-degree heat. Also missing: the personality, specifically the sense that a bar is part of a tradition and the fabric of a city, and not just another gap-filling exercise in some shitty leisure mall. Oh, and let's not forget the lack of that legendary *Cheers* live-before-a-studio-audience laughter, or indeed any sort of laughter at all, come to think of it. What about the similarities, I hear you ask. Well, for a kick off it did have a stump-dumb barman. In fact it had several. It had a scattering of the Kirsty Allie syndrome - lasses you might have chucked one up when they were young and slim, but would be a bit more reluctant to now they're twenty bloody stone. Also in attendance: plenty examples of that fuck-awful short-arse wife with the perm, thinking she's god's gift to comedy and the scathing putdown, when it's plainly obvious most people have seen funnier jokes in a Christmas cracker. Christ, it was rotten. Paddling through the internet looking for a picture of the place - my cacky digital camera doesn't work too well in the gloom of The Gate - I found one other similarity. As with the plethora of identical '*Cheers*-branded' bars springing up to cater to fuckwits the world over, it seems that Bannatyne is also part of a chain, though whether that includes the health clubs of the same name run by him off *'Dragon's Den'* is anyone's guess. It fucking wants to, judging by the clip of the lardies in here.

For: I'm hearing that, rather than being a *Cheers* tribute, Bannatyne is actually supposed to be a Moroccan theme bar. Blimey, that was design money well spent, wasn't it? Casting my mind back, I did see some sparkly curtains and what looked like a fortune-teller's booth in the corner. 'I see your future. I see you drinking up and getting the fuck out of here.'
Against: The weakest beer pumps in the northern hemisphere. You could watch two episodes of the TV smug-fest in the time it took to pour our pints.

I will be Prime Minister one day. There's no point in arguing; the job is mine. And when I'm in power, I will outlaw the piss-dribbling beer taps that are so frustratingly commonplace in our bars, and in their place will be the Parisian rocket-fuelled version. *Schoomf-spatula-serve, all in under ten seconds: that's how it'll be when I'm at Number 10. A nation will rejoice.*

Beyond
The Gate, NE1 5RE
'Cheap'

Well, nobody can say I haven't tried to give Beyond a fair crack of the whip before I stick the boot in. I've been here on numerous occasions over the years, with different people, under different circumstances, and it's always, always been cack. Despite the change from its original virginal white to standard pub-issue purple, this place still retains, and will always have, all the cosy ambience of a chain hotel lobby, and it fair takes me back to the times I've stood in cheap European reception areas arguing in hopelessly inept French with a poor teenager on the minimum wage. Over-friendly bar staff with League Two footballer mullets serve up shockingly-priced beer to unsuspecting after-work punters whose only crime is fancying a change from their usual venue, while evenings bring in the sort of arsewits who like to give off an air of sophistication, as if getting ripped off in a leisure mall bar makes you some sort of debutante. The teat who served me last time had an unnerving habit of winking at me; whether he was trying to communicate 'I understand your order', or 'Mmm. Good choice of terrible beer', or 'Meet me in the shitters in five, handsome' is not something I want to ponder too deeply. I wasn't going to go back for another round to find out, that's for sure. And now that the pocket-plundering restaurant to the left of the bar has been ditched and walled off, each peak time has the same number of people as before, but jammed into a smaller space, with every one of them obeying the first rule of group drinking: you always have to put up with what the biggest cunt in the group wants. And bearing in mind that even the most normal member of these groups is still a fucking mallrat, a fool who'd tolerate any number of shit bars as long as they didn't get rained on going between them, then this place doesn't really strike me as somewhere I'd want to strike up a casual conversation with a stranger. Add some grinning dickhead of a toilet attendant pouncing on you and showering you with Eau de Donkey's Dong every time you go for a widdle, and you really have got an experience to rival root canal surgery. It's 'Beyond' the fucking joke.

For: I liked that strange shaped glitterball. But that was all.
Against: This is the future of the pub. All bars will be like this unless we join together and take a stand. And I mean it.

I didn't see this, but my missus tells me that when she was on her way to the bogs, she saw the lasses behind the bar were doing all that 'mwah, mwah' air kissing on shift change over. You're a barmaid in a mall in Newcastle, love. You are not Kate Moss. Please try to understand that.

Hide

The Gate, NE1 5RF
'A shining example'

I was once of the opinion that Hide was the only bar in The Gate leisure complex with any merit. That was based on an impromptu pint after work on a Tuesday, and bears no relation to what we found on our prime time Friday night refresher. Hide is appalling. Situated in the Dockside area of The Gate, at least a mile from the nearest waterway - unless you count Newgate Street's legendary flash flood zones in the pissing rain - Hide is a shining example of how to create a bar with no character, no depth and no pride. Run by a chain, designed with disdain and staffed with no real interest, this is a shocker even for a mall bar. And from what I can remember of the last time I was here, it looks like people have been pinching stuff since it opened, leaving only the glued-down black and white tiles and the leather pouffes, the ones nobody with a spine would ever find comfortable enough to steal. There aren't even any real punters to discuss, just an endless parade of spotty, gum-chewing adolescents in hoop earrings and cropped sportswear, scowling their way to the bogs and back out again. I'm looking at their pasty faces as they pass, and suddenly I realise why the English are getting progressively uglier. This is why: the good Lord in His wisdom has provided for the people the miracle of public transport. In His omnipotence, He bestowed upon mankind the intelligence to make use of the Earth's natural resources, like oil and metals and rubber, and He trusted us to use His gifts with care. The trouble is, by the time the average teenager on an English estate - yours, mine, anyone's you care to name - has realised that the big moving thing with the wheels and windows is there to take you to other places, and not just for hurling rocks at, they're already the proud parent of seven puking, dribbling kids with their equally rodent-faced next-door neighbour. Those children are outside in the mall, and their mothers are in here, getting on my fucking tit ends. Finally, I have to see what the hell is so fascinating back there, so I disentangle my legs from the booth and hobble to the lavs. And this is what I see while I'm splashing my wages into the trough: a huge price comparison chart above the urinals, like a breakdown of the weekly shop, totting up how much you'd save if you bought every item on the drinks menu here instead of in Tiger Tiger or Mood. Well, that's me convinced. That's the only way I could stay here for more than a solitary jar, by working my way through the list until the tears flowed and I no longer knew or cared about who I used to be. What a fucking night that'd be. Is next Saturday OK for you?

For: Why not take up their special offer and hire your own booth for that big sporting occasion?
Against: And then sit wedged in and cramped, with your face an inch off the TV screen, until the Deep Vein Thrombosis kicks in.

Hoop earrings and natural resources: some thoughts. Can there be greater evidence of the stupidity of the human race than the concept of 'precious' metals? How can one sort of metal dug from the ground be of more value than another? Why isn't, say, tin stashed away in the vaults? Yes, I understand its rarity, the nature of status symbols and 'Do you know how much this costs?' But why? How did it become so sought-after in the first place?

What does it do? I'll tell you: it does nothing, except say 'I am rich and I am flaunting it,' or 'I am poor and I'm trying to look like I have something to flaunt.' And when Mammon's carefully constructed economic fabric rips at the seams, when hyperinflation hits and we're all carrying home piles of worthless currency in Netto bags, who will be the ones with the smug grins and the deluxe pizza menus? The ones with the lump of fucking yellow metal buried in the allotment, that's who.

Keel Row

The Gate, NE1 5RE
'Kids are scum, too'

The Wetherspoon chain specialising in cod-authentic traditional bars has an offshoot catering for the more discerning, upmarket customer under their Lloyds No.1 brand. And this place, the Keel Row, is an example of how they hope to make their riches. Take one carpet off-cut from the colour-blind range, add a selection of self-assembly, black ash effect furniture from the Argos catalogue, circa 1985, and then turn the lights down really low and hope that people don't notice how shoddy everything is. Fair enough, it's nice to have a bit of gloom and atmosphere in a bar, but when you can't see where you're going, it tends to be a bit of a health hazard. Take that barely visible spindly branch thing, like an upturned witch's broom, on the wall by the quiz machine. The damn thing nearly took my fucking eye out and I'm not lying just to get the sympathy vote. Like a dying man heading for the bright light at the end of the tunnel, we made for the crappy *Saturday Night Fever* dance floor on the off chance of actually being able to see something. Oh, we saw something, alright: reams upon reams of menu pages advertising vodka-Red Bull combinations and child-sized food portions available in the - blink, blink, shit it's real - family area at the back of the bar. Look, I might as well spell this out since nobody else seems willing to do it: anyone who takes kids to the pub is obviously scum. There can be no argument about that. And their kids are scum, too. You turn up at the pub expecting a relaxing pint and some adult conversation, and what happens? You get irritating little bastards barging their way past you to their tables, screaming the bloody place down 'cause they can't have another Coke and their fish fingers haven't got peas for eyes like it said on the menu, and then being dragged back out by the wrist after they've shown Mummy and Daddy up. You little fuckers. I don't care if you are top of your class: you spill my pint and you get a slap in the face. Christ almighty, this bar is shite. Not even the dirt-cheap beer is enough to bring me back here again.

For: The seats outside have an unrivalled view of an escalator and a cash point.
Against: If you sniffed the contents of a vacuum cleaner bag, puked on the floor, left it to dry, hoovered it up, then sniffed it again, you still wouldn't come close to the awful smell we encountered by the tables to the right the last time we were in.

The Keel Row is the darkest of bars in the darkest of malls. I hate the dark. Not like Mummy-leave-the-light-on, but in that pathetic Seasonal Affective Disorder way, the one that gives me carte blanche to act like an utter twat from October to March. I only mention this because I'm sitting here at work, skiving, and across the other side of the office they're covering the windows up with the panels from the air conditioning. No matter where you toil, you're subjected to a constant penny-pinching squeeze, with corners cut and luxuries slashed to make the brand lean, mean and more obscene. Bring your own coffee, I can understand. Pay for your own parking, yes. Chip in for your protective clothing, maybe. But provide your own fucking daylight? Now that's just taking the piss.

Mood

The Gate, Newgate Street, NE1 5TG
'Someone is gonna get lamped'

So, I walk through the portals and survey the decor, and I'm thinking, 'Mmm, yes. Heavy Gaudi influence, with strong elements of Gothic and Moorish, coupled with striking wrought iron and almost breathtaking use of catenary arches.' My mind races as I try to remember which of Gaudi's works this most closely resembles: is it the secular splendour of the Palau Güell, or the fairytale façade of Casa Batlló? Maybe this incredible interior is most redolent of the little-known but supremely sumptuous Puerta de la Finca Miralles. And then my learned companion captures the very essence of the building with his carefully worded summary: 'Wha-hey! It's just like Noel's House Party in here!' He's right, you know. The staircase looks just like the one the bearded goon used to bound down every week, before his wilderness years and subsequent *Deal Or No Deal* resurrection. On first impressions Mood is better than any bar in a shopping mall 'village' has a right to be, and scores extra points for letting in any old riff-raff, which is more than can be said for fucking Tiger Tiger out the front. The beer's cheap enough, at least in the afternoon, and there's a complete absence of the over-officious 'touch NOWT' stupidity you get in some bars. The communal bathroom area is a novelty, though how it'll pan out at pissing in the sink time when the pub turns into a club after 11 o'clock is anyone's guess. I can guarantee someone is gonna get lamped by the bog doors, though. Two floors provide plenty of space for all manner of punters, from strimmer-cut fashion victims to tanked up match goers; from office girls after work to shopping families. That gives me an idea: why not pull up a stool and listen to bag-laden pensioners trying to explain away the huge abstract images of ladies' front bottoms on all the windows to their inquisitive young charges? I can see it now: 'Well, Connor, they're just lines to try to hide the escalators outside and to make the beerbar a nicer place to sit in.' Little Connor thinks for a minute, and then pipes up: 'Cor, Grandma, you know tons! And I thought they were twenty foot high fannies, an' all...'

For: The massive screens for live sports are way, way over the head height of even the lankiest twat.
Against: The constant stench that is beyond mere vomit and into human decay.

I think I've whinged before about my problems with depth perception, and about how I have real bother walking into glass because I just can't see it. Coming out of Mood before the match, slightly the worse for wear, I see what I think are two doors and, seeing my mates go through the one on the right I look at the one on the left and think, 'Right. These bastards aren't going to get me this time. That's an open door and this is a window.' So I sidle up to it, practically checking my barnet in my reflection and, would you believe it, there's nothing there. No glass, no nothing. I'm pressing thin air like some two-bit mime artist and the bouncers are pissing themselves. What the hell is wrong with me?

Opera Piano Bar

The Gate, Newgate Street, NE1 5RE
'Tremendous'

I am in hell. I am at the bar of a pitch-black pub in the already dismal Gate complex, and I am standing underneath a mirrored ceiling, peering over at the finest quality Dralon upholstery. The barmaid is struggling vainly with the cocktail menu, and she has just told the lad being served before us that this is the bar with no beer. Not as a general policy, you understand: opening time just took them by surprise again, and the draught's off. So, I pay through the nose for our bottles of Belgian-brewed Mexican lager and, pausing only to wonder how a bar this dark can safely be strewn with nigh-on invisible glass tables, I slump down in my seat. There's a couple in the corner. They're forty-odd; he's like a whippet with a traffic cone on its muzzle, and she's like a gable end. And they're snogging. Not just a delicate peck, or a respectful loving embrace, but a full on neck-fest, like two hooligans in a bus shelter, ripped to the tits on Diamond White. I think he's getting his tops, too. It's horrific, and heaven knows how I'm going to make it to the end of my overpriced Corona without fetching up my lunch. Inevitably, there's a lull in our conversation, and I realise that what I had initially taken for the hum of the air conditioning is actually the bar's choice of music. In the absence of a real piano player it's Omar, it's the Brand New Heavies, and it's ambient lounge-jazz. Tremendous. All I need now is a bit of M People and blood will be shed. Outside there's a commotion. I can see they need to leave the door open to make passers-by realise that there's a bar here and not just a dark, empty retail unit, but just listen to those clowns out there in the mall. There's not one of them who wouldn't benefit from an iron bar right in the kisser. Staring really hard at the promotional literature I notice the buzzwords for the Opera experience. Finest cocktails? Ambient atmosphere? Class? I snort, derisively and justifiably. This is the sort of place you'd struggle to find 'classy' if you'd just done a twelve-stretch at Her Majesty's pleasure, pissing in a bucket and drinking rainwater. It's awful. Christ, my eyes. Surely they could have put in something other than a wall full of illuminated bottles to lift the murk. I head to the toilets, hoping to relieve, in addition to my bladder, the tension behind my poor straining lenses. And this is when I find that Opera shares the pissers with Beyond next door. It's not even a separate bar! It's clearly just the failed restaurant bit of Beyond given a fresh coat of paint and a new sign to hoodwink the punters. What an absolute debacle. Imagine if I offered a bike rack for sale on eBay and then, when the poor sap with the winning bid paid up, said, 'Sorry, it's not technically bicycle storage: it's actually my arse.' There'd be a fucking rabbit off, wouldn't there? How come this lot can get away with it, then? C'mon, tell me. It's a gyp, a sham and an absolute fucking disgrace, and we fell for it, like the sad, grasping losers we are.

For: Go in through Opera, use the bogs out the back, and leave through Beyond. No shame, no embarrassment, no charge.
Against: Every time a new bar opens in the frigging Gate, I always think, 'Well, it can't get any worse.' Tiger Tiger, Bar Bannatyne, even the Keel Row, you have my humblest apologies. THIS bar is clearly rock bottom.

This disgusting Gate complex was built on the site of the old Mayfair Ballroom, a venue that was thriving until some cunt demolished it specifically for the purpose of building the mall. If you were to drop a plumb line from the bar in Opera, while you might not hit where the stage used to be, you'd certainly leave it hanging somewhere near the merchandise tables. The Mayfair: scene of legendary gigs and landmarks in my musical history, from the Sigue Sigue Sputnik swindle to Nirvana just as they broke. And what does the fucking Gate - and Opera in particular - have as entertainment? Sinatra tribute acts. Whoever gave the planning go-ahead should be publicly castrated.

Players

The Gate, Newgate Street, NE1 5TG
'Copyright-be-damned'

There's an old Newcastle tradition of fingering the latest craze amongst the kids, churning out cheap copies and then flogging them from a barrow or amongst the seagull shit at the Quayside market. From Rubik cubes to Sudoku; from 'Frankie Says' T-shirts to Crazy Frog hoodies; from Tamagotchis to Roboraptors; they've all been there under a grubby tarpaulin, and they're all as tacky as fuck. One thing you can guarantee is that whatever's fashionable will be exploited for the masses, regardless of whether the original was any bloody cop, and while you or I may think, 'Eh?! Why?', rest assured there'll be some fucking idiot along in a minute keen to part with his readies. And this bar, Players, this shameless cash-in, is no more and no less than a piss-poor, toxic paint, fall-apart-in-your-hands version of the already-hopeless Sports Café on Grainger Street, together with a few copyright-be-damned bits from other equally rank places. It truly is fucking awful. Fair enough, they boast the biggest telly in Newcastle, but two things marred my viewing enjoyment just a tad. One, the pain-in-the-arse yappy - as opposed to chin-stroking - DJ shouting endless shite about drinks promotions (Foster's is not a premium lager, you fucking chump); and two, the antics of the Players All-Stars dancing girls on the high podium in middle of the bar and right in front of the bastard screen. Laugh as I might at the desperateness of the dirty dancing - you could have dragged in two lasses at gunpoint from any bus queue you care to name for a better performance - when I'm in a sports bar I want to see Ameobi's Greatest Hat-tricks on DVD and not some dumb bints gyrating over-enthusiastically for a quid an hour. A bit less 'Tits oot!' and more 'Siddoon!' wouldn't go amiss. And the dancers are the best part of the whole sorry experience. If you're looking for something out of the ordinary in the rest of the bar, then forget it; it's just a big round room with two floors, the gallery above having as little to recommend as the non-entity below. If you want pool tables, go to a snooker hall; if you want dance floors, go clubbing; and if you're after ever-changing lighting effects, then drink Domestos and whack yourself with a mallet. You can get everything you get here just by sacking off the insulting facsimile and going elsewhere. Believe me, you'd feel less ashamed afterwards. There it is then; and you're welcome to every last over-polished inch of it. You can keep the laminate flooring and the massive padded cell effect on the TV wall. Help yourself to the wall covering that's so godawful it's hard to tell where the bogs end and the bar begins. Take it all and shove it. And if this place actually is your thing, then you'd better get along sharpish, since some other type of bar will be trendy in a few months, and all this bandwagoning crap will be out the back in the skip. Until then, though: Get yer white sports socks, three pairs for a pound.

For: It's impossible to come up with a 'for' when this bar aims to combine the very worst bits of Shearer's and Sam Jacks.
Against: I don't think this is the final piece in the horrifying Gate jigsaw. I'm sure there's just enough room to cram in one more terrible bar.

For all their pouting and hip-grinding, those hapless lasses on the podium reminded me of nothing so much as Boyzone's legendary non-singing debut on Irish TV's Late Late Show with Gay Byrne. Just in case you've so far had enough of a life to avoid all those Ladgeful Telly Moments rundowns, here's a brief précis of the performance. 'Ah, yer a fine lookin' bunch o' lads, so ye are. Have ye got a song for us?' No. 'What about some anecdotes?' Not really, Gay. 'Sure, what can ye do for us?' Well, Gay, we can chuck ourselves about like tits on a trampoline on live television. 'Grand. Off ye go'. Picture Ronan Keating bodypopping with his flat cap on sideways: these girls weren't far behind in the embarrassment stakes, I'll tell you now.

Sam Jacks

The Gate, Newgate Street, NE1 5TG
'Kick the cunts when they're down'

In writing the Burglar's Dog I've done my level best to visit and have a drink in every boozer in Newcastle. I've wasted a day's wages in the luxury bars by the station; I've chanced permanent hearing and eyesight damage in the Bigg Market fun pubs; and I've even risked life, limb and genitalia in the radgie alehouses on a Friday night. But if there's one bar that I haven't been able to abide since its depressing slide into debauchery, it's the self-appointed 'good time educator' Sam Jacks. Believe me, I've tried. Many times I've given a determined 'alreet?' to the bouncers, hopped up the stairs into the main room, only to stand aghast at the terrible scenes before me and then fuck off before reaching the bar. Formerly a quaint, innocent, gingham-and-cowboy-hat bar with emphasis on comfort and relaxation, Sam Jacks has somehow become just like all the other venues in this inexplicably popular area of town, a blackened, throbbing, standing room-only disgrace. And, clearly pissed off that they were NewcastleGateshead's second saloon theme bar, a microwaveable version of Buffalo Joe's, they've decided to tone down the Wild West motif and just go straight for the stag, hen and student market, in the process descending into the hideous, tits-oot-for-the-lads embarrassment that ranks this town just behind Blackpool in the arsehole magnet stakes. I suppose I should have known, when the windows became covered over with adverts, that something bad was going on inside. I'd guess that the Council had instructed them that their appalling behaviour was fine, just so long as they kept it out of the view of any sensitive types on their way to the cinema or Asperger's Casino out the back. Major changes? Out: the arty displays of antlers on the walls. In: big screen tellies to plug the drinks promotions. Out: the fully clothed and choreographed dancing girls, smilingly recreating Madonna's moves in that stupid cowgirl video. In: astonishingly inept pre-match strippers and piss-away-your-self-respect drinking competitions. Out: the bucking bronco, which has clearly done the only sensible thing and legged it in shame. And in: 'amazing' breakdancers. Fucking breakdancers? In a pub? The only time I'm even prepared to tolerate tits like that is when I'm on holiday, hobbling around some mediaeval market square after being on the move all day, with feet too sore to kick the cunts when they're down. And if that wasn't enough, they're plugging the spirits-down-your-neck-in-the-dentist-chair idea as being an original novelty gimmick more than ten years after Gazza brought shame on the nation with it. The real pisser for me is that you can't even just bypass Sam Jacks and pretend that it doesn't exist, since every time I walk by on my way to the match, it's spilling out into the street. There'll be some wizened old boot – the manager's grandmother, probably – with blonde extensions, leather kecks and furry leg-warmers, marching up and down Newgate Street with a pint of HRT in one hand and whopping great Sam Jacks sign-on-a-stick in the other. And that's supposed to tempt people into one of the most deliberately unpleasant bars the city has ever seen? I really don't understand what is happening here, or to society as a whole. I'm aware that, from the cradle to the grave, from the classroom to the dole queue, being stupider than the next person is now seen as a badge of honour. But how the fuck did it come to this?

For: I would have said the cheap beer, but imagining the place stuffed full of whooping arseclowns off their faces on two-for-one makes my skin crawl.
Against: If you fancy doing a bit of research or preplanning on their website, then be aware that the fucker is two years out of date. If there are any glaring inaccuracies in the review – surely they must have scrapped the breakdancers by now - it's their fault and not mine.

Much as it made me weep to do so, I used the appalling name

NewcastleGateshead simply because Buffalo Joe's is on the other side of the river. That's the way the box-tickers in committee-land want you to refer to the two distinct places from now on: all one word with a capital G in the middle, as part of a pitiful attempt at a Budapest-style merger. Think what we'll become: pointlessly but inexorably linked, every mention of the proud city of Newcastle will be tarnished by what amounts to no more than the geographical Schnorbitz, with the scabby mutt dragged forlornly behind on a leash. Great.

Sinners

63 Newgate Street, NE1 5RF
'Crying like Paris Hilton'

Giving much-needed euthanasia to the bed-ridden and drooling tragedy that was Lennon's Music Bar, Sinners is attempting to inject a new lease of life into the premises. And in keeping with the fucking appalling name and the inevitable concept that goes with it, I'm going to quickly run through a list of the seven deadly sins and see if I can superglue them to various aspects of the bar. Wish me luck. First up: LUST. Well, there's plenty of that, with pot-bellied, middle-aged blokes in teenagers' T-shirts trying to embarrass the knickers off the young fluff. GREED we can pin on that self-same fluff, blackmailing another half-dozen rum 'n' cokes and the taxi fare home from their back-tracking suitors with the threat of a call to the wife whose number they 'accidentally' found on his mobile when he went for a slash. Next, the GLUTTONY is pretty much self-evident, as legions of the city's binge drinkers pile out onto the rooftop terrace, puff on an entire box of twenty in the open air, before scrambling back inside for another litre or two of vodka and pop. Then you've got ENVY from innocent customers forcibly dragged in on some cunt's birthday bash, jealous of the warring adolescents being manhandled into the police van outside in preparation for a quiet night behind bars: I'm sure they'd swap an evening in here for a few contemplative hours on a wooden bench and an £80 fine in the morning. After envy comes SLOTH, or more accurately the designers' attitude of, 'Shall we attempt something new, or shall we just do another Perdu-themushroom-Quilted Camel travesty of faux-glamour?' How many sins is that? Five? The PRIDE is plain to see, etched on the faces of defiant old boilers mouthing the words to the self-help anthems that sum up their lives, shortly before slumping in a corner and crying like Paris Hilton. And finally there's WRATH which, needless to say, comes from yours truly, kicking in phone boxes all the way home and screaming, 'Why? Why? WHY?' at the terrified passers-by. Is that all seven done, then? Champion. To be honest, I don't see a rosy future for this place. I can't see a major transition from the scruffy sham- bles that was once there into the prestigious luxury in the Sinners business plan. As a dog returns to its vomit, so a fool repeats his folly: the Lennon's hellhounds will be back with a vengeance, the topless dancers will be on before the match, and the building will be shaking like Ozzy Osbourne on an oscillator quicker than you can say 'Come On Eileen'.

For: Seven impoverished students or out-of-work actors were paid good money to get clarted up in green paint and Halloween costumes, and then sent out to stand with placards listing the sins at twenty-yard intervals on the Tyne Bridge. A fine way to pro- mote a bar, don't you think?

Against: This is not an 'against' for the pub, but for Go-Ahead buses. Thanks to their paranoiac security measures, the Perspex shield between the driver and I prevented me from grabbing the wheel and mowing all seven of those fuckers down in a nice, neat line.

The review was done while the place was still in bits pending the grand opening. I just made up a load of stuff based on my usual intolerance, thinking that if I was right, then you'd see that my frequent claims to genius were justified, and if I was wrong we'd just chalk it up to experience: let's face it, I couldn't look any more of a dick than I do already. Went in last night for a 'Stop Press' to see the finished article and, although I'd missed out the tacky red backlit curtains and the curry vodka, everything else was spot on.

Tiger Tiger

The Gate, Newgate Street, NE1 5RE
'Denim's fighting fabric'

One of many branches of a national chain, Newcastle's Tiger Tiger achieved notoriety in its earliest days with the most spiteful door policy the city had ever seen. There wasn't a week went by without another 'ruined birthday' exposé in the papers, stories of poor souls being refused entry for any number of farcical reasons. Whether it was for being too young or too old, too fat or too skinny, too gay or too straight, if the ballbag on the door felt like acting the cunt there was nothing you could do about it. It probably won't surprise you to know that one unfortunate sod was barred simply because the doorman 'did not like his smile', or that their dress code was as baffling as it was draconian (I hear they once denied admission to one of their own bar staff because his company-provided uniform wasn't up to scratch). I recall that back in the days before you were nobody without a £200 pair of maker-ripped jeans, they had a right arse-on about denim. Fair enough, if you're carrying a machete, or you're blind drunk or bollock naked, then they have every right to stop you, but excluding the punters on the grounds of the material they're wearing does seem a little bit bloody childish. 'Sorry, son: denim's fighting fabric.' Maybe they were right, though. When I'm wearing dress pants or, like, a nice fresh pair of chinos, I'm an honest and upstanding member of society, but once I pull my jeans on, I start eating orphans and making replica B-52 bombers out of my own turds. No such bother tonight, though: for once, I've made it past the doorman and I'm gawping around to see if the place can justify its boasts about sophisticated style. Now, I'm not entirely thick: I understand the nature of exclusivity, and of aspiration, and I'm aware that the world would be a dreary place if every bar was exactly the same. But I expect to get what I pay for, and it has to be said, repeated and underlined that, for a so-called luxury bar, Tiger Tiger is absolutely fucking woeful. The decor is poodle piss-poor, with acres of fuck-all enlivened by fashionable (three, maybe four years ago) feature walls of garish red wallpaper. And while I know the importance of having per. And while I know the importance of having hardwearing surfaces in licensed premises, is there really any need to laminate the bloody walls too? Leaving our lass to get the beers in, I nip for a piss and nose around in the bogs – always the dipstick of true luxury - to check whether there are actually any knickers under the Tiger fur coat. Knickers, yes, but the elastic's gone and there's a stubborn stain that just won't play ball with the Vanish, since the toilets have been utterly trashed, with a half-severed tap here and a dozen tiles off over there. Have the fucking cheapskates never heard of reinvestment? Returning to the bar, I find the wife still hasn't been served, and I'm just about to raise Cain when I remember the billion-and-one tales I've heard of obstreperous bar staff and their painstaking incompetence. And I can see the evidence right in front of me, as some razor-cut imbecile puts the cock into 'cocktail' and the twat into 'of the first water' for the benefit of his equally surly customers. Finally served with our overpriced and sticky premium pilsner, we head to one of the few remaining sofas along the wall that backs onto Sam Jacks, sofas so disproportionate that even Peter Crouch's feet wouldn't touch the bloody floor. I stare past the sudden deluge of weekend millionaires and into the area where the rest of the furniture used to be. And that's when I realise that there is no hope for mankind. Weigh up the evidence. There are hundreds of people outside and they are swarming in this direction. They are checking their reflections in the windows and they are looking to impress. They have waited all week for this, and they are ready to 'party', cheek to cheek and jowl by saggy jowl. I say this: accelerate climate change, trigger nuclear meltdown, let the GM crops run riot. Bring 'em all on, because if the human race is not only prepared to tolerate this, but is actually willing to queue up for entry and encourage it to thrive, then the human race does not deserve to live.

For: You can be excused for having one pint, since you've got to have some reward for the mind-games with the bouncers...
Against: ...but if you go back to the bar for so much as a little bendy straw, you want a bullet in the back of your skull.

I only went into the ground floor bar bit, and not the nightclub, or the VIP bar, or the restaurant with its jack-of-all-trades 'fusion' menu, so I can't justifiably bellyache about those. But I was once physically dragged to one of the corporate function rooms upstairs, and stood in absolute astonishment that the god-awful brown and orange contemporary '70s kitchen that I ripped out the second I moved into my house had been recreated right down to the last detail in this supposedly sleek modern bar.

12

Bigg Market

'A disgusting melange of vomit, pizza boxes, and bottle tops between cobbles; a shameful display of boarded up restaurants, eight-inch stilettos and nightly carnage; a veritable blot on the landscape. This is the area that is unaware of the dividing line between tantalising midriff and fat fucking gut. This is the epicentre of Newcastle's legendary nightlife. And this is enough to make a grown man weep. Screw this: you're not paying me anywhere near enough to put up with this crap. I'm offski.' - Norman Undercroft, Historian.

Balmbra's Reflex
5 Cloth Market, NE1 1EE
'Clueless Brummie fuckers'

I haven't been to Balmbra's for ages following the embarrassing furore there a couple of years ago; embarrassing for Mitchells and Butlers, that is. It's not very often you get a motion in Parliament to stop a pub chain from pissing around with stuff - more's the pity - but the saga of this place tells where it all kicked off. And here, in lieu of a review, I'm going to explain how. Once upon a time those clueless Brummie fuckers at Mitchells and Butlers decided that, to satisfy their brand value of 'social responsibility' (see their website - I'm not making this up), the former music hall concept of Balmbra's was redundant, and that the area would be better served by a shitty '80s theme bar called Reflex. And even though they obviously they hadn't been in for a while, since it already WAS a shitty '80s theme bar in all but name, this got the politicians up in arms, yelling about the 'blatant disregard for Tyneside' and about how the proposed changes were 'deeply resented by the people of the area'. M&B then stated their case, sort of along the lines of, 'Tough. The kids who pay their money don't give a fuck about history, so why should we?' And you can see their point: how could over a hundred years of North East tradition - immortalised in the song *The Blaydon Races*, sung by 52,000 every other week at St James' Park - compare with the cultural might of a hit by Birmingham's own Duran Duran? Still, anxious not to shoot themselves in the shitter, M&B hammered out a compromise of paying the sign writers a couple of hours of overtime to prefix the tacky wire puzzle-effect logo with the word 'Balmbra's'. This, apparently, meant that the whiners would be happy while the 'well-recognised and popular Reflex branding [would be] there to reassure our existing customers and to attract new ones'. Oh aye, and they agreed to keep the blue plaque in the doorway. The bottom line is, though, that they still fucking got away with it, and there it sits today, forlorn and tainted with derelict shite either side. I'm not going to claim any sort of nostalgia for what was there before. I hated it when it was still just Balmbra's, and I could list any number of complaints about unpleasantness I encountered, like the toilet troughs full of broken glass, and the pig-fucking-obstinate bar staff who seemed to think that a pub full of punters wearing Toon shirts would rather listen to Atomic Kitten than hear live reports on Sunderland getting relegated. Even before the Mitchells and Butlers debacle, the place had been wrecked, mangled, battered and desecrated beyond all hope of salvation. But it's the principle that counts, and without principles where are we? Up a lap-dancer's pole with a feather up our arses, probably.

For: Old time music hall is the equivalent of the modern DJ bar, which means that, sooner or later, with the passing of time and a change in fashion, we'll be rid forever of the dicks with the decks.

Against: Could have been a legend, chose to be a fun pub. What a fucking waste.

The bar stinks like the time I drunkenly made the mistake of peering into the sanitary bins in the unisex bogs in the missus' halls of residence. I could never forget that stench. Well, that's me skipping the jam roly-poly for pudding, then.

Bar 24

24 Cloth Market, NE1 1EE
'Generation Missing Syllable'

The public house at 24 Cloth Market has had a bit of a chequered past to say the least, and when the Dog first became aware of it, it was known as Bewicks, a scruffy little reprobate that was clearly up to no good. Inevitably it fell further in with the wrong crowd and, through a combination of malevolent influences and Social Services neglect, it degenerated into the notorious Cage Bar, a place famed for drug abuse, ear-biting, stabbings and mayhem. Obviously a pub as downright nasty as that couldn't be allowed to flourish, not even in the debauchery of the Bigg Market, so it was only a matter of time before the bizzies stepped in and laid down the law. Next came a caution, a whack on the arse with the plimsoll of justice and the opening of the baffling Fizz Fun Bar, although what the fuck happened to that, I don't know. One minute it was there and the next it wasn't, like the Nokia you left on that park bench, just before you saw those lads in the caps running like the wind. And now look at it. Spruced up and gleaming, the newly re-christened Bar 24 looks all sweet and innocent, as only a repeat offender up before the beak can. Look how much effort it's put into its appearance: Book cases! Logs! Carpets! Aw, what a good lad! And what about those old pictures on the walls? Look at the one of the under-construction Tyne Bridge, looming over the Tuxedo Princess when it was still a steamship and it was All You Can Drink for two-and-sixpence. And as with all delinquents, it expects serious compensation just for behaving in a civilised manner, so that'll be the reason for the three quid Foster's. But - and I'm trying to see the bigger picture here - it's made the effort to turn over a new leaf, and for that it should be applauded. The trouble is, though, will anyone be able to take it seriously? The people who looked down their snecks beforehand will still approach it with the same prejudice, while the pestilence who got it in its former state will refuse to associate with it until they've brought it back down to their level. Fair enough, it looks respectable now, but before you know it, it'll be back to its old ways, riding the Metro with a four-pack of Skol, Pinky & Perky on the ringtone and wading into bystanders for not sparking them a tab. Wazza and Dazza will scratch their calling cards into the windowpanes, while Natlie and Nicla - the tragic children of Generation Missing Syllable - yank each other's hair out over who's got the cushest electronic tag, swear to god. And it'll be fucking this and fucking that and fucking the other, ye daft radgie cunt. The language of kids today. It just breaks my heart.

For: It's the Bigg Market, which means there WILL be one, but I didn't see any evidence of his presence and that's good enough for me, so I'm going to put 'No DJ' as the 'For:'.
Against: Yes, I'm whining about DJs again. How many times is that now? There's one thing that's been troubling me, though. See Santa Claus aka Santy aka St Niclaus? And see DJ Schmoov aka DJ Smoove aka DJ Smooooth? Notice the similarities? Lots of slightly different names for the same person: we've all heard the stories, but do either of them even exist? I think they're both just a cruel invention to keep the kids in line. 'If you're not a good boy, DJ Schmoov won't spin you any choons this year...'

Rowdy charvers on the bus are a pain in the fucking arse, I'm sure we're agreed. But it's not their fault: they're shite and they know no better. When I'm on my way home after the match, wedged in upstairs without so much as my knackered old Walkman to keep me company - I refuse to buy an iPod because I don't want to be mugged by a twelve-year-old – I get to experience the flipside of the coin. Educated and well-spoken, and with a healthy allowance to boot, tomorrow's doctors, lawyers, chemical engineers and makeover stylists show me the benefits of their upbringing, at full volume, front to back of the entire top deck. 'I was, like, so, like, ohmygod, and she was like, so, like, ohmygod, and he was, like…' Is that the best you can manage, you floppy-fringed fucktards? That's what makes you so, 'like', alternative? Just bloody button it, will you? And pull your fucking pants up, an' all.

Beehive Hotel

2 High Bridge, NE1 1EN
'Eat, drink, sleep and shite'

If you judged the Beehive purely on its decor, you'd have a fine example of a well-kept heritage pub, with Burmantoft tiling, ornate carved ceilings and tons of authentic historical detail. You can guarantee, though, that when the man from the tourist board arrived with his clipboard he'd be told to fuck off in no uncertain terms, and his photographer would be buzzing the office for an insurance form before he'd even got his lens cap off. The Beehive is - and there's no getting away from it - a wee bit on the rough side. But don't let me put you off. After all, there's rough and there's rough, and I've never had any grief in here, despite my condescending manner and my supremely punchable face. It really depends on when you go, I'd say; for my money, as long as you arrive at a time that the price list classes as Level 1 - Monday to Thursday - then I think the emphasis tends to be on cheap beer, best of order, and very little fighting. (This might just be a load of bollocks that I've invented to fill up space; I can't imagine anyone paying a Level 2 premium to get their head stoved in.) If you're that bothered about personal safety, you can get a good idea of what to expect from the outside, through the huge windows lined constantly with haggard old bastards who look like they eat, drink, sleep and shite on their stools, although that isn't the full punter range by any means. While I can honestly say we were standing next to a honking old duffer on his own, muttering down the sleeves of his demob suit, that would be to ignore the generous helping of chatting couples, fact-packed quiz-jockeys, young lasses sipping wine and, over in the corner, Frank N Furter and Janet Weiss on their way to the Theatre Royal. You know, this place isn't all that bad, and it's a hell of a lot better than what you've feared in all the years you've been passing it by. Fair enough, maybe the first thing you notice is that maybe it looks a bit tatty in places, but it still remains an atmospheric little boozer serving a good pint at a sensible price, with no fucking about or inescapable beats. And if the jukebox choices are rubbish or there's sod all on telly, you can always sit and watch the blokes from the council cleaning up all the shattered glass and broken teeth in the Bigg Market from the night before.

For: A down-to-earth traditional pub. You know, the type that people - as any leisure chain will tell you - apparently don't want any more.
Against: The toilets were absolutely minging, and that was noticed from outside the bog door. Jesus, what a Judi Dench.

And speaking of lavs, there's a view from the Beehive's upper level of the Bigg Market's public toilets. These loos - according to the campaigners who want to see them afforded listed status - are some of the best still-functioning Victorian conveniences in Britain today. It's a valid point, I suppose, but I don't support their preservation as a matter of aesthetics, but as one of simple financial sense. The Bigg Market needs public pissers to stop it turning into a torrent of wee at closing time, from KFC down to the job shop, but installing the fancy new ones would just attract enraged spotty hooligans and kebab-clutching fornicators, eager to trash them on general principle. As for the ancient underground ones, well, have you been in them lately? Unwreckable doesn't even scratch the surface.

Blackie Boy

11 Groat Market, NE1 1UQ
'I simply cannot be arsed today'

In 1967, high on amphetamines and full of despair, the late Johnny Cash crawled into Nicajack Cave in Tennessee and waited to die. 'If I crawled in far enough,' he said, 'I'd never be able to find my way back out, and nobody would be able to locate me until after I was dead'. I feel like that whenever I hobble into the Blackie Boy although, admittedly, I have a fair bit extra in the way of creature comforts and nothing more troublesome on my mind than making it through the hangover to the three o'clock kick off. The Blackie Boy is my post-Friday night, pre-Saturday match boozer, and it's far and away the darkest, gloomiest bar the Bigg Market will ever know. I can think of no better pub opposite the back of the Pig & Whistle for when you've got a head like a Wurlitzer, a creak in your bones like a ship in a storm, and a sadness in your soul that says, 'I simply cannot be arsed today.' You slump in the armchair beside the roaring fire, stare vacantly at the stained glass fittings, and grumble yourself back to health. And as your body starts to thaw and your eyes regain focus, you might pull a weighty tome from the dusty bookshelves, before putting it straight back in disgust and reaching for a wetwipe. Your pint is soothingly poor, the atmosphere comfortingly dead, and your fellow punters want nothing more than a nod of recognition that you are brothers in pain. It's blissful. Of course, this is MY Blackie Boy I'm describing, in the way that only I see it. You, on the other hand, think I'm on about a completely different pub, don't you? The Blackie Boy you know is the heaving meat market on a Saturday night, but I'm ever so tired and I'd rather you didn't make me think too hard about that. And in my fragile state I'd prefer not to remember that everyone knows someone who's been tempted into the adjoining back lane and engaged in an impromptu act of knee-buckling love over the wheelie bins, before returning, breathless and spent, to rinse away the evidence with ice from the Smirnoff bucket. Oh, that lane! It's so romantic! Who needs oysters, champagne or springtime in Rome, when that tart, pissy aroma is the only aphrodisiac your heart could desire?

For: The signs on the toilet doors: 'Dick' and 'Fanny'.
Against: Pick the wrong chair to collapse into and you'll break your arse in three.

You're interested in the Blackie Boy's bookshelves? You like stories? Then here's an apocryphal tale you might just enjoy. Once upon a time, there was a big, bad boss who worked for the street cleaning department at the council. The big, bad boss couldn't control his big, bad bladder and, after drinking heavily in the Blackie Boy's function room one night, was nabbed urinating - some say in the street, some say down the stairs - by a handsome prince from, you've guessed it, the street cleaning department at the council. And he was bollocked and spanked and disciplined by the king, and they all lived happily ever after. Sorry, did I say this story was apocryphal? It's apocryphal in as much as the Chronicle had it splashed - huh huh huh - all over their front page, with suitably lurid headlines. Me, I'd have rubbed his fucking nose in it, too. Dirty dog.

City Vaults

13-15 Bigg Market, NE1 1UN
'I just miss the seediness'

I'm not really sure what the owners' plan was for this place when they did the refit: they spent billions doing it up, making it into a swish, modern, chilled lounge bar, and then ruined it all by letting the usual Bigg Market riff-raff back in. Like something out of London's Covent Garden, the City Vaults has been brought up to date with space enhancing mirrors, and stylish-yet-functional decking, and then wrecked by grunting morons dressed head-to-toe in snide Fred Perry gear. What they've done here - if you remember the old Vault - is glass in the piss-stinking alleyway at the side, and make the whole thing into one big bar. There's a big drop-down screen in the old ramp bit, most likely there to give a central focus to people watching the match on Sky. I take it that idea was meant for evening kick-offs, since you can see bugger all on it during the day, the light shining through from behind giving an effect not entirely unlike watching a pair of beige curtains for ninety minutes. Or Sunderland. Ho ho ho. Carried forward from the old bar's previous lifetime are the 'shock' DJ, looking like he'd rather be anywhere than shouting the same nonsense to the same losers week after week, and the legendary topless totty, giving a half-hearted frug and a quick flash of the norks to whatever's clogging up the charts this week. They've moved the stage to one side instead of at the end of the pub, but it's still a bastard to see what's going on unless you're in the front row. It's not all bad, though: you mightn't get much of an eyeful of strippers, but it's an absolute fucking godsend when it comes to avoiding seeing that idiot Geordie Dancer making an arse of himself every weekend. So why do I keep dodging the place, then? Maybe I just miss the seediness of what was the stickiest floor in the city. Or maybe I just can't bear to admit that - what with the Toon being so bleedin' awful to watch lately - that seeing some bored girl take her top off to a Britney Spears 'classic' is the highlight of a match day. Terrible state of affairs either way.

For: The old Vault really was a shitehole.
Against: Trying to get served when you're looking at bosoms is an absolute nightmare.

The Geordie Dancer, in case you're unaware, is a fat, specky bloke with a mullet and a Toon shirt, and his high-kicking, belly-flopping antics have been amusing pre-match drunks for a few years now. The thing is, though, if you watch the many online clips of him in chronological order, you can see his initial cheeky enthusiasm giving way to a pained grin that ponders why ap-plause gets louder the lower you sink. I feel we have a lot in common.

Flares

31-33 Mosley Street, NE1 1YF
'The staff canteen on Monday lunchtime'

Look, I might as well come clean here. I've been in Flares once, whilst very, very drunk, and even though I'm normally a stone-faced snob, I think I enjoyed it. Ah, here, if you're not going to take me seriously... I also think that I may have pre-empted Ricky Gervais' terrible dancing from *The Office* by a good eighteen months, so it must have been a while ago, but that hardly ex-cuses my actions, does it? Still, it's out in the open now, anyway. The shame of it: I think I'd be less embarrassed telling my folks I'd fallen in love with a goat than owning up to having a half-way decent time in Flares. I don't know what the fuck we were thinking even stepping through the doors, to tell the truth. Let's look at the evidence: it's part of a chain, it's a '70s-themed, groovey (Flares website's own spelling) fun pub, and it was absolutely rotten when it used to be Circus Circus. What on earth possessed us? I obviously don't remember much of what was there or what went where, but that really doesn't matter in a bar like this; what does matter is how fucking mental the overall atmos-phere is, especially to sneering, broom-up-the-arse miseries like us. So aye, the '70s theme: the headfuck lights, the Don't Walk: Boogie signs, the mirror balls, the platform heels, the wigs and the glitter. It's all there. I seem to recall you can even buy tons of costume stuff from behind the bar to make your night go with a real swing, but I'll fight to the death anyone who says I even considered putting my hand in my pocket for anything other than the beer. You get the staff dancing all over the place, in the windows and that; you get really cheesy DJs, and I'm talking about mobile disco standard and not the git-beard elitists from your average lounge bar; and you get all the annoyingly infectious tunes you thought you'd purged from your mind. And the punters: hen nights with their amusing pseudonyms – Anal Angie? Blowjob Barbara? Oh, my sides - and stag parties with their attendant violence-for-dignity trade-ins, plus the usual after office forty-something crowd for whom self-esteem is but a distant memory.

Ain't gonna bump no more (with no big fat woman), especially not if she's gonna be in the staff canteen on Monday lunchtime. It is, to all intents and purposes, hell on toast. So, did I and would I ever go back after the review visit all those years ago? No. Did I really, unapologetically, enjoy it? Yeah, I suppose so. Maybe that's where we've been going wrong all these years. Maybe we should just put our sad little notebooks away and start strutting our collective stuff. Maybe. More like maybe not.

For: As Thomas Beecham once famously wrote, you should 'Try everything once except folk dancing and incest.' Can't argue with that.
Against: Why does seeing the word 'fun' in print or on the screen make me want to weep?

Right, this is the last time I'm going to try to get this through your thick skull. Flares used to be Circus Circus, but when the Flares that was up the road changed to Reflex, the concept was shipped down here. The place that was Reflex then became Boom! when the people behind Reflex tried to muscle in on the Balmbra's legend, shortly before being told to fuck off in no uncertain terms, hence the appallingly named Balmbra's Reflex just up the hill. What a fucking carry on, and what a fucking waste of time and energy. All of those bars are shite.

Kiss
18 Cloth Market, NE1 1EE
'Includes major surgery'

In the heart of Newcastle's legendary Bigg Market, [insert name of bar here] has been happily serving gassy swill to problem drinkers and borderline psychotics for a good while now. Under-dressed teens and their shame-free mothers shimmy on down to endlessly pounding holiday disco music, while hollering block-heads whip up a storm behind the turntables. An abandoned wreck of overstuffed wheelie bins by day, [insert name of bar here] comes alive after 8pm, the times when only a lunatic with a death wish would set foot in the Bigg Market without a Kalash-nikov. Gangs of brainless turds pile in, squeal and rage over their cut-price alcopops, and flood back out again, pausing only to make obnoxious eye contact with their prospective sparring partner come the chucking-out time free-for-all. It's hideous, it's embarrassing and it's very, very worrying. Welcome to Faliraki on Tyne. I can honestly say the review visit was one of the worst experiences of my life - and that includes major surgery - and it'll be a long time before I darken the doors of [insert name of bar here] again. Dump.

For: Ample opportunity for Mr Plod to wade in and crack some craniums.
Against: Fuck me, why didn't I think of this one-size-fits-all reviewing technique before we suffered the rest of the Bigg Market hovels?

My dictionary clearly states that 'Party' is a noun and not a verb. Party is something you have, and not something you do, trust me. The disgraceful appropriation of the American usage by the crème-de-la-shite of our once-proud nation - we invented the fucking English language after all – tears me apart, it really does.

Liquid
32-36 Cloth Market, NE1 1EE
'Exposure to blinding lights lowers the sperm count'

If they stuck you in Liquid and faced you away from the beer pumps, you'd be hard pushed to recognise this as a bar. You would, I'm certain of it, make the mistake of thinking that this stinking, echoing dump was some sort of slaughterhouse, half-heartedly hosed down for the next truckload of wide-eyed rumi-nants. You won't be far off, though. Liquid is a horrible single-room bar, devoid of anything whatsoever except walls, floor, pillars and ceiling. I'm not even going to try to describe the paintjob, since it seems to defy classification; I can't see a colour, only shadows, as if Dulux have brought out a range off the edges of the visible spectrum. The last time I came in here - young, foolish and irresistibly handsome - I remember they had some bubble lamps scattered around, as a sop to the 'liquid' theme. Returning now, saggier round the cheeks, eyes and buttocks, and with a hint of an arthritic limp, I find those lamps are nowhere to be seen. They're gone, smashed, and drained, and the only liquid that decorates the place these days is the sloshed beer and the sticky globules of fuck knows what, both inevitable when you allow dangerously stupid people to move about uncuffed and unmanacled. For such a notoriously raucous bar - you can hear it from the other side of the planet, never mind across the road - I have to admit I'm shocked to see miserable fuckers sitting around at the back of the room, like reluctant greyhounds in the traps. I needn't have worried, because soon it all kicks off, and people start hurling themselves around to what passes for tunes in bars of this terrible ilk. Stick on any late-night schedule-filling TV show, then wait for the adverts, and you will hear what I am hearing now, only at a less lethal volume. Watch in bemusement as yet another compilation of 'darnce anthems' and 'classics from the cluuuubs' is paraded for your indifference by the horrible yappy voice that is mandatory for that type of crap. At least on the adverts the fools shimmying on down are reasonably good looking; in here you just get a parody of Ibiza glamour, with spelk-thin boys circling dirigible-fat girls in an interminable hobble of lust. His weedy biceps display - in footballer-aping Olde English script - tattoos reading Mam & Dad, while sticking out over her see-through white pants is not so much a muffin top as a whole fucking patisserie. And, looking at the blossoming of their courtship, I'm praying that exposure to blinding lights lowers the sperm count. Fucking hell man: how is this volume legal? Why are the Old Bill not outside waiting for the signal to charge in and break it up? I know I'm cracking on a bit, but I've had my fair share of racket. I've been in the front row at a Metallica gig - twice - god damn it. But this is just ridiculous. Why do I put myself through this? I don't stay to finish the pint, never mind long enough to write a thesis, but just have one last peer through the glare to confirm my prejudices, then scarper before the windows finally blow out. Incredible. And I mean that literally.

For: Now I'm stone deaf and registered as disabled, I don't have to pay to go on that sign language course.
Against: That's offset against the bribes I had to offer my mates to even cross the doors.

If you're on the dancefloor in some £100-in Ibiza superclub, pilled up or on one or whatever the fuck they call it, you're doing your 'thing', and out of the corner of your eye you see someone else doing your thing, what do you do? Do you challenge them for stealing your moves, or do you inch over to them and gimp in their ear, 'Do you want to be my frieeeend?' Freaks on pharmaceuticals; the only chemicals they deserve are ones given American justice style, intravenously, while strapped to a bed in the presence of the warders, the doctor and the priest with his last rites fact sheet. See what sort of a fucking buzz they get off that.

Pig & Whistle

Cloth Market, NE1 1EE
'A gift-wrapped body bag with a broken zip'

Resurrected in summer 2005 after the three-week spell when it was known as just plain Whistle, the Pig & Whistle has always been one of the shoddiest bars in Newcastle. And guess what? Now it's worse than ever. In addition to being host to the dregs of both ends of the drinking age spectrum - from fresh-faced felons to pensionable pissheads - they're now promoting 'For Your Eyes Only dancers and bikini barmaids before every Newcastle home game!' Go on, go in. Watch in horror as a parade of desperately unhappy exotic dancers whip their knockers out and climb shiny poles like drunken monkeys up the rigging. Stand astonished as your bottle of expensive-yet-piss-weak lager turns out to be plastic, and think what that says about their trust of their customers. And punch yourself, repeatedly, in the face, genitals and solar plexus, for being dim enough to enter, let alone hand over your entire soul in the search for entertainment. You want me to elaborate on those punters - and why not, since there's absolutely fuck all in the way of decor or anything else to discuss? Fair enough. Look at the junior end of the scale for starters; berks who think it's perfectly acceptable to wander the town with no fucking shirt on from March to October, yet would whine that they'd freeze to death if you asked them to remove their baseball caps. And while I swear to you now that I will never, ever go in after dark to see the older, night-time clientele, I've seen what traipses up and down the Bigg Market and into places like this; it's that whooping, saggy-titted, fight-starting, overpainted dog mess that we all know and avoid like the chlamydia. For the love of god, when these women are getting ready and they say to their mates or their husband or whoever, 'How do I look?' why, instead of saying, 'You look nice, dear,' can someone not say, 'Christ, sort yourself out. You look like Eddie Izzard'? It's like this: you get Daytime TV fashion spots where they wheel out some old trout for a makeover, slap too much blusher on her mush, spruce up the beans-on-toast perm, and stuff her into some horrendously inappropriate black and gold dress. 'Eeeh!' they say, 'I might get a (giggle) Toy Boy! I look a million dollars!' No, love: you look like a gift-wrapped body bag with a broken zip. And you're making me feel sick. Now stamp your feet, pull your knickers up, pick up your tabs, and fuck off.

For: The advert that I got handed on the way out has a convenient pocket-sized fixture list on the back.
Against: Ah, man. Where do you start?

There's a Pig & Whistle in Stockholm. There is: I saw it with my own eyes. I would have nipped in for a Spendrups or a Pripps, but with even Swedish cooking lager heading for four and a half quid a pint, the name alone was enough to put me off. I'm obviously aware that the whole fucking world has already seen it, but if you search one more time on Google for 'sthlmvip' and 'pig & whistle' you will come across the pictures that show the contrast between Sweden and here, all nicely packaged in a PowerPoint presentation. And while I know the Stockholm pics weren't taken in their Pig & Whistle, there's no harm in having one more chuckle at the expense of the typical Bigg Market punter.

Popworld

14 Bigg Market, NE1 1UW
'The stylish café-bar with pavement terrace'

A few years ago a bunch of bright sparks made a big hoo-hah about smartening up the Bigg Market. Was it the council, or was it private investment? I dunno, but some flaming half-a-job outfit gave the area a much-needed facelift, improved the quality of life by putting in new seats, restored the fountain, and tried to bring it more into line with the Grainger Town regeneration around the corner, only to then wreck it all by allowing this place to open up slap-bang in the middle. Maybe it was lack of funding, maybe it was internal politics, or maybe some lazy get just pissed off early on a Friday night before the paperwork was finished, but somehow the stylish café-bar with pavement terrace from the original blueprint failed to appear, and instead there's now a loathsome pop nostalgia pub. From the outside Popworld is an insult to the building that houses it, and from the inside it's an affront to everything I've ever held dear. Here we are having a shocking time, wondering exactly why we've just been charged festival prices for standard lager in a shit-tip like this. These punters are really annoying me tonight, pillocking about to some minor chart entry from yesteryear, one that was abysmal when it first went down and tastes no better now it's being burped back up. And they're staring at us - not glancing but glaring outright - with expressions that quiz, Why are you so miserable? Why are you not having fun? Whoo! C'mon! Why? I'll tell you. I'm here because I have to be, because I need to cross this fucker off my list. I'm surrounded by some of the most appalling disco decor I've ever seen, with terrible pop star cartoons and a whole gallery of glitter wigs and those frigging cowboy hats. This being the Bigg Market's closest thing to a gay bar, there is a fifteen stone mohicaned lesbian rampaging about, knocking people flying; none of them seem to mind, though, because it's a FUN pub and accidents will happen, even if they require surgery to put right. I'm propping up this padded rail because I'm knackered, and because there are no chairs of any description. And I'm miserable because I'm being danced at by a mother-and-daughter team, who I can just smell are looking for love and are clearly not fussed who gets the beef and who gets the dripping. What the fucking HELL was that? That gimpy twat DJ - him, over there on the dancefloor in an oversized Christmas ornament from the saddest tree in the street - has just upped the bass on his system and literally bounced me off the rail and up against the claggy table. I've taken all I can stand of this. There is no need for this enforced jollity when I could be more happily occupied being tortured in a third world death camp somewhere. Here, mate: do you want this pint? I've barely touched it, swear down. You can have it. We're fucking out of here.

For: Nothing.
Against: The cocktails are so knowingly dire that the menu's admission of 'comes with a straw' is seen as a major selling point.

Dancing is a bloody ridiculous pastime. If we're such intelligent creatures, then how come evolution hasn't stamped it out yet? I know it's a throwback to the dawn of time when we were just another species struggling for survival and maybe a bit of domination as a bonus. I know it's a prelude to mating, that it's supposed to be erotic, and that the attraction of drumbeats is that they replicate the increased heart rate of the sexual act. I know all that, but I'm still having trouble tying it in with the vision before me, galumphing about with her elbows wedged into her waist and her wrists hanging limply in front. I can't decide which she more closely resembles: is it a Tyrannosaurus Rex, or is it Tommy Cooper in drag? Either way, I have no desire to breed with the pedal-pushered troll.

Pumphreys

44 Cloth Market, NE1 5UF
'Cheapskates and bandit-slaves'

For all my incessant and frankly tedious carping about how bars should be left alone, looking at the state of Pumphreys these days, it appears I might have to have a rethink. Because this pub, this grubby, neglected, stinking hovel of decay, is what Balmbra's down the street might have been like if it had remained untouched by the soft, healing hands of those loveable pub chains. With a carpet that leaves sticky standing at the bus stop and is roaring off towards sodden, everywhere you look the bog-standard - for 1918 - English pub decor is starting to look more than just a bit tatty. And while I'm never going to appear on Life of Grime tsk-tsking about the squalor of the nation's cities, I always worry when the wallpaper on the sloped ceiling directly beneath the toilets is peeling off and sliding down the necks of the punters below. Who is responsible for this? And which idiot designed those toilets? Wee Jimmy Krankie? Seriously, if you're over four feet tall you'd be better off running up the street to the Beehive or the public bogs, because if you unleash the beast in these pissers, you'll splash your bloody chin never mind your trousers. Look, I know I'm basing this on a selective viewpoint; I'm clearly not fucking mad enough to go at night when the rest of the Bigg Market piles in and starts setting about the fixtures and fittings. But every time I've been in here before the match, practically dragged in by cheapskates and bandit-slaves, there's always been an unbroken line of watery-eyed old wheezers, clinging onto the bar for dear life like it's some sort of Touch The Truck competition. What the fuck are you so scared of, Grandpa? The man on the other side of the room wearing your jacket and your greasy flat cap? It's a mirror, you silly old fool. Jesus, what the hell is that smell? I'm sure I know it from somewhere. It's... it's... it's like I've been scratching my nadbag on a hot summer's day, fresh from a three mile run in my nylon shorts. That's what it is. And it ain't pleasant.

For: I came in here the day Shearer broke Milburn's record. Abysmal though it is, Pumphreys will always be a part of my mental image of that day.

Against: Has anyone got the number for Mitchells & Butlers? I think I might have a suggestion for their next compulsory purchase.

Pumphreys used to have a bloke behind the bar who bore - if you'd just spent an hour staring at the sun - a faint resemblance to Chris 'fucking' Moyles. It's a shame he doesn't work there anymore, because it robs me of the opportunity to set down in print my opinions about the self-appointed saviour of Radio One. Actually, bollocks to that. I will not be denied by the turnover of bar staff. I'd like to state this here, clearly, both on and off the record. Moyles: cunt. His toadying hangers-on: bigger cunts. And anyone who's put up with any of his prattle and thereby kept him in a job all these years: the biggest cunts of all.

Rewind
31 Groat Market, NE1 1RE
'By kids for kids'

Now on its fourth incarnation in my drinking lifetime, Rewind is aiming to succeed where Macey's, Lord Chancellor's and Pop! at this site have all obviously failed. Once again I have to haul my sorry arse down the Groat Market to try to spot the tiny changes. And you know what? I can't even be bothered to get annoyed about it. Instead, there's just a bored indifference, like some poor bloke stuck outside the changing rooms in Top Shop, witnessing an endless parade of interchangeable yet wholly unsuitable jeans emerging from behind the curtain. What about these, he's forced to consider. Yeah, whatever, is the half-hearted reply, knowing fine well that there'll only be three months' wear in the bloody things anyway. Look, there's just no point in raging about this place any more. It's clearly not meant for the likes of me. It's a bar run by kids for kids. That's just how it is. They say your heart beats more slowly as you grow older, and your perception of time changes accordingly; that an hour to a child seems like forever, but to a bitter, thirty-summat, hacked-off pub reviewer, it's only the time it takes to mix a cocktail in some pompous, gloomy wankbar near the station. And that must be the reason why this bar sees no problem with the idea of Rewind-ing all the way back to the golden age of Girls Aloud six months previously and making a fucking theme out of it. That's the only logical explanation I can find. Like I said, I'm not in the mood to take the piss, so the sub-Mondrian geometric patterns and the horrible purple paint will have to go un-ridiculed. Likewise the bulbous orange lights and the white daubs on the walls outlining the silhouettes of people dancing and livin' it up. Actually, scrap that. They're not slipping that one past me. Those white lines would have been ones of chalk, marking where the fuckers had been put against the wall and pumped full of lead, if this was my bar. Dancing? In the sodding pub? Summary execution's what they really want.

For: Decent pint, strangely enough.
Against: '...plus drinks, sweets and games to bring back those fond memories.'

I'm standing in the toilets in Rewind, badly drunk, half asleep and thoroughly cheesed off. I've somehow had black marker on my face since early this morning, there's beer down my shirt and some little shit's chewing gum is rapidly fastening me to the floor. I calculate that I'm twice the age of the management here, never mind the bloody punters, and I am sick, sick, sick of what remains of my life. I'm looking at the condom machine on the wall, merrily blinking its blue lights into the pissy mist of the urinals, and I'm reading the promises of the products it's trying to make me buy. Thrillseeker; Erotomax; For The Ultimate Pleasure. And I don't know whether to shrug, scoff, cry or rip the damn thing off the wall and take it to the head barman to explain what age and bitter experience have taught me all too well: if you seriously want to give someone the 'ultimate pleas-ure', then just shut the fuck up. It's really that simple.

Index

	Page
Adelphi	120
Akenside Traders	13
Apartment	60
As You Like It	177
@Home	63
@ONE	237
The Attic	64
The Bacchus	122
Balmbra's Reflex	273
Bar 24	275
Bar 42	124
Bar Bannatyne	254
Barluga	126
Baron & Baroness	239
Beehive Hotel	277
Bernaccia	66
Beyond	256
The Black Bull	180
The Black Garter	127
The Blackett Arms	129
Blackie Boy	279
Blue	15
Bob Trollop	16
The Bodega	68
Boom!	131
Box	133

The Bridge Hotel	70
Buffalo Joe's	18
Butlers	135
Camp David	240
The Carriage	182
Centurion	71
The Charles Grey	137
Chase	19
City Vaults	280
Clear	73
The Cluny	215
Coco.V	75
The Cooperage	21
Crow's Nest	184
Crown Posada	23
The Cumberland Arms	216
Destination	76
The Dog	241
Dog & Parrot	78
Duke of Northumberland	138
The Duke of Wellington	140
The Eagle	243
Eclipse	244
Egypt Cottage	24
The End	245
Enigma	142
Exchange	26
Eye on the Tyne	27
Fever	30
Fitzgeralds	144

Flares	282
Fleet Street	80
Fluid	185
Flynn's	32
The Forth	82
Free Trade Inn	218
Fusion	145
Gengis	83
The Globe	85
The Goose	188
Gossip	247
Gotham Town	87
The Hancock	189
Head of Steam	89
Hide	257
Hoko-10	147
The Hotspur	191
Idols	149
Jimmyz	34
Keel Row	259
Kiss	283
The Lane	151
Liquid	284
The Living Room	153
The Lodge	155
Logic	219
Long Bar	91
The Lounge	92
Luckies	193
Mr Lynch	195

Madisons	196
Market Lane	156
Martha's	35
Mood	260
Moot	221
themushroom	158
New Bridge Inn	223
Newcastle Arms	198
Newcastle Hero	94
North	95
Northumberland Arms	160
O'Neill's	97
Offshore 44	37
The Old George	161
Old Orleans	199
Opera Piano Bar	262
Pacific Bar Cafe	201
Percy Arms	202
Perdu	257
Pig & Whistle	286
Pitcher & Piano	38
Players	264
Popolo	163
Popworld	288
Pumphreys	290
The Quayside	40
Quilted Camel	41
Rafferty's	101
The Red House	43
Revolution	102

Rewind	291
Rose & Crown	165
Rosie's	204
Sam Jacks	266
Secco	166
Sgt Pepper's	206
Shearer's	207
The Ship Inn	225
Sinners	268
Six	226
The Slug & Lettuce	44
The Sports Café	104
The Star	106
Stepney's	228
Stereo	47
Strawberry	208
Switch	248
Tanners	230
The Tavern	210
Tavistock	48
The Telegraph	107
thirty 3i8ht	50
Three Bulls Heads	211
Tiger Tiger	270
Tilleys	108
Tokyo	110
The Trent House	213
Trillians	169
Twist	250
The Tyne	231

Union Rooms	112
Vineyard	170
Waterline	52
The Yard	252
Yates's	113

Read more from Tonto Press:

Jonny Kennedy

The Story of the Boy Whose Skin Fell Off
As told to Roger Stutter, Foreword by Nell McAndrew
Tonto Press 2007, ISBN 9780955218385, paperback, £9.99

Jonny Kennedy was the star of the unforgettable Emmy award-winning documentary The Boy Whose Skin Fell Off. He was an extraordinary character determined to live an ordinary life despite being born with the agonising condition Dystrophic Epidermolysis Bullosa (EB), which meant that his skin could literally fall off at the slightest touch. It was a daily struggle he faced with courage, determination and wit, offering inspiration to millions around the world. Tragically, Jonny was just 36 when he lost a final battle to skin cancer. This is his moving, honest and uplifting story.

The Rocketbelt Caper

A True Tale of Invention, Obsession and Murder
by Paul Brown
Tonto Press 2007, ISBN 9780955218378, paperback, £8.99

When three friends set out on a quest to build a real-life Buck Rogers-style flying machine, their obsession with the Rocketbelt 2000 shattered their friendship and set in motion an astonishing chain of events involving theft, deception, assault, a bizarre kidnapping, a ten million dollar lawsuit and a horrifically brutal murder. From sci-fi to reality, this is the incredible true story of the amazing rocketbelt. 'A delight to read. Genuinely stranger than fiction. Recommended.' - Popular Science .co.uk. 'Reads like good movie material' - BBC Focus.

Available from bookshops and www.tontopress.com

Read more from Tonto Press:

Wor Al

A Fans' Tribute To Alan Shearer
Edited by Paul Brown and Stuart Wheatman
Tonto Press 2006, ISBN 0955218330, paperback, 192 pages, £7.99

Shear class: 206 goals for Newcastle, 173 more for Southampton and Blackburn, plus 30 for England. A total of 409 goals in 733 top-level games - Alan Shearer's record speaks for itself. But what do Alan's many fans have to say about their hero? This unique tribute to the England hero and Geordie legend looks at Alan's brilliant career through the eyes of fanzine, website and terrace writers. Crammed with goals, games and wonderful memories, it is a fantastic celebration of a true football great - Our Alan, Wor Al.

Coming soon from Tonto Press:

Stephen Miller

The Autobiography
by Stephen Miller, coming summer 2008

Stephen Miller is one of Britain's most successful athletes. Record-breaking Stephen, who has Cerebral Palsy, has won three Paralympic gold medals, plus dozens of other international accolades, in the club and discus events. A writer and poet, Stephen's inspirational autobiography tells of his struggles and triumphs, and is told with refreshing honesty and infectious humour. Stephen is currently preparing for Beijing 2008 and his attempt to win a fourth-straight Paralympic gold.

Available from bookshops and www.tontopress.com